WELFARE POLICY

WELFARE POLICY

[feminist critiques]

edited by Elizabeth M. Bounds,
Pamela K. Brubaker, and
Mary E. Hobgood

The Pilgrim Library of Ethics

THE PILGRIM PRESS, *Cleveland, Ohio*

To all those who work to make this society
a better place for women and children

The Pilgrim Press, Cleveland, Ohio 44115
© 1999 by Elizabeth M. Bounds, Pamela K. Brubaker, and Mary E. Hobgood

The chapter "Poor Women, Work, and the U.S. Catholic Bishops" by Mary
E. Hobgood is reprinted by permission of Journal of Religious Ethics, Inc.,
from the *Journal of Religious Ethics,* vol. 25, no. 2 (fall 1997): 307–33.
Copyright © 1997 by Journal of Religious Ethics, Inc.; all rights reserved.

Printed in the United States of America on acid-free paper

04   03   02   01   00   99   5   4   3   2   1

Library of Congress Cataloging-in-Publication Data

Welfare policy : feminist critiques / edited by Elizabeth M. Bounds,
    Pamela K. Brubaker, Mary E. Hobgood.
        p.   cm.
    Includes bibliographical references.
    ISBN 0-8298-1305-5 (pbk. : alk. paper)
        1. Public welfare—Religious aspects—Christianity.   2. Poor
    women—United States—Social conditions.   3. Public welfare—United
    States.   4. Feminist theology.   I. Bounds, Elizabeth M., 1956–   .
    II. Brubaker, Pamela, 1946–   .   III. Hobgood, Mary E., 1946–   .
    BT738.48.W44   1999
    261.8'32—dc21   98-53434
                                                                  CIP

Contents

PART ONE
Theological and Philosophical Ethical Frameworks

PART TWO
Race, Class, and Family Values

PART THREE
Analysis of Responses of Churches and Activists

Afterwords

Foreword

Beverly W. Harrison

THE PUBLICATION OF *Welfare Policy: Feminist Critiques* is for me an occasion for rejoicing. Grounded in the present public controversy over so-called welfare reform, the ten chapters published here, along with afterwords from noted womanist and *mujerista* theologians, model a genre of feminist ethics, informed normatively by radical reading of Christian or related religious traditions. However, the distinctiveness of this book lies in a theological perspective that is also profoundly and unapologetically political, rooted in advocacy for a policy that aims at women's well-being, a position situated outside the mainstream of current public policy debate.

Readers who do not follow the subtle shifts of academic theology and ethics in the academy may be surprised to hear me say that this wonderful collection of chapters is the first of its genre, but that it also could (if trends continue) be the last of the genre as well. Why is this so? Ours is a time when new and sometimes subtle forms of neoliberal theology and ethics are impacting every area of theological and religious studies, including feminist work in women's studies. While producing often-artful cultural criticism, much newer feminist theology is nevertheless dismissive of positive claims to religious or moral knowledge and is subtly antipolitical. Today's cultural critic (postmodernist jargon for any and all intellectuals who reread established intellectual traditions) frequently aims to deconstruct political, moral, and religious interpretations as such. Some recent feminist theology, and even some feminist religious ethics, rereads in ways remote from the actual dynamics of our historical situatedness in a political economy which, as never before, is restructuring the lives and life conditions of every man, woman, and child on little planet earth.

Such a retreat into apolitical feminist work follows a neoliberal enthusiasm for the erasure of politics and relegates cultural criticism to academic enclaves where the presumed rites of cultural radicalism go on. Much such academic work supposes that novel speech-acts uttered in classrooms or published in books are a sufficient politics of change. In this new neofeminist world, participation in public policy debate itself is often taken as a symptom that one has not understood the profundities of postmodernist critique. Imbibing the socially constructed right-wing attack on political correctness, enthusiasts for postmodernism often leave us without comprehension about this present world, where now everything is left to market forces. The current ideology of welfare reform itself is suffused with neoliberal moral and theological assumptions, including the deep and libelous assumption that private business can solve problems that the state heretofore has only mismanaged. Happily, the essays in this volume help unmask such welfare reform by locating these reforms in relation to global economic shifts that go unnoted in most of the public debate on the welfare question.

In their introduction, the volume editors provide a valuable account of the methodological assumptions that set these authors apart from ahistorical and antimaterialist genres of cultural criticism which I find so disturbing. As they note, the genre of feminist ethical work presented here is liberationist, not liberal. It seeks to address the concrete patterns of human suffering, not only to illumine gender injustice but to show how the interstructuring of racism as cultural supremacy and class/economic privilege, and labor exploitation interact with gender/sex oppression to shape ongoing public discourse.

Exposing the duplicity in welfare reform is not easy. It is central to the goal of this feminist ethical work to challenge the imposition of neoliberal ideology, so triumphant in the Reagan-Bush era and proceeding apace under President Clinton. The rhetoric of welfare reform aims to persuade us that serious efforts are being made at restructuring government spending. Welfare reform is a rhetorical concession that Clinton has tossed his right-wing critics to prove his fiscal caution and his commitment to less government.

The contention here—that the state should address more vigorously issues of justice and undertake new initiatives at distributive justice—has an almost quaint ring in this political climate. The media fill the airwaves with analyses that suggest that state-initiated efforts at solving social problems simply do not work. Welfare creates bureaucracy, it is said, and can do little else. Such arguments are merely propaganda, however, and they are wrong historically. The facts are that federal government initiatives can work and have done so consistently, reshaping society in a more democratic direction. Here and in every liberal western democracy where public policy has aimed at change, state programs have made important differences. Most justice-centered programs do what they were designed to do.

The problem is that the United States, unlike many European welfare democracies, never intended to do much for dependent children or poor women! It is a truism that the original Aid to Dependent Children in our now downsized welfare program was created intentionally to be bureaucratic. Our nation, with its fierce tooth-and-claw-like work ethic, creates all social programs with rigid standards for eligibility so as to require administration by experts to discern entitlement.

Because we believe that it is necessary to ferret out ruthlessly malingerers and the undeserving, public welfare American-style is an endless, tangled process of demonstrating and documenting need. Is it not "the American Way" to make the process of applying for public assistance so demeaning and so stigmatizing in itself that only the most desperate will ask for help? Needless to say, in the past, many welfare democracies (including Canada and most European nations) had programs in which moderate child-welfare subsidies were paid to each and every child born into the society. Such universal programs do not require costly administration and were the preferred pattern in most countries. Persons with disabilities, those receiving unemployment compensation or retirement benefits, can be benefited by programs that are designed to reduce administrative cost. By contrast, U.S. programs are created to search out and destroy unworthy claimants.

No one denies that there was an urgent need for reform in our former AFDC system. As the authors of these chapters make clear, however, the one thing that has never been tried is an approach that makes the survival and well-being of poor single mothers and their children a central value in the policy process itself. When the smoke clears from the present restructuring of AFDC, we may safely predict that this downsizing, said to be required by fiscal responsibility and the need for less government, will merely have further shifted the costs of bearing and raising children to poor and poorly educated women and to voluntary organizations such as churches and private agencies. The tiny savings in the federal budget garnered from ending federal programs will turn out to have been only an occasion to shift costs to state and local governments. Nor will these costs be accurately counted. Increased homelessness and poorer health and education will have a social cost that politicians will deny. Welfare reform is merely redistributing the cost of our social-moral contempt onto those already victimized by a death-dealing neoliberal theology that God rewards only those who help themselves.

So long as deeply racist, antidemocratic values prevail in this public debate, and so long as the debate is shaped by skepticism that political solutions can work to enhance the common good, the welfare debate itself will further poison our already hate-filled society. In such an atmosphere, concern for real commitment to the common good will appear as naively idealistic, a holdover of an outmoded liberalism which threatens the enterprise, ingenuity, and creativity of deserving elites. In such an environment, issue-oriented, publicly concerned theological and ethical discussion, which this volume represents, can be easily brushed aside.

Readers should be clear at the outset that the crisis we face is not a crisis in our welfare system. The crisis is a loss of moral decency and fairness in the broader society. The authors of these chapters see this point clearly. Targeting poor women and their children and making them the issue is a way of evading the truth: that the problem is a political-economic system that privileges the wealthy and obscures its own profoundly antidemocratic value system by victim-blaming.

What follows here should be read against a backdrop that insists that what government does shapes all our lives, for better or worse. All of us must learn to reread welfare reform as a matter that is addressed in every act of Congress, in every bill enacted into law. All tax policy and all appropriations are also public welfare decisions. Every public expenditure is the use of government for someone's welfare, and every wealth-producing activity left untaxed (read: profit-making) is wealth accumulated without attaching social costs.

If the feminist ethical goal is a full rereading of our national welfare policy, then it is time for us to ask: Why is the Pentagon budget so privileged and central to our national welfare? Why are the defense industries, the banks, those who own wealth-producing wealth allowed to live so free of any social accountability for the use of that wealth? What are we missing when we are forced to name the elimination of AFDC "welfare reform"? What is going on when welfare reform becomes the occasion for the muddled middle (not a class), who do indeed pay most of the taxes, to blame those who carry even more of the social costs for the wealthy than do the middle? The rhetorical ploys of the current debate quite erroneously lead those of us in the middle to suppose that the federal government is actively looking out for us rather than rapidly accelerating the overprotection of our corporate-welfare system.

Any Christian or religious acquiescence to the rhetoric of welfare reform is deeply wrong, it is racist, sexist, and class-distorted nonsense. Our real agenda should be to recall federal, state, and local governments back to their responsibility for shaping policies that provide minimum conditions for human dignity. Those least well placed to earn the ever-growing amount of cash required to buy human dignity in this society are not the enemy. We can devise better and more creative ways to support poor women and their children than the old model enabled. But we had better not do so until we grasp the truth clearly that poor women and their children are not the problem.

The problem is an antidemocratic economy that rewards those who already have wealth while, more and more, closing off conditions of economic access not only to mothers who stay at home with young children but to most working people as well. The middle sector of this society is being hurt by the same downsizing policies that punish poor single women. The same dynamics that are brutally reordering poor women's lives and punishing their children are those shaping ours as well. No amount of prosperity for the few can obscure the connections between the neoliberalized zeal for blocking state initiatives for welfare and the growing welfare system for the rich that this state currently enacts daily.

We have never needed serious, overtly political feminist liberation theology and ethics more than we need such work today. So join me in resolving that this new liberation feminist reader on public policy will be only the first in a long line of such volumes.

Acknowledgments

ALL BOOKS REQUIRE NETWORKS IN ORDER to emerge. Much of the pleasure in creating this book came out of continuing connections. The original source of this work was our professional network, the American Academy of Religion, where some of these chapters were first presented at a session on welfare organized by Carol S. Robb for the Women and Religion Section, and others at a session sponsored by the Ethics Section. Our thanks go to the organizers, especially Carol.

The special network that brought the three of us together for this project comprises students, friends, and mentees of Beverly W. Harrison. Since Bev was the first one to tell us that our papers had to be a book, it gives us joy to acknowledge her support and to offer our work as one of the many honors for her retirement.

The actual production of this book required a network of contributors, helped by e-mail, mail, phone, and fax. Thanks to all of them. Thanks also to Timothy Staveteig of The Pilgrim Press, whose enthusiasm for this project has been a great support. And thanks to Michael T. Bradley Jr. for his editorial assistance at a very crucial point. We are also grateful to Sara Goldreich of the New England Welfare Reform Initiative for help with the resource list.

In addition, Liz would like to thank Candler School of Theology for providing resources (especially the help of Aimee Delevett and Tami S. Groves); Pam acknowledges gratefully California Lutheran University's help through grants and library assistance; and Mary thanks the College of the Holy Cross for a junior leave in the spring of 1997.

Contributors

Gloria H. Albrecht is associate professor of religious studies at the University of Detroit Mercy, Detroit, Michigan. She is the author of *The Character of Our Communities: Toward an Ethic of Liberation for the Church* (Abingdon, 1995).

Elizabeth M. Bounds is associate professor of Christian ethics at the Candler School of Theology, Emory University. She is the author of *Coming Together/Coming Apart: Religion, Community and Modernity* (Routledge, 1997).

Pamela K. Brubaker is associate professor of religious studies at California Lutheran University. Her publications include *Women Don't Count: The Challenge of Women's Poverty to Christian Ethics* (Scholars, 1994).

Beverly W. Harrison is the Caroline Williams Beard Professor of Christian Ethics at Union Theological Seminary in New York City. Her publications include *Our Right to Choose: Toward a New Ethic of Abortion* (Beacon, 1983) and *Making the Connections: Essays in Feminist Social Ethics* (Beacon, 1985).

Mary E. Hobgood is assistant professor of religious studies at the College of the Holy Cross, Worcester, Massachusetts. Her publications include *Catholic Social Teaching and Economic Theory: Paradigms in Conflict* (Temple University Press, 1991).

Ada María Isasi-Díaz is associate professor of ethics and theology at Drew University. Her publications include the edited volume *Hispanic/Latino Theology: Challenge and Promise,* with Fernando F. Segovia (Fortress, 1996). She is the author of *Hispanic Women, Prophetic Voice in the Church: Toward a Hispanic Women's Liberation Theology,* with Yolanda Tarango (1988; 2d ed., Fortress, 1993); *En La Lucha: Elaborating a Mujerista Theology* (Fortress, 1993); and *Mujerista Theology: A Theology for the 21st Century* (Orbis, 1996).

Janet R. Jakobsen is associate professor of religious studies and women's studies and co-coordinator of the Committee for Lesbian, Gay, and Bisexual Studies at the University of Arizona. Her publications include *Working Alliances and the Politics of Difference: Diversity and Complexity in Feminist Ethics* (Indiana University Press, 1998).

Ellen Ott Marshall is a doctoral candidate in religion, ethics, and society at Vanderbilt University.

Carol S. Robb is the Margaret Dollar Professor of Christian Social Ethics at San Francisco Theological Seminary. Her publications include *Equal Value: An Ethical Approach to Economics and Sex* (Beacon, 1995).

Joan Sakalas is a doctoral candidate in Christian social ethics at Union Theological Seminary, New York City, and works with welfare recipients.

Ruth L. Smith is associate professor of religion and philosophy at the Worcester Polytechnic Institute in Worcester, Massachusetts. Her publications include articles in *Cultural Critique* and the *Journal of Feminist Studies in Religion*.

Emilie M. Townes is professor of Christian social ethics at Saint Paul School of Theology in Kansas City, Missouri. Her publications include the edited volumes *A Troubling in My Soul: Womanist Perspectives on Evil and Suffering* (Orbis, 1993) and *Embracing the Spirit: Womanist Perspectives on Hope, Salvation, and Transformation* (Orbis, 1997). She is the author of *Womanist Justice: Womanist Hope* (Scholars, 1993), *In a Blaze of Glory: Womanist Spirituality as Social Witness* (Abingdon, 1995), and *Breaking the Fine Rain of Death: African-American Health Issues and a Womanist Ethic of Care* (Continuum, 1998).

Traci C. West is assistant professor of Christian ethics and African American studies at Drew University Theological School. Her publications include *Wounds of the Spirit: Black Women, Violence, and Resistance Ethics* (New York University Press, 1999).

Welfare "Reform": A War against the Poor

Elizabeth M. Bounds, Pamela K. Brubaker, Mary E. Hobgood

Digna Jimenez could not find new child care after her baby sitter slapped her daughter. When her welfare caseworker refused to help, Ms. Jimenez withdrew from workfare, preferring to reduce her welfare support by nearly 20 percent than risk her children's well-being.

RACHEL SWARNS, "MOTHERS POISED FOR WORKFARE FACE ACUTE LACK OF DAY CARE," *New York Times*, APRIL 14, 1998

A homeless woman in a workfare program filed a sexual harassment claim saying her supervisor continually made comments about her body and had once said he would help get her a job if she would go to a motel with him. "His conduct made me feel embarrassed and worthless, and affected my ability to do my job," she stated.

DAVID L. LEWIS, "WORKFARE WOMAN CLAIMS SEXUAL HARASSMENT," *New York Daily News*, MARCH 12, 1998

Keisha, a 28-year-old mother of two, was delighted to be accepted for nurse's training. But in order to qualify for childcare under the Ohio Work Program (a workfare program), she could not spend more than 10 hours a week in training while also working 20 hours a week at a job. Keisha may have to forgo training for a better job, and stay in a lower paying job to abide by the new welfare rules.

ARTHUR JONES, "NEW LAW MEANS MORE POVERTY," *National Catholic Reporter*, APRIL 17, 1998

1

Rosa Dolone goes by subway from food pantry to food bank in the Bronx, begging for groceries. As an immigrant, albeit legal, she has been dropped from the food stamp rolls. Even though one church food pantry won't accept her without a referral and another has run out of food, she keeps going, since "My children have to eat."

RACHEL L. SWARNS, "DENIED FOOD STAMPS, MANY LEGAL IMMIGRANTS SCRAPE FOR MEALS," *New York Times,* DECEMBER 9, 1997

These stories, women's stories, are the reason for this book. Recent welfare legislation has profoundly affected the lives of poor women in the United States. Feminist ethical work, accountable to promote the well-being of women, is required to respond to this situation. This accountability may even be greater for feminist Christian ethicists (the location of most of the contributors to this volume), since they also speak out of strands of Christian traditions that have called for justice for the poor and the most vulnerable members of our society.

The 1996 welfare legislation effectively dismantled the over-sixty-year legacy of federal responsibility for poor families in the United States. The Personal Responsibility and Work Opportunity Reconciliation Act (PRWORA) has initiated a historical restructuring of U.S. welfare policy by the federal government, states, and counties that is affecting the well-being of millions of women, children, and poor men. Our purpose is to expose critical assumptions that inform the welfare reform discussion and to explore some resources for shaping a policy discussion more accountable to the needs of women and children. Such work is urgent, we believe, as the current law will be reviewed by Congress in 2002.

In recent years, welfare dependency has emerged as a focus of public policy debate in a national economy that is booming but whose benefits accrue primarily to a small portion of the population. The majority suffers from economic insecurity, resulting from an increase in downsizing, low-wage work, underemployment, and the stagnation of real wages. Those at the bottom sectors of the economy, disproportionately women and people of color, suffer these effects with the greatest intensity. However, moral rhetoric about the poor is always careful to shift public attention away from critical analysis of the political economy, which has been radically restructured in the past quarter-century as capitalism becomes a global system. Public attention continues to be maintained now, as in the past, on the regulation of individual behavior, especially female sexual behavior, cast as "personal responsibility."

All of the chapters in this book resist this focus, insisting that ethical approaches to welfare policy must include critical feminist analysis of the political economy and of religious and other cultural ideologies that support the status quo. It is this perspective that distinguishes our work from that of some other recent work in Christian ethics, such as that done by the Center for Public Justice. While we share their Christian affirmation of human dignity, multifaceted responsibility, and a government called to establish public justice, we note the reluctance to identify the specific condition of poor women and the silence on the destructive impact of global capitalism.[1] We understand current welfare legislation in the United States to be part of the larger restructuring of late twentieth-century neoliberal corporate capitalism, which we will discuss in greater depth in the next section. In light of this understanding, we are especially concerned with the lack of attention to the economy in the welfare discussion. In this country, when we are electing presidents who can affect the well-being of the comfortable, we can cry "It's the economy, Stupid," but when we talk about welfare, the concern is economizing rather than the economy itself.

Thus, our purpose is to bring together in this volume progressive feminist religious voices that seek to make the economy and its complex effects more visible. While we highlight the exploitative power of economic forces, we simultaneously emphasize the complex interconnections with the historical forces of race and gender. Some authors focus more on macroanalysis—the big picture; others on microanalysis—details of the legislation. Some advocate major transformation of the political economy, others incremental change. While some are more focused on economic questions and others more on questions of race, sexuality, or ideological formation, all focus on the root causes of poverty.

We ourselves, the editors of this volume, speak specifically from materialist feminist Christian perspectives which draw on feminist and Christian traditions that are critical of the economy and on legacies of movements for social change.[2] Even though not all of the contributors would identify themselves in this way, we find each piece represented here makes a contribution toward the common goals of critiquing oppressive structures that thwart the well-being of poor women and their families and calling for new policies answerable to their needs.

In the remainder of this essay, we will offer some resources helpful for engaging the work of this volume by providing introductions to neoliberal economics, recent welfare legislation, and feminist Christian ethical approaches to public policy questions. Each of these sections will provide some basic information for readers new to these areas while further articulating the assumptions underlying our approach. They reflect the work of feminist Christian ethics, attentive to material realities while in dialogue with critical moral norms.

Welfare and Neoliberal Economic Policy

We understand welfare dismantling to be part of the larger system of neoliberal structural adjustment policies which are intensifying poverty for the majority of the world's population under the new conditions of the capitalist global economy. In the previous three decades, the post–World War II economic expansion by the United States has been replaced by fierce economic and financial competition among U.S.-, Japanese-, and Western European–based corporations. Although 85 percent of industrial output is still produced by national corporations, global production is increasingly dominated by relatively few corporations and mobile financial institutions. Investors no longer find themselves accountable to the communities and regions where they do business and can roam the planet for the best business deals (or, even more frequently, can threaten to do so). Class power has shifted with the "exit threat" of capital, which holds governments and workers hostage to its demands.[3]

These demands include nonrestrictive access to world markets, massive reductions in international and domestic labor costs, and increased state subsidies for the other costs of corporate profit making. This is accomplished through such neoliberal economic policies (often called economic "reforms") as free trade agreements, privatizing the public nonprofit sector, and "downsizing" the private sector. On a global scale, these policies promote the mechanization of higher-skilled work traditionally monopolized by men, the proliferation of low-wage labor increasingly dominated by women and children, and massive cuts in state spending for social welfare and environmental protection. They encourage foreign ownership of Two-Thirds World economies through short-term investments that can be pulled out abruptly at the first sign of lowering returns on profits. The economies cannot protect themselves against capital fluctuation, creating the need for massive bailouts and more severe adjustment policies as seen recently in Mexico and east Asia. Side effects of these polices include increased trafficking in armaments, which is profitable to countries like the United States, while also providing weaponry to repress resistance to the impact of these economic policies. Intensive and mobile industrial development has also severely impacted environments throughout the globe, from the depletion of rain forest resources to the dangerous pollution of many Two-Thirds World cities.

As a result of such policies which serve the profit-making interests of relatively few shareholders, income inequality is growing within as well as among nations. National and state legislatures find themselves competing with each other to subsidize jobs that may soon become lost altogether to technology, or are deskilled and devalued. Governments find themselves vulnerable to the demands of big business because it is often the only economic game in town and/or because they need relief from the escalating debt that plagues their economies.

The new so-called efficiency of neoliberal economic policy is, in large part, simply reflecting the shifting of costs from a paid labor force onto the invisible backs of women in the household. The theory of economic structural-adjustment policy is that an economy will be stronger if it is structured to serve a world market which makes profits for relatively few investors, with no consideration of social needs. States are supposed to assume that the experiences of belt-tightening due to higher prices for necessities, lower wages, and higher unemployment will be temporary until "trickle down" from long-term growth takes effect. Structural adjustment includes reducing the role of the state (by defunding environmental protection, education, and other social services) and increasing the role of the market. Such austerity plans have been initiated by the International Monetary Fund and the World Bank in the Two-Thirds World as a condition for refinancing a country's loans. In the United States, we have been experiencing deregulation, regressive tax policies, the dismantling of welfare, and moves to privatize increasing sectors of the economy like Social Security, Medicaid, public education, and transportation. We have seen a radical restructuring of the labor market, where 80 percent of workers have lost 20 percent of buying power over the last two decades and where over one-third of the work force (predominantly female) does contingent labor. The overall effect of these policies, in both the Two-Thirds World and the United States, has been a significant increase in women's work as they seek to "bridge the gap" between the needs of their families and the income available.

In a possible reversal of thirty years of small but measurable economic progress for women (as well as for many men), most women's overall situation has deteriorated since the onset of structural-adjustment policies. As governments cut education, health clinics, hospital stays, food subsidies, transportation, and other social services, household labor must increase to fill the gaps. Not only does unpaid domestic labor intensify as women care for the sick, educate the young, and try to grow more of their own food, but female employment increases exponentially. This is true not only in the United States but throughout the globe as women drop out of education and enter the expanding sectors of informal and low-wage labor, often in an effort to replace earnings from the better-paid jobs lost to men. As men migrate in search of employment, the number of female-headed households depending on their unstable and insufficient resources increases. As companies pressure one another to keep costs down in order to win the competitive game by making the highest profits, there is little doubt that women—especially poor women— have borne the brunt of neoliberal economic policy.

In this process of economic transformation, however, the neoliberal policies of late capitalism also threaten to erode other structures that historically have been important in maintaining the status quo in the United States. These include the male-dominant traditional family, the racially segregated labor market, and social expenditures in health, education, and welfare which historically have protected people from the worst fallout of the economic system. As female-headed families replace male-dominant ones, as whites join diverse peoples of color at the expanding lower rungs of labor markets, and as economic insecurity increases for larger sectors of the population, rising cultural anxieties and the need to protect relatively few shareholders at the top lead people to search for scapegoats to explain and justify these radical inequalities.

Welfare for poor families becomes a likely target, since historically it has provided the symbolic social space to assemble and reinforce racist, class-elitist, and gender-polarized religious and cultural values which have served to maintain the social order. If the behaviors of poor women, especially poor mothers of color, can be identified as the reasons for family instability, deepening poverty, and increasing economic insecurity for the majority, then the actual structural dynamics that systematically reproduce these outcomes remain invisible. Also escaping notice are the increases in women's unpaid domestic labor, which must remain unlimited and free in order for structural adjustments to "work."

As women throughout the globe underwrite its costs, neoliberal economic policy intensifies the inequalities promoted by class, race, and gender structures. It is these structures and the ideologies they promote that this book seeks to address and evaluate. In a time of escalating unmet domestic needs and increasing numbers of jobs that pay less than a living wage, welfare and other social services that provide people with some meager alternatives are being dismantled amidst intense attack. It is our contention that politicians, conservative think tanks, and the media use welfare issues as a foil for the economic interests they serve and the religious and cultural beliefs that maintain the status quo.[4]

Welfare Policy

Capitalism has always reproduced poverty and has struggled to contain its effects. During the Depression era, the Roosevelt administration realized that poverty could no longer be managed at the state level. The New Deal initiated a two-track federal welfare system. The first track, offered to those who were "independent" workers, included social insurance programs like unemployment and old-age insurance and offered aid as entitlements. Second-track public assistance programs like Aid to Dependent Children (ADC), which later became Aid to Families with Dependent Children (AFDC), were constructed as charity to those deemed "fit and proper"—at first, only white widows and their children. Welfare rights advocates organized in the 1960s to change the terms of welfare programs and to expand coverage. It was during this period that AFDC became a legal entitlement: if you met the financial criteria, you were entitled to assistance. As welfare beneficiaries came to be perceived as undeserving members of different racial and class groups, demands for "reform" began, which, in the context of increasing global economic pressures, have eventually developed into the current welfare legislation.

PRWORA, the Personal Responsibility and Work Opportunity Reconciliation Act of 1996 (Public Law 104-93) was a deliberate departure from the heritage of these policies. PRWORA dismantled welfare programs for poor families by, among other things, ending the federally mandated entitlement status, which ensured at least provisional benefits for anyone across the country who fell below a certain income level. It abolished AFDC, JOBS (the work and training program for welfare recipients), and Emergency Assistance to Families with Children (a program that provided emergency help to families with children).

All of these programs were replaced with Temporary Assistance for Needy Families (TANF), a block grant of federal funds distributed to the states. PRWORA requires states to operate welfare programs but gives them flexibility in allocating TANF funds—a percentage of which may be transferred into child care and development, community service jobs and employment incentives, or social service block grants. States were given increased authority to determine eligibility and to administer cash assistance, employment and training, and child-care funds in accordance with federal guidelines. These require that most parents must participate in work activities within two years and that individuals who have received aid for more than two months do "community service," unless a state opts out of this requirement. States were required to assess recipients' skills and could develop "personal responsibility plans" for individuals. Families were limited to a lifetime total of five years of cash assistance, although states may grant hardship exemptions to up to 20 percent of the average monthly caseload. States could deny cash benefits to children born to welfare recipients (the "family cap"). Food stamps for noncitizens were eliminated. Overall, cuts in federal funds for these welfare programs were projected to be a total of $54 billion over six years.

The Balanced Budget Act of 1997 made some adjustments to the 1996 legislation. Minimum-wage protection was to be applied to required jobs. A $1.5 billion "welfare-to-work" grant program was created to be distributed to the states in fiscal years 1998 and 1999, for use through 2001. Although further funds were added in the 1997 budget, the total is still not adequate to cover the cost of these programs. Recent increases in funds for child health and child care enacted by the federal government and some states are also insufficient to address needs.[5] The 1997 act and further 1998 legislation restored food stamps to certain categories of legal aliens, leaving many still without access to food relief.

One critical outcome of PRWORA was to change welfare from a program administered under common federal guidelines to programs that could vary widely according to different state mandates. Thus, assessing the impact of PRWORA requires a state-by-state analysis, which will take several years. The Children's Defense Fund issued a report in the fall of 1997 as an initial assessment of state programs developed in response to the federal legislation.[6] According to the report, twenty states have revised PRWORA's five-year maximum lifetime limit by allowing shorter stays over a longer period or by selecting various time limits of less than five years. The report indicated that advocates in some states have been successful in creating programs that are beneficial to poor children and help families go to work. States recognized for positive programs include Minnesota, Utah, Illinois, New York, and Ohio. Other states, however, are taking steps that will increase the severity of the new federal rules as they allow thousands of families to lose aid (fifteen states have implemented two-year time limits on welfare provision). Especially high termination rates have been observed for families in Mississippi, Massachusetts, Iowa, South Carolina, Virginia, and Wisconsin.[7]

The report noted that approximately one-third of families nationally (3.4 million out of 10.7 million) have been dropped from the rolls since 1993. It is estimated, however, that only 15 percent of these 3.4 million families left the roles because of increased parental earnings. It appears that most closings were due to a failure to comply with welfare rules, indicating that many families may be falling into increased immiseration. A New York state survey found that only 29 percent of those who went off New York welfare rolls from July 1996 through March 1997 found full-time or part-time work in the first several months without assistance. Between October 1997 and October 1998, the Wisconsin rolls fell by 70 percent. However, a University of Wisconsin study found that 75 percent of those who left for new jobs lost these jobs within nine months.[8]

It is not hard to be dropped from the system. The rules vary from state to state and may not even be uniform across a state. Often they are so confusing that welfare workers in the same state may often give clients different and contradictory information.[9] Minnesota case managers found that up to 75 percent of adults who had been sanctioned had at least one barrier to employment: either domestic violence, physical disability of parent or child, depression, or substance abuse.[10] A newspaper reporter accompanying a woman whose inability to find child care qualified her for exemption from the work requirement found that the social worker threatened her by stating falsely that the law had changed.[11]

Counties also have flexibility to develop their own programs within the bounds set by federal and state legislation. Los Angeles County in California has the largest welfare system of any county in the nation and is also larger than that of many states. In early 1998, more than 1.6 million county residents received some form of public assistance, with 768,000 enrolled in TANF, the largest cash-assistance program (which replaced AFDC). The Los Angeles County welfare program, adopted by county supervisors at this time, exempts mothers of children under one year old from work requirements, as permitted by state legislation. However, other single parents are required to participate in thirty-two hours of work or related activities per week to maintain their eligibility for a cash grant.[12] Los Angeles County's welfare-to-work program has received a national service excellence award. However, 85 percent of welfare recipients placed in employment remain on the welfare rolls because they cannot earn enough to provide their families with the minimum necessities.[13] A survey conducted by Diana Pearce for Wider Opportunities for Women found that mothers in urban California must earn two to three times the minimum wage to escape the need for government assistance and just to cover housing, child care, transportation, and medical needs. An adult with one infant would need $12.24 an hour, or with one infant and a preschooler, $16.24 an hour. In western Massachusetts, the Pearce study found that a woman with two children would have to earn $13.98 an hour, or almost $30,000 a year, in order not to have to choose between basic necessities, for example, between housing and health care.[14]

What will happen to these families when they reach the maximum five-year period for receiving benefits? The state of California did pass legislation that assures "continued but reduced assistance to children" once the family's time limit is reached (using state dollars since federal dollars cannot be used for this purpose).[15] But what will happen when this time actually comes, particularly if the state is in another period of recession?

Observers have already seen an increase in the numbers of the working poor seeking food aid. A survey by the U.S. Conference of Mayors reported that 86 percent of cities surveyed noted an increased demand for emergency food assistance, rising an average of 16 percent. And 38 percent of people seeking this assistance are actually employed, up from 23 percent in 1994. An increase in the number of working poor seeking food aid does not bode well for the success of welfare reform if our criteria for success is lifting people out of poverty. Nor does an increase in the number of women with children among the U.S.

homeless. An October 1998 survey by the International Union of Gospel Missions found a dramatic increase in the number of homeless women with children—from 46 percent of homeless families in 1991 to 66 percent in 1998. One-fifth of homeless families surveyed had lost AFDC and/or food stamps in the past year.[16]

While the purported major objective of PRWORA was making people "responsible" by bringing them into the waged work force, recent studies of workfare programs, which place welfare recipients in jobs, are extremely troubling. In an economy where thirty-year-old white, male high-school graduates have seen their real wages drop 35 percent in the last twenty years, workfare increases the competition for these low-wage jobs, potentially throwing even more workers into welfare poverty. According to the Children's Defense Fund, there are only enough new jobs nationwide to employ 54 percent of welfare recipients. The Midwest Job Gap Project discovered that in Ohio in 1997, there were four job-seekers for every low-skilled job; twenty-three potential workers for every low-skilled job that paid at least poverty-level wages ($12,278 annually); sixty-six for those that paid at least 150 percent of poverty level wages ($18,417); and one hundred for every one that paid what was estimated to be a living wage for families with children ($25,907).[17]

Nor can workfare jobs be seen as stepping stones to better-paying work. Restrictions on education and training enacted in the 1996 law were greatly tightened by the 1997 federal Balanced Budget Act, which makes it nearly impossible for adult welfare recipients to acquire the skills for decent-paying jobs. In contrast to prior welfare programs, TANF does not consider higher education to be work, only vocational education. And even if a woman pursues vocational education, work requirements permit only 30 percent of those on state rolls who are classified as working to be engaged in vocational education and only twelve months of support are allotted. Although women might try to attend college on their own time, there is little time left after work requirements and family needs are fulfilled. Indeed, there has been a dramatic decrease in the numbers of welfare recipients enrolled in community college, university, and adult education programs.[18] A *New York Times* report on the Work Experience Program, a New York City workfare program, remarks that "Much of the work is so menial that it offers few, if any, skills that employers demand," such as cleaning city offices and picking up trash in parks.[19] Further, workers are forced to do this unsanitary, sometimes dangerous, work under inhumane conditions, including lack of access to toilets and lack of basic equipment such as coats and boots for street sweepers.[20] It seems that work requirements are creating a "permanent underclass of workers that will be a source of slave labor for both public and private sectors."[21] A hopeful sign is efforts by some employers to work with job training programs, but these experiments are still rare.

Welfare reform may also make women more vulnerable to various forms of abuse and endangerment. Since many women enter welfare programs in order to leave abusive male partners, decreased access to benefits may compel them to remain. Strengthened paternity identification requirements, while encouraging paternal responsibility, can also force women to have greater contact with violent partners. Teenage mothers are required to live with their parents, which in some cases may expose them to further sexual abuse and also make their whereabouts known if they are in danger from violent partners. Women and their children may also be physically endangered if family cap rules discourage them from seeking prenatal care.

Since the 1996 welfare bill was not constructed with careful planning, foresight, or reasoned debate but rather was based on stereotypes, myth, and political ideology, no one has a handle on what may lie in store for poor families in the years ahead. Despite seven years of almost uninterrupted growth in the U.S. economy since 1989, the 13.7 percent official poverty rate for 1997 was higher than in 1989. Many analysts believe that these official figures would be much higher if they reflected the actual cost of living and after-tax income. In their 1986 pastoral letter on the economy, the U.S. Catholic bishops stated that perhaps one-fourth of the population was living below "any reasonable standard" of need.[22] Some studies estimate that 50 million Americans, or almost one-fifth of the population, live below the national poverty line, including one-fourth of U.S. children under the age of eighteen.[23] Yet while thousands of families are leaving the welfare rolls for greater immiseration and the poverty rate for children of workers is on the rise, experts on state fiscal affairs predict that at least one-half of the states will enact substantial tax cuts in 1998.[24] Even with the severe cuts in taxes for the wealthy (for example, the corporate share of tax revenue has decreased from 20 percent thirty years ago to 12.5 percent now),[25] most states are sitting on sizable tax surpluses. Such surpluses are unlikely to be redistributed to the poor and working class. For them, average weekly earnings have declined by almost one-fifth since 1973. The income gap is increasing everywhere in the nation. In New York state, for example, the gulf between the top fifth and bottom fifth of families has increased 127 percent since the 1970s.[26] Richard Freeman, a Harvard economist, fears that given these shifts and the elimination of the welfare safety net, any downturn in the economy will mean "that the bottom will literally fall out for Americans at the bottom of the income distribution."[27] In our future may be what Freeman has called the "apartheid economy," divided between the privileged "haves" and the destitute poor.

Feminist Ethics and Public Policy

Neoliberal economic policies and "reforms" such as welfare dismantling create social structures and systems that make the liberty of the market and profit for investors the unchallenged social priority. These structures channel funding from the bottom and middle sectors in the economy to those privileged at the top, and are unassailable in the media and dominant cultural ideology. Corporate and labor market structures, among other forces, systematically reproduce routinized inequality and injustice which fly in the face of principles of social ethics, especially feminist social ethics.

Feminist Christian ethics has something to say about welfare dismantling because it draws upon theological traditions and moral resources that are pertinent to the public policy debate. As Christian feminist ethicists, we find ourselves equipped with a rich set of resources as well as traditions that need to be challenged for considering questions of public policy such as welfare. We recognize, as Ruth Smith's discussion of Christian attitudes toward poverty shows, that Christian traditions have often used the poor as objects of charity, enabling the salvation of others through the economic and political perpetuation of poverty. And as both Janet Jakobsen's and Elizabeth Bounds's discussions of the Christian right demonstrate, contemporary conservative Christianity is actively engaged in constructing poor women (and men) as dangerous bodies, requiring moral regulation and rehabilitation. However, while acknowledging these oppressive strands, we also find that as we put feminism and Christianity into dialogue, transformative places emerge which strengthen the seeking of justice. We will point out a few of these transformative places in the formation of Christian feminist public ethics, noting their presence in the different chapters included in this volume:

Engagement and Accountability

Feminist ethics seeks not to be one more academic conversation but tries to follow the heritage of women's movements which have sought to change their communities. Christian ethics (although by now endowed with plenty of academic discussions), at heart, is also practical, seeking to discern the activities of Christian persons in the world. Such practical concerns mark every contribution in this volume from Ellen Marshall's suggestions for reforming Individual Responsibility Plans to Traci West's suggestions for antiracism work in the churches and Joan Sakalas's suggestions for developing a just, faith-based outreach support.

The practicality arises from a sense of accountability. Feminist policy proposals are not constructed while considering a generalized group of citizens but in engagement with the concrete struggles of women and of the men and children surrounding them. Feminists see themselves accountable to those within their own communities (evident particularly in the works of womanist and *mujerista* ethicists) and to women elsewhere in the nation and the world who struggle against exploitation and domination. Such accountability demands taking these women's experiences as central to the doing of ethics and considering their well-being as the focal point for policy making. It intersects with strands of Christian liberation theologies, which have sought to keep the poor at the center of moral and theological reflection.[28] This accountability is most vividly present in Joan Sakalas's reflection on a group of women in New York City, struggling to determine their lives. Her focus—to move, as she puts it, "from margin to center"—can be discerned in all the essays in this volume, which, regardless of the scope of their concerns, always keep at the center the present sufferings of women who are forced to rely on welfare.

Staying with the Concrete

Although feminist ethics may speak in a variety of voices, using many different theoretical modes, it is always attentive to the concrete, starting with the complexity of women's stories. As Beverly Harrison has explained, "A treatment of any moral problem is inadequate if it fails to analyze the morality of a given act in a way that represents the concrete experience of the agent who faces a decision with respect to that act."[29] The chapters in this volume construe the concrete in all of its multilayered complexity. Traci West, for example, looks at the ways in which the media and the government distorted the concrete realities of poor, black teenage mothers through inaccurate and unjust stereotypes. Gloria Albrecht uses women's experiences to reconstruct notions of dependency as she shows how the economy has had a profound effect on current family life. And Ada María Isasi-Díaz insists upon the centrality of *lo cotidiano* (the everyday) as the "first horizon" of *mujerista* ethics.

Complex Standpoints

Although it may seem paradoxical, careful attention to and analysis of the concrete requires, ultimately, complex and multifaceted theoretical frameworks. Close analysis of any particular moment leads to consideration of the contradictory and multiple forces that constitute that moment. This recognition has been slow in coming for white feminism, where pressure to shed a diverse consciousness encouraged a virtually unidimensional focus on gender.[30] However, challenges from women of color both within and outside of the United States, poor women of all races, lesbian women, disabled women have all shifted the single lens to a kaleidoscope which can encompass the multiple structures at work. As Nancy Fraser remarks, "The task facing feminists is formidable. If we are to have any hope of understanding just what it is we are up against, we need...frameworks that are sensitive to specificity, but that nevertheless permit us to grasp very large objects of inquiry, such as the global economy. We also need approaches that promote our ability to think relationally and contextually."[31]

While no single one of us can ever accomplish this task, the variety of lenses used here demonstrate a common understanding that only multidimensional theories are equal to the task. This complexity reveals itself in an acknowledged insistence on engagement with multiple dimensions of social reality—as when, for example, Traci West keeps race, class, and gender in tension in her analysis of the stigmatizing of black women or when Ada María Isasi-Díaz points to the intersecting social and economic forces constituting both Cuban and U.S. realities. It also reveals itself in a less-acknowledged assumption that feminist ethics is interdisciplinary, drawing on a variety of disciplines to get the fullest possible account of the problem at hand. For example, in order to comment on wage proposals for women, Carol Robb draws on both feminist moral theories and feminist economic theories to show that gender socialization shapes moral rationality in economic decision making. Janet Jakobsen's discussion of the regulation of sexual morality shaped by a restructuring postmodern capitalism uses both poststructuralist and postcolonialist theories. Mary Hobgood draws on class theory in her analysis of the intensification of poverty, racism, and sexism to evaluate the strengths and limitations of the U.S. Catholic bishops' response to the welfare reforms.

Critical Perspectives

While drawing on multiple perspectives and disciplines, feminist ethics does not content itself with a liberal pluralism but rather seeks to find vantage points that both illuminate and criticize. The possible location of such emancipatory criticism is a topic of debate in current feminist theory, as postmodern and poststructuralist theorists point out the ways in which criticism may avoid the exclusions and limitations of its own position.[32] While we recognize this problem of location, our concern here is to provide some perspectives other than those most widely heard in the welfare debates. All of our authors hope to provide insights into the mystification of economic and social power and the scapegoating of poor persons. Using differing theoretical frameworks, they subject welfare policies to sharp criticism, pointing to places for resistance to the status quo. Ruth Smith traces the limitations of approaches to the poor and poverty from early Christian history to contemporary social theory and liberation theologies that maintain spiritual and economic hierarchies. In Smith's discussion of poverty and Jakobsen's exploration of freedom, we see how ideologies weave a cloth of "common sense" that hides the seams of struggles and inconsistencies. Gloria Albrecht challenges assumptions of liberal and communitarian discussions of family and poverty. Mary Hobgood reveals the oppressive structures of current economic policies and the weaknesses of moral and theological statements that seek to alter them. Emilie Townes names the forces behind our "age of spectacle."

Relationality, Dignity, and Autonomy

There are a variety of moral norms shared by feminist and Christian ethics. First, there is both an ontological and a moral insistence on the relationality of all things. From Paul's image of the body of Christ to the U.S. Catholic bishops' statement that the human person is social and has obligations to all of society, Christianity has affirmed the relational nature of human life. Similarly, feminist work consistently stresses what Beverly Harrison calls "the centrality of relationship...the reality that our moral-selves are body-selves who touch and see and hear each other into life."[33] Emilie Townes insists upon the fundamental relationality of the African American community, "interactive and interdependent in a spirituality of wholeness."[34]

Such relationality seems little acknowledged in a welfare debate that defines individual responsibility as complete self-sufficiency, in ways antithetical to feminist and Christian thought. The autonomy of "personal responsibility" (a slogan of the welfare debate) is assessed in light of ideologies that ignore our basic interdependence. Elizabeth Bounds notes how women's dependence on men always has been the other side of male-defined self-sufficiency, which has enabled poor black women to be labeled as "improperly dependent." Gloria Albrecht points to the ways in which the economic well-being and status of affluent families have always been dependent on the unpaid labor of poor persons. Stepping outside of this dichotomy of independence/dependence, Pamela Brubaker tests current welfare reform in light of *inter*dependence, a theo-ethical norm derived from an acknowledgment of relationality. Joan Sakalas demonstrates a program that seeks empowerment through the strength of interdependence.

Yet feminist and Christian ethics do not reject autonomy when viewed within a context of responsible interdependency. Christian traditions have continually stressed the worth of the individual, created in God's image. In discussing reproductive rights, rape, and domestic violence, feminists have called for a women's right to body autonomy, to control what happens to her physical and emotional self. The valuing of the human—particularly here the female human—leads to assertion of the importance of enabling one to live with dignity and with the ability to shape as much as possible the circumstances of one's life. The question for feminists is how to balance the goods of autonomy and relationality. As one possibility, Ellen Marshall draws on Amartya Sen's notion of "freedom to achieve" as a form of autonomy that understands the individual as not isolated but as a person in society.

Connections of Public and Private

Both contemporary feminist and contemporary Christian ethics have struggled with a privatized location. In modern U.S. society, the church and women have been relegated to the feminized private sphere. In contrast, men are understood to inhabit a secular public sphere, conceptualized as a place where individual citizens make policy through the exercise of power. Over the past few decades, there has occurred a realignment of private and public. Persons and their issues from the "hidden" public of the black community and other marginalized racial/ethnic communities entered the public arena through civil rights legislation. Feminists brought into public discussion what were previously considered issues with few or no public moral dimensions: marriage, domestic violence, rape. Gay and lesbian persons continue to try to make sexual identity a public question involving rights and responsibilities.

For feminists, the public and private spheres must always be held in tension. From the early feminist insistence that "the personal is political" to Beverly Harrison's insistence that we connect "personal pains" to "the wider dynamics of the social system,"[35] feminists have examined the ways in which private and public intersect in the issues that concern us. Welfare, our subject here, is a wonderful example of the complexity of this interconnection. On one hand, it is clearly a public issue, subject to debate in the media and in the legislatures. On the other hand, what have been considered private issues—family, sexuality, race—have been very much part of the debate, as many of our contributors demonstrate. Janet Jakobsen, Gloria Albrecht, and Elizabeth Bounds all show how anxiety over the private world of family has been a central theme in welfare reform. Traci West shows how racialized and sexualized stereotypes profoundly affected public policy making.

Justice as Solidarity

Justice and love lie at the heart of Christian traditions. Feminism, which emerged around calls for justice for women, continues to have justice at its heart. Certainly in the welfare discussion *justice* was not a popular word. One key dimension of justice is the claiming of rights as part of the assertion of the dignity and well-being of persons. By removing the federal responsibility for welfare, the U.S. government removed the possibility of claiming welfare as a right. The emphasis instead was on "personal responsibility," a renunciation of collective obligations and a preoccupation with the morality of individual poor persons.

While we see rights as essential (since they are basic recognitions of the worth and dignity of persons), we do not, as both Christians and feminists, work with highly individualized notions of rights, preferring to see rights in the context of our basic relationality. As a norm, justice participates in many of the transformative places we have already discussed. It is a relational word, denoting accountabilities to others. Iris Young remarks that reflection on justice "begins in a hearing, in heeding a call,"[36]—that is, in response to the needs of others expressed through our relationship to them. In the welfare debates, this notion of justice as a mutual negotiation of needs was silenced in favor of an individualist model where, if one could not be "responsible" for providing for one's own needs, one should turn to charity. Yet charity, as Ruth Smith and Joan Sakalas point out, is preeminently a relationship among unequals, where the givers enhance their power and moral "goodness" and the receivers are considered dependent and morally inferior.

Justice as a relational category also requires attention to values of caring. Although no one in this volume draws upon the recent discussions concerning a distinctive feminine ethic of care,[37] we find that this discussion at its best highlights the importance of certain aspects of justice, such as mutuality and the creation and sustenance of positive human relationships. Attention to care also requires us to consider the realm of ordinary daily life where persons (primarily women) tend through caring labor to the daily needs of those around them. The degree of justice offered by any proposal for welfare policy must be measured in terms of its impact on the possibilities of providing care under conditions supporting the dignity and self-esteem of both the caregiver and the recipient.

Justice demands a full analysis of the social forces involved, so that we can understand just what needs to be changed and why. It is a norm of engagement rather than passivity. Such structural analysis, as found in these essays, is necessary, although not sufficient, for solidarity and coalition building. As Janet Jakobsen says, alliance politics is the very basis of an alternative possibility once we work to unearth the structural links among diverse oppressions. Speaking of Latinas, Ada María Isasi-Díaz writes, "Justice for us refers not only to what we receive but also to our active and effective participation in making justice a reality."[38] We find this a call to all of us to engage in the alliances necessary to transform unjust welfare policies.

Looking Ahead: Initial Policy Proposals

Whether stated or implicit, justice is perhaps the primary normative commitment uniting all of the contributors to this volume. While we acknowledge the ways a renewed language of "the common goal" may also orient people toward forms of mutual responsibility and common welfare, we insist that such language can perpetuate exclusion and domination if there is no attention to justice. The impetus behind this work is our hope that it will contribute, in at least some small way, to the realization of greater justice for poor women and their children than is possible under current welfare policies. We recognize the complexity of policy making, which is particularly evident in the post-PRWORA state-by-state variations in welfare law. Thus, we cannot pretend to advocate a clear set of specific policies, as these will have to emerge on a local basis.

What readers will find here are some base points, some fundamental moral considerations for constructing social policy for persons in poverty. What is morally at stake is the ability of women to achieve some measure of dignity and self-determination to provide for their own well-being and the well-being of those they love and for whom they are responsible. Proceeding from these feminist ethical values, we would like to enumerate, not a comprehensive program for social justice, but some components of what might comprise authentic welfare reform aimed at empowering poor women:

1. Our society needs to redefine work to include the socially necessary labor of caring for children, the sick, and the elderly, a task requiring the rethinking of the relationship of the public and private spheres. The mental, physical, and emotional caring labor that is absolutely necessary to maintain life and enhance its quality should secure for every household a tax-free income up to the actual cost of a decent standard of living. It should also include publicly subsidized high-quality child care. Public child care and the work of nurturing in the home can be remunerated out of public revenues secured through a more equitable tax code, including restoring more progressive corporate taxes and taxing household incomes above the decent standard of living level, regardless of their source, at progressively increasing rates.

2. Virtually full employment at above poverty wages and in conditions that support human dignity needs to be created to provide work for all who are able. Employment for all able to work can be achieved by shortening standard work time and creating additional work by publicly sponsored, socially necessary production. (Full employment does not exist now primarily because the competition for work among un-

employed people is necessary to decrease wages and increase profits.) Making work support human dignity means making work enhance self-respect, social recognition, and a sense of contributing to the commonweal. As work increasingly takes on these kinds of qualities, people do not have to be forced to do this work since it fulfills basic human needs for security and a sense of belonging to a community.

3. We need to provide a social context that sustains human communities. Such a context would include the publicly sponsored provision of socially necessary goods and services, such as affordable housing, universal health care, education, environmental protection, public transport, and infrastructure maintenance. Since these goods and services are considered "external costs" and unprofitable, they are not provided by our market-oriented, profit-making capitalist system. Policies preventing discrimination on the basis of race, gender, sexuality, age, and disability would also be a part of a supportive context.

4. We need a system of social security for all those not doing caretaking work in the home or attached to public labor. People unable to work include those involuntarily unemployed while searching for work, students, and people whose capacities for work are limited or nonexistent because of age, disabilities, and ill health.

5. We need to develop a policymaking system that draws upon the experience of past and present welfare recipients and includes them in program formation and policy evaluation. The formation of just policies requires the participation of all who are affected by their outcome.

Although we believe that only programs that include these five components can promote true "well fare," we also recognize that what may be offered instead are adjustments to basically unjust policy. Within this limited framework, we would call for the following:

- elimination of the five-year lifetime benefit limit or development of a more flexible exemption policy
- abolition of the family cap
- adoption of the family violence exemption as a federal mandate
- increase in the minimum wage to better approximate the wages required for adequate family provision
- more realistic work participation goals respecting the needs of adults to parent children
- provision of adequate health care and child care
- better evaluation of state performance to ensure that states are rewarded for promoting real self-sufficiency, not merely reducing welfare rolls

- promotion of education as an alternative to work, and more adequate job training
- monitoring of the health and safety of work conditions in workfare programs, including attention to any racial and sexual harassment[39]

We hope that the work in this volume, through its analysis of structural powers and its engagement in moral reflection upon welfare questions, will offer resources for evaluation and action for those both within and outside the Christian churches who work for a welfare system that ends rather than reproduces poverty. To seek authentic reform we need to engage in specific analyses as we forge alliances across boundaries of income level, gender, and race to create policy that will alter the welfare system and *stop this war against the poorest in our society.* We seek a world where no more Rosa Dolones travel the streets saying, "My children have to eat."

Notes

1. See "Appendix: A New Vision for Welfare Reform" in *Welfare in America: Christian Perspectives on a Policy in Crisis,* ed. Stanley W. Carlson-Thies and James W. Skillen (Grand Rapids, Mich.: Eerdmans, 1996), 551–79.

2. For an introductory discussion of materialist feminism, in relation to other forms of feminism, see the introduction to Rosemary Hennessy and Chrys Ingraham, *Materialist Feminism: A Reader in Class, Difference, and Women's Lives* (New York: Routledge, 1997), 1–14.

3. William Tabb, "Globalization Is an Issue, the Power of Capital Is the Issue," *Monthly Review* 49, no 2. (June 1997): 22; Frances Fox Piven and Richard A. Cloward, "Eras of Power," *Monthly Review* 50, no. 1 (January 1998): 20; Ellen Meiksins Wood, "Class Compacts, the Welfare State, and Epochal Shifts," *Monthly Review* 50, no. 1 (January 1998): 31, 41.

4. The argument in this section relies on M. Patricia Connelly, "Gender Matters: Global Restructuring and Adjustment," *Social Politics* 3, no. 1 (spring 1996): 12–31, and Pamela Sparr, ed., *Mortgaging Women's Lives: Feminist Critiques of Structural Adjustment* (London: Zed, 1994), 1–36, 183–201.

5. Children's Defense Fund, *Summary of the New Welfare Legislation,* Sept. 1996 (updated Oct. 22, 1997), 1–2.

6. Children's Defense Fund, *Special Report: Welfare to Work,* Oct. 1997.

7. Ibid., 5–9.

8. Raymond Hernandez, "Most Dropped from Welfare Don't Get Jobs," *New York Times,* March 23, 1998, A1; Jason DeParle, "Wisconsin Welfare Experiment: Easy to Say, Not So Easy to Do," *New York Times,* October 18, 1998, A1, A24.

9. *Survival News* 11, no. 1 (spring 1997): 34–36.

10. Children's Defense Fund, *The New Welfare Law: One Year Later*, March 1998.

11. Rachel L. Swarns, "Mothers Poised for Workfare Face Acute Lack of Day Care," *New York Times*, April 14, 1998, A20.

12. Carla Rivera, "County Supervisors Approve Bare-Bones Welfare Plan," *Los Angeles Times*, January 7, 1998, B8.

13. Leonard Schneiderman, "Perspective on Welfare," *Los Angeles Times*, January 9, 1998, B13. (Schneiderman is professor emeritus at the UCLA School of Public Policy and Social Research.)

14. Virginia Ellis, "Study Tracks Pay Women Need to Escape Welfare," *Los Angeles Times*, January 28, 1997, A3; Diana Pearce and Laura Russell, "The Self-Sufficiency Standard for Massachusetts," *Wider Opportunities for Women* (September 1998): 8.

15. Children's Defense Fund, *New Welfare Law*, 2.

16. Melissa Healy and Judy Pasternak, "New Face in Line at Soup Kitchen: Working Poor," *Los Angeles Times*, December 27, 1997, A14; *Religious News Service Digest*, November 23, 1998.

17. Children's Defense Fund, *New Welfare Law*.

18. "Welfare Reform and Post-Secondary Education: Research and Policy Update," *Welfare Reform Network News* 2, no. 1 (April 1998): 1–2.

19. Alan Finder, "Evidence Is Scant That Workfare Leads to Full-Time Jobs," *New York Times*, April 12, 1998, A8.

20. Ibid., A1.

21. *Western New York Peace Center Report* (Mar.–Apr. 1997): 4.

22. National Conference of Catholic Bishops, "Economic Justice for All: Catholic Social Teaching and the U.S. Economy," *Origins* 16, no. 24 (November 27, 1986): 411.

23. Holly Sklar, *Chaos or Community: Seeking Solutions Not Scapegoats for Bad Economics* (Boston: South End Press, 1995), 5, 12–13. See also Arloc Sherman et al., *Welfare to What: Early Findings on Family Hardship and Well-Being* (Washington, D.C.: Children's Defense Fund, 1998).

24. Kevin Sack, "Eager and Flush, Many States Plan Yet More Tax Cuts," *New York Times*, January 4, 1998, A1.

25. "Underground Economy," *The Nation*, January 12–19, 1998, 3–4.

26. Ibid.

27. Richard Freeman, "Unequal Incomes," *Harvard Magazine*, January–February 1998, 64.

28. For an introduction to Latin American liberation theologies, see Penny Lernoux, *Cry of the People* (New York: Doubleday, 1980), and Maria Pilar Aquino, *Our Cry for Life: Feminist Theology from Latin America* (Maryknoll, N.Y.: Orbis Books, 1993). For a focus on the liberation of Hispanic Ameri-

can women, see Ada María Isasi-Díaz, *En la lucha—In the Struggle: A Hispanic Women's Liberation Theology* (Minneapolis: Fortress, 1993).

29. Beverly Harrison, *Making the Connections: Essays in Feminist Social Ethics*, ed. Carol Robb (Boston: Beacon, 1985), 123.

30. Janet Jakobsen, *Working Alliances and the Politics of Difference* (Bloomington: Indiana University Press, 1998), 65.

31. Nancy Fraser, "Pragmatism, Feminism, and the Linguistic Turn," in *Feminist Contentions: A Philosophical Exchange*, ed. Seyla Benhabib et al. (New York: Routledge, 1995), 159.

32. For a good introduction to this debate, see the exchange in Benhabib et al., *Feminist Contentions*.

33. Harrison, *Connections*, 15.

34. Emilie Townes, *In a Blaze of Glory: Womanist Spirituality as Social Witness* (Nashville: Abingdon, 1995), 66.

35. Harrison, *Connections*, 247.

36. Iris M. Young, *Justice and the Politics of Difference* (Princeton, N.J.: Princeton University Press, 1990), 5.

37. Two key tests in this discussion are Carol Gilligan, *In a Different Voice: Psychological Theory and Women's Development* (Cambridge: Harvard University Press, 1987), and Nel Noddings, *Caring: A Feminine Approach to Ethics and Moral Education* (Berkeley: University of California Press, 1984). See also Barbara Andolsen, "Justice, Gender, and the Frail Elderly," *Journal of Feminist Studies in Religion* 9, nos. 1–2 (spring/fall 1998): 127–45, and Grace Clement, *Care, Autonomy, and Justice: Feminism and the Ethic of Care* (Boulder, Colo.: Westview Press, 1996).

38. Ada María Isasi-Díaz, "*Un poquito de justicia*—A Little Bit of Justice," in *Hispanic/Latino Theology: Challenge and Promise*, ed. Ada María Isasi-Díaz and Fernando E. Segovia (Minneapolis: Fortress, 1996), 237.

39. We are indebted to *Is It Reform? The 1998 Report of the Welfare and Human Rights Monitoring Project* (Boston: Unitarian Universalist Service Committee, 1998) and to David Gill of Brandeis University, "Toward Constructive Alternatives to the Welfare System," unpublished manuscript, 1997.

PART ONE

THEOLOGICAL AND PHILOSOPHICAL ETHICAL FRAMEWORKS

[1]

Making Women and Children Matter

A Feminist Theological Ethic
Confronts Welfare Policy

Pamela K. Brubaker

"We're already turning back people who need emergency food and it is going to get worse. I come from a poor family, and I know what it's like to not have food on a continuous basis—the feeling of not knowing where your next meal will come from. It's very disheartening, very frustrating. It's fearsome. It's scary. I've been tossing and turning in bed, . . . knowing there will be more poor people we can't help. But most people are not concerned because they have food security." —Herman Pena, manager of San Bernardino County Food Bank.

Los Angeles Times, MARCH 2, 1997

"The lowest you can get for rent is $450. I [have been] receiving $493. With the Pampers you have to get, the clothes you have to get, you're basically living on $20 a month. We are the guinea pigs of '97. They come out with these ideas to see if they're going to work and they try it out on us people without knowing what the result is going to be." —Yvonne Parris, twenty-six, living temporarily in a homeless shelter with her nine-month-old son because of eviction; monthly welfare payment reduced to $467 as result of federal welfare reform.

Los Angeles Times, JANUARY 1, 1997

One in five American children lives below the poverty line: 20.5 percent of children under eighteen years of age, 22.7 percent of children under six. Families with children under eighteen are three times more likely than families without children to be poor. This is particularly true of female-headed families. A majority of children (58.8 percent) under six living in female-householder families are poor.[1] Welfare programs such as Aid to Families with Dependent Children (AFDC), food stamps, and Medicaid, have been ways in which many poor children's basic needs are met. Without these programs, many children's life chances will be even more severely diminished. Thus, proposals for welfare reform must be evaluated from the perspective of these children and their families. Will their basic needs for food, shelter, clothing, education, and health care be adequately met?

Despite studies predicting that proposed legislation would throw more than 1 million more children into poverty,[2] Congress passed and President Clinton signed into law the Personal Responsibility and Work Opportunities Reconciliation Act (PRWORA) in August of 1996. This act dismantled AFDC and replaced it with Temporary Assistance to Needy Families (TANF). As of January 1, 1997, poor families are limited to a maximum of five years of federal cash assistance. Recipients are required to work within two years of signing up for welfare. No longer is there a guarantee of cash assistance to every eligible poor family with children. Cash welfare has been converted to block grants for states, which have more freedom to develop their own programs to move welfare recipients into jobs and are penalized if they do not.[3] With this federal legislation in place, the struggle has now moved to the state level.

Welfare reform is hotly contested terrain in the current political climate. Conservative critics charge that welfare programs erode the work ethic and traditional values and cause welfare dependency, rising rates of illegitimate births, teen pregnancy, and various social ills. It seems not to matter that there is little factual basis to the charges that welfare programs are the cause of these social ills.[4] Poor women and their children are convenient scapegoats for complex social and economic problems. Clearly, the well-being of children is not a central concern for conservative advocates of welfare "reform," for whom welfare is both a defense of traditional "family values" and an attack on government social spending. The lack of concern for families is evident in suggestions made by some conservatives that children whose parents cannot support them be taken away from them; equally evident is the lack of consideration by conservatives and liberals alike for the impact of cuts in benefits on children.

Why is it that poor children seem not to matter? Norton Grubb and Marvin Lazerson identify several factors in their book *Broken Promises: How Americans Fail Their Children*. Historically, family structure has changed from a predominance of extended families, with shared responsibility for children, to the nuclear family and the evolution of childrearing as a private responsibility. These developments have reinforced the tendency to differentiate sharply between one's own and other people's children. Structural inequalities along racial, class, and gender lines also affect and shape family relationships and children's opportunities, as well as public attitudes. "Class and racial biases harden the negative perception of other people's children." Grubb and Lazerson conclude that it is difficult to maintain a belief that children are a group deserving specific attention in a society with severe inequalities. When there are vast differences in income, advocacy of public responsibility for children seems to imply redistribution of resources from rich to poor, thus confirming the perception that "other people's children are costly liabilities."[5]

The gap between the wealthy and the poor in the United States continues to grow. Median family income showed the first statistically significant increase in six years in 1995, when it rose 2.7 percent. However, this was still below the median rate for 1989. In the period from 1974 to 1996, median income has increased just 1.6 percent, while in the period from 1947 to 1973, it doubled. Furthermore, the gap between the wealthy and the poor in the United States continues to grow and is the widest such gap in any industrialized country. By 1994, the top 1 percent controlled almost 40 percent of net worth. The top 10 percent owned 71 percent; the remaining 90 percent shared the other 29 percent.[6] This disparity in income and wealth, coupled with the stagnation in many families' incomes, is a factor in pressure for dismantling the welfare system.

A crucial factor in the calls for welfare reform, though, is political leaders' scapegoating of welfare recipients to deflect attention from the structural sources of economic inequality, such as the globalization of capital, changes in the labor market, and regressive taxation. Some citizens respond to stereotyping and scapegoating by asking why they should work and pay taxes to support people who are perceived to be irresponsible and lazy. However, polls show that children's issues—safety, health and education—are a top priority for voters, some of whom have expressed concern about the impact of welfare reform on poor children.[7]

The welfare debate is, among other things, a struggle over changing family structure, roles of women, caregiving, race, citizenship, and the state. At stake are different conceptions of the common good and the responsibility of the state for the general welfare. The term *welfare* at one time referred to the common good. The Preamble to the U.S. Constitution declares that the federal government was formed, among other reasons, "to promote the general welfare." I want to reappropriate this meaning of the term in order to develop an ethical conception of the common good in which poor women and children matter. I undertake this task in this chapter by presenting a theological ethic of compassion and solidarity, from which I develop criteria to evaluate conservative and liberal welfare reform proposals. Progressive public policy proposals grounded in conceptions of the common good in which women and children matter conclude the chapter.

A Feminist Ethic of Compassion and Solidarity

> To struggle against oppression, against alienation, is a matter of ongoing personal conversion that involves effective attempts to change alienating social structures. This personal conversion cannot happen apart from solidarity with the oppressed. . . . Who are the poor and oppressed for whom we must opt, with whom we must be in solidarity? They are the ones who are exploited, who suffer system violence, the victims of cultural imperialism. The poor and oppressed are those for whom the struggle to survive is a way of life.
>
> ADA MARÍA ISASI-DÍAZ, *Mujerista Theology*

A Theological Ethical Stance

My ethical stance is rooted in a Christian ethic of neighbor-love which has been deepened by the work of women of other racial/ethnic groups. I am a middle-strata, Anglo/white woman, the divorced mother of two grown sons. *Mujerista* theologian Ada María Isasi-Díaz teaches us that solidarity is a primary expression of love of neighbor. She calls those of us with some privilege to become friends of the oppressed, to join with them in the struggle for justice, liberation, and reconciliation.[8] I have found that compassion—the capacity to "feel with"—enables authentic solidarity. Through dialogue and friendship, compassion and solidarity are developed.

In a similar vein, womanist theologian Delores Williams challenges those who call themselves Christian to be in solidarity with suffering black people who struggle for survival/quality of life, including those "living in dire poverty, the poverty-stricken single parent trying to raise children."[9] Those like myself in positions of relative class, racial/ethnic, and/or gender privilege are summoned to see other people's children, as well as our own, as part of our community—or to speak theologically, to see them as part of the "kin-dom of God."[10] Isasi-Díaz's felicitous reimaging of the realm of God as an extended family is particularly appropriate to an ethic of compassion and solidarity. Additionally, it invokes Jesus' blessing of children, declaring that "it is to such as these that the [realm] of God belongs" (Mark 10:14), a blessing given despite the protests of the disciples, who wanted to keep the children out of the way.

Feminist biblical work also upholds an ethic of solidarity. The narrative of the Syro-Phoenician woman may be rhetorically invoked as a biblical metaphor for an ethical stance that embraces all children. This woman came from a different and despised ethnic group. She came to Jesus and begged him to cast the demon out of her daughter. Jesus said to her: "Let the children be fed first, for it is not fair to take the children's food and throw it to the dogs," emphasizing the distinction between the "chosen" children and "other" children. She responded, "Sir, even the dogs under the table eat the children's crumbs." In saying this, she disrupted sharp distinctions between children. Jesus told her, "For saying that, you may go—the demon has left your daughter" (Mark 7:24–30; also Matt. 15:21–28). Biblical scholar Laurel Schneider points out that the Syro-Phoenician woman "persisted in the face of overwhelming rejection." She suggests that although the woman seemed to accept Jesus' characterization of her people as dogs, by coming to Jesus she envisioned "the laying of a new table to which all are invited, under which none must grovel."[11] This narrative is a biblical remembrance of suffering, compassion, and solidarity.

Relevant Moral Principles

A feminist theological ethic may also articulate moral claims that are formulated in nontheological terms. These facilitate our ability to build alliances with nonreligious people in working for social justice. Two claims are particularly consequential for a more adequate conception of a common good in which women and children matter. These are: (1) the need to recognize interdependence as characteristic of our social relations and (2) the need to recognize the economic value of caregiving work. Both claims challenge androcentric and individualistic assumptions which undergird mainstream notions about dependency and economic value. In the following discussion, I will show that such assumptions do not adequately reflect our socioeconomic reality and are harmful to the well-being of poor women and children.

Interdependence

Assertions that social programs such as AFDC create welfare dependency have been a primary rationale in calls for welfare reform, which would end entitlement status for poor women and children. Empirically this claim is questionable: states with the lowest benefits tend to have the highest number of welfare recipients. Yet the claim is rhetorically effective in stigmatizing welfare recipients. Feminist social theorists Linda Gordon and Nancy Fraser charge that the term *dependency* "leaks a profusion of stigmatizing connotations—racial, sexual, misogynist, and more."[12] It is meant to conjure up an image of a "welfare queen"—a promiscuous, poor, black woman with several children sitting home and watching soap operas. (See the chapter by Traci West.) In the context of this debate, dependency is a morally reprehensible condition.

A careful examination of the meanings of dependency unsettles any such moral certainty. Historically, there has been a significant shift in the meaning of the word. Fraser and Gordon point out that at one time *dependency* meant gaining one's livelihood by working for someone—a situation in which many men were considered dependent. Today wage labor bestows independence, while counting on charity or welfare bestows dependency. These shifts reflect in part what Fraser and Gordon call "progressive differentiation of the official economy," the development of increasingly complex corporations (such as transnationals) and the expansion and segmentation of markets for commodities, labor, and capital.

> Before the rise of capitalism, any particular dependency was part of a net of dependencies, a single, continuous fabric of social hierarchies. Although women were subordinated and their labor often controlled by others, their labor was more visible, understood, and formally valued. With the emergence of religious and secular individualism, on the one hand, and industrial capitalism, on the other, a sharp, new dichotomy was constructed in which economic dependency and economic independence were opposed to one another. A crucial corollary of this dichotomy, and of the hegemony of wage labor in general, was the occlusion and devaluation of women's unpaid domestic and parenting labor.[13]

In other words, with the rise of capitalism, laborers who had been seen as economically dependent were now seen as independent. In the feudal system which predated capitalism, laborers were dependent on their masters, who in turn were dependent on someone above them in the social hierarchy. In this system, although women were subordinate, women's labor was visible and valued. With the development of wage labor under capitalism, women's household labor became invisible and devalued. While their wage-earning husbands were now perceived as "independent," they remained "dependent."

Diana Pearce, the activist and scholar who coined the term "feminization of poverty," also questions this valuation of dependent and independent. She rightfully argues that paid workers' perceived independence is possible because of "the hidden and unrecognized dependence the workers have on others," such as housewives and day care centers. Pearce suggests that we rehabilitate dependency as a valuable, even normal, human quality.[14]

Fraser and Gordon express caution about such an approach, noting that welfare recipients themselves saw the existing conditions of AFDC as wretched and damaging. They make a useful distinction between "socially necessary dependence,...the need for others' care that is an inescapable feature of the human condition," and "surplus dependence...rooted in unjust and potentially remediable social institutions." They further advocate transcending the dependence/independence opposition entirely, recognizing that in the contemporary world ever-higher relations of interdependence are created, based on ever-increasing divisions of labor. This necessitates a redefinition of work to include nonwage-earning labor, "such as housework and childcare, children's activity in attending school."[15] Our social reality is clearly one of interdependence.

Caregiving and Economic Value

Feminist social theorists Hilda Scott and Marilyn Waring pointed out over a decade ago that traditional women's work of caring is not given economic value unless it is commoditized—exchanged within the market. Even when commoditized, its value is low.[16] The devaluing of such work is questionable on both economic and ethical grounds. Economic theory is not value-free. It constructs reality, and, as now developed, theories of economic value do not value caregiving. Thus domestic labor such as food provision and preparation, child care, and family health maintenance are not counted as part of gross national product. This practice influences public policies and has a negative impact on women, children, and families, as was demonstrated by numerous studies during the United Nations Decade for Women (1975–85).[17]

Some feminist economists are now challenging reigning definitions of economic value, too. (See Carol Robb's chapter for a critical assessment.) Several members of the American Economic Association published a volume of essays, *Beyond Economic Man*, which its editors describe as the first of its kind, in the hope that it will lead to improving economic practice. Julie Nelson contends that economics has been too narrowly construed as the exchange of goods and services. She notes that Adam Smith, the founder of mainstream economics, understood economics to have a twofold focus: how society was organized by exchange and how society was provisioned. However, mainstream economics has focused solely on the organization of exchange—buying and selling. Nelson argues that economics should reclaim this concern for provisioning and engage itself "with the study of how humans, in interaction with each other and the environment, provide for their own survival and health."[18] Such a shift in focus would likely assure that unpaid caregiving activities are given economic value.

In this same volume, Diana Strassmann charges that limiting what counts as economics to buying and selling silences important objections to the "primacy of self-interested individualism and contractual exchange which reflect a male-centered and Western perspective on selfhood and individual agency." She cites Harvard economist Amartya Sen's questioning of the reliability of economic analyses based upon the story of the benevolent patriarch, a key component of mainstream economic theory. This story maintains that the male head of household makes choices that are in the best interest of his family, which is treated as an individual agent. Sen points out that the failure of many family patriarchs to act altruistically calls into question claims about the efficiency or optimal results associated with the workings of the market. Strassmann questions the "story of free choice," another key component of mainstream economic theory. She points out that there are constraints on choices—particularly for the young, women, and the elderly. She asks whether policy failures, "particularly the undue suffering of infants and children, may be partially attributable to the current thinking, of economics, which coheres with the American story of resources going to those who work for them and deserve them."[19] This belief is a corollary of the story of free choice, claiming that those who make good choices are rewarded and those who make poor choices suffer.

The insights of these feminist social theorists and economists on interdependence and the value of caregiving resonate with feminist theological criticisms of individualism and androcentrism. For instance, in her study of women's poverty, family policy, and practical theology, Pamela Couture critiques principles of personal responsibility and self-sufficiency as the basis for public policy. She offers instead the principle of shared responsibility, which she connects to interdependence and caregiving: "An ethic of care through shared responsibility allows room for the psychic empowerment of self-sufficiency by locating it within the larger context of interdependence." As a principle for public policy, shared responsibility would recognize that national policies "create conditions which impoverish women and children" rather than looking only to personal responsibility. With this recognition, policies would be developed to provide care for poor families and individuals on the basis of need to meet the basic needs of all for food, shelter, health care, and education.[20]

I draw on these principles of interdependence, valuing caregiving, and shared responsibility to develop criteria for evaluating current welfare reform proposals, the task of the next section. Are these proposals adequate in illuminating socioeconomic reality to account for sources of concrete suffering? Do they adequately meet basic needs and recognize the value of caregiving? Are they appropriate to our vision of a common good in which poor women and children matter?

Whose Welfare Matters? Analysis of Welfare Reform Proposals

"What's out there? McDonalds? Del Taco? I don't see how we're going to get off welfare and stay off welfare if we move on with no skills. We'll be right back where we started. We are scared our dreams might be taken away." —Luisa Ruiz, thirty-one-year-old community college student, high-school dropout, welfare recipient, and part-time worker.

Los Angeles Times, APRIL 13, 1997

Background

Since the New Deal in the 1930s, the United States has had a liberal form of welfare capitalism. Political scientist Gosta Esping-Anderson describes this as a residual welfare state which only reacts to what are perceived as market or family failures. Assistance is limited to marginal or especially deserving social groups.[21] As originally conceived, Aid for Dependent Children (ADC) was limited to dependent children of widows who maintained what was considered to be a proper middle-strata lifestyle. It was part of a two-track welfare system created during the New Deal.

The first track of the New Deal welfare system, according to Nancy Fraser and Linda Gordon, was social insurance programs, which included unemployment and old-age insurance. These programs offered aid as an entitlement to people with certain employment histories, "without stigma or supervision and hence without dependency." They were intended to replace temporarily the family wage. Few women and minorities were included in these programs, since domestic and agricultural workers (predominantly women and minorities) were exempted from them. Second-track public assistance programs like Aid to Dependent Children, which later became AFDC, were quite different from these first-track programs. They continued the practice of private charities which supported only those deemed "deserving." Because these programs were funded from general tax revenues instead of earmarked wage deductions, it seemed that recipients got "something for nothing." There were entirely different criteria for receiving aid: "means-testing, morals-testing, moral and household supervisions, home visits, extremely low stipends."[22]

Welfare rights advocates organized in the 1960s to change the terms of welfare programs and to expand coverage.[23] Beneficiaries came to be perceived as undeserving members of different racial and class groups. This was a significant factor in calls for welfare reform, which culminated in the dismantling of AFDC as of January 1, 1997. As states shape their own welfare programs, both conservative and liberal proposals are under consideration.

Conservative Proposals

Most of the policies supported by conservatives were incorporated into the adopted federal legislation (PRWORA). The most significant were ending the entitlement status of AFDC, putting a time limit on welfare benefits, and requiring recipients to work outside the home. Additional conservative proposals are not required by federal guidelines but may be instituted at the state level if conservatives have their way. Conservatives want now to abolish welfare altogether for unwed teen mothers. Also, states have the option to deny additional cash aid to welfare recipients who have children while receiving benefits. Some states have adopted these provisions.

States are also working out policies for meeting the federal work requirement, which mandates that states place at least 25 percent of cash welfare recipients in jobs or work programs by 1997, and 50 percent by 2002. Some conservative governors, such as Pete Wilson of California, have proposed that new mothers be required to go to work after only twelve weeks. He also proposed that recipients have twenty days for an up-front job search and that single parents must be in approved job activity thirty-two hours a week.[24]

Conservatives' proposals are based in a belief that poverty is a result of personal irresponsibility. This idea is a consistent theme in the debate on welfare reform in America, according to Joel F. Handler and Yeheskel Hasenfeld. They contend that "from the brief experiment with rehabilitation through social services (Eisenhower and Kennedy) to the concentration on the various work strategies, the focus has been on reforming the individual rather than on addressing the structural conditions of poverty."[25] This focus is consistent with conservative notions of the common good.

Conservatives generally envision the common good as being best served by a combination of an unregulated market, traditional families, and private charity. Each of these spheres is perceived as an autonomous, yet complementary, arena for the exercise of personal responsibility. In keeping with conservative views, there is no significant role for government in promoting the common good. Market efficiency, family discipline, and reform efforts of private charity are supposed to promote the common good. From this perspective, poverty is seen as a result of personal irresponsibility, not a failure in structural organization or institutional practice. At its crudest, this perspective is a form of social Darwinism: those who do not make it are considered unfit to survive.

This perspective does not adequately account for sources of concrete suffering. The separation of family and economic arenas from the political in conservative discourse biases this conception of the common good toward the advantaged. Nancy Fraser explains this dynamic in her discussion of the politics of needs interpretation. How do we decide what needs are legitimate and who has responsibility for meeting them? Needs are depoliticized when the political is separated from the domestic and the economic in social discourses about needs. Rather than recognizing that needs are interpreted and negotiated through political struggle, it is assumed that individuals identify and meet their own needs. In contemporary American society, this has the effect of advantaging dominant groups which have more political power to identify, legitimize, and fulfill their needs.[26] Thus, those in the capitalist, managerial, and entrepreneurial classes are understood to flourish because of the good choices they have made, not because of public policies such as mortgage interest deductions and corporate welfare, which benefit them. Likewise, poor single mothers, whether employed or not, are understood to suffer because of the poor choices they have made rather than public policies that make their needs invisible and provide no concrete opportunities to meet them. (See the chapter by Ellen Marshall.) Such an interpretation obscures rather than discloses the sources of concrete suffering.

Furthermore, market efficiency, family discipline, and private charity do not adequately redress the suffering of poor people. Unregulated market economies, particularly in a context of structural inequality such as exists in the United States, exacerbate poverty and economic injustice. For instance, poor people are not able to create sufficient demand for low-income housing, which is not as profitable for developers and the construction industry as other housing and real estate development. Nor are wages set by the low end of the labor market adequate to bring many poor people out of poverty.[27] Many poor people are employed, some full-time. The number of children in working poor families grew 30 percent, to 5.6 million, between 1989 and 1994. According to the Annie Casey Foundation, children in these families are "less likely to be fully immunized, less likely to enter school ready to learn, less likely to graduate and less likely to attend college."[28] Clearly, unregulated markets do not reduce poverty; they likely exacerbate it.

Nor do traditional families provide guarantees against poverty, as is evident from the number of two-parent families living below the poverty line.[29] Donald Hernandez found that although the overall poverty rates of children might have been 2 to 4 percentage points lower without the rise in mother-only families that has occurred since 1959, "more than 80 percent of children would still have been poor." Furthermore, Hernandez found that "economic insecurity and need also apparently contributed substantially to the rise in separation and divorce, at least after 1970."[30] Family stability is dependent in part on economic security. Social policies advocated by some conservatives that would threaten the poor with economic insecurity and coerce pregnant women into marriage or make divorce prohibitive for poor people are questionable as a means of reducing poverty. Social policies targeting fathers—such as tightening child-support enforcement and developing comprehensive programs for young fathers—may contribute to children's well-being, but research has shown that these programs alone do not remove the majority of families with young children from poverty.[31]

Although private charity has a place in a vision of the common good, it clearly is not capable of meeting the socioeconomic needs of poor and low-income people. When Congress began considering substituting private charity for welfare benefits, 115 charities jointly notified Congress that they would not be able to meet the needs of the poor if the government significantly cut benefits. Fred Kammer, president of Catholic Charities, said in Congressional testimony that religious charitable programs are primarily there during times of crisis when they drag small amounts of cash from limited funds to help people. He insisted that "What none of us [does] is to provide regular income to poor families. I speak here for everybody—Catholic, Protestant, Salvation Army, Jews, evangelicals. None of us [has] that kind of money." The bulk of the money for many of these programs comes from government funds—federal, state, and local. For example, Catholic Charities USA receives nearly two-thirds of its operating budget for its fourteen hundred programs from government funds.[32]

Public policy experts Handler and Hasenfeld charge that charity makes little real difference in alleviating poverty. "While specific acts of charity provide real benefits to some, charity is, by and large, myth and ceremony. It does little to relieve poverty; at the same time, it confirms the status of the donor and the recipient."[33] In other words, charity affirms the moral superiority of the donor, who is perceived as having funds to give because of individual choices and merit, and the moral inferiority of the recipient, who is "needy" because of some personal deficit, whether poor choice, ability, or luck. (See the chapter by Ruth Smith.)

The conservative vision of the common good—grounded in the market, traditional families, and private charity—and its attendant dismantling of the residual welfare state is actually a form of social Darwinism. Those with the most power, privilege, and resources thrive; the rest struggle to survive. Although a few do rise up the income ladder, as is to be expected in any Darwinian system, many more struggle to maintain a basic standard of living. Its assumptions are not congruent with the dynamics of socioeconomic reality, nor is its vision of the common good appropriate to a theological ethic of compassion and solidarity.

Liberal Proposals

More liberal proposals for welfare reform include education and job training as part of an effort to reform welfare. President Clinton's proposed 1994 Work and Responsibility Act included such provisions, but the act he signed into law in 1996 did not. It is up to states to include such provisions in their welfare legislation. Liberals see a positive role for government, both in providing a safety net for family and market failures and in providing what former Secretary of Labor Robert Reich calls a "springboard" to a better quality of life. While recognizing the appropriateness of notions of personal responsibility, liberals are aware of constraints on personal choice. Their proposals for welfare reform attempt some redress of inequalities in educational and economic opportunities.

Democrats in the California Assembly, for example, proposed a longer period for receiving benefits than Governor Wilson's proposed two-year limit: three years for those requiring training and five years for those requiring training and substance abuse, domestic violence, mental health, or other treatment. They also proposed that work training or treatment assignments could substitute for work requirements. Wilson's proposal makes no provision for training or treatment.[34]

Theoretically, such proposals have some merit, but to be effective, particular types of support, training, and reform are required. For instance, analysis of experimental job-training programs indicate that "you can, in fact, achieve very real gains if the programs permit AFDC recipients to invest in college education, which is the only reliable road to above-poverty wages for women."[35] A second caution in regard to education and training programs is that there must be sufficient jobs for those who complete such programs. Seldom, though, is this the case. Without a full-employment policy or a federal jobs program, the value of these programs is debatable. (See the chapter by Mary Hobgood.)

A primary purpose of training programs is to ensure that work pays a living wage, so that families are indeed lifted out of poverty. Another proposal for making work pay is increasing the Earned Income Tax Credit (EITC), so that low wages are supplemented by a sliding-scale tax credit. Some expansion of this program did take place during Clinton's first term. EITC has lifted some families out of poverty. However, the Institute for Women's Policy Research (IWPR) found that even proposed increases in the EITC do not necessarily bring women out of poverty. Using current recipients who combine work and welfare, they found that many would actually be worse off if EITC is substituted for their AFDC benefits. The average estimated annual EITC benefit would be $1,250, while the estimated loss of AFDC benefits would be $2,350. IWPR concluded that further increases in the EITC or a change in employment patterns would be necessary to make up for the loss. Their research shows that many women who receive AFDC during a two-year period do work in paid employment. This is particularly true of those with a high-school education, job training and work experience, no work-inhibiting disability, and who live in a state with a low unemployment rate. However, the jobs available to these women tend to be low-level service or clerical jobs, usually temporary.[36]

If the problem to be solved is not welfare dependency but *poverty*, additional strategies are needed. IWPR researcher Roberta Spalter-Roth concludes that it is quite unlikely that women will get out of poverty without additional sources of income support (from other family members or child support, which most do not receive) or without substantial reform of the low-wage labor market. To begin this reform, she advocates policies such as "raising the minimum wage, instituting pay equity, and enforcing anti-discrimination policies and unionization."[37] These strategies would also benefit working poor two-parent families. Obviously, the minimum-wage increase referred to would be significantly greater than the recent small increases from $4.25 to $4.75 to $5.15, which have not even restored the purchasing power that the minimum wage provided twenty years ago.

Welfare reform, whether from conservatives or Clinton's "New Democrats," has been promoted in the context of budgetary savings. The truth is that a comprehensive federal training and employment program would, in its initial years, necessarily burden the budget significantly rather than provide savings. Ignoring this reality means that the budget is to be balanced at great cost to our poorest citizens, as is the case with the balanced-budget agreement reached by President Clinton and Republicans in Congress in May of 1996.

Toward a Common Good in Which Women and Children Matter

"What is in the community interest is in our self-interest. The safety of children. The health of children. That's what we are advocating whether they're our children or somebody else's children. We will all suffer if they're not cared for. And we will all benefit when they are." —Sara Moores Campbell, minister and activist.

Los Angeles Times, FEBRUARY 9, 1997

Progressive Proposals

Proposals such as Spalter-Roth's, coupled with universal health care, affordable housing, and accessible and affordable quality child care, begin to move from a residual type of liberal welfare capitalism to what Esping-Anderson identifies as universalistic and egalitarian social democratic institutional states. Such states are proactive rather than reactive and intend to meet the welfare needs of all population groups.[38] These progressive proposals resonate with parts of the U.S. Catholic bishops' pastoral letter "Economic Justice for All," which advocates a new American experiment, through the guarantee of minimum conditions for human dignity economically for everyone.[39] These proposals are grounded in a more adequate analysis of the sources of concrete suffering and are more appropriate to a theological ethic of compassion and solidarity than either conservative or liberal proposals. Yet they do not yet fully address the needs of children for care or women's economic vulnerability grounded in their caretaking responsibilities.

The valuing of child care and other family labor is a critical element missing from conservative, liberal, and some progressive welfare reform proposals. This is an element crucial to the well-being of children and those who care for them. Although most mothers work in the paid labor market, many choose to work only part-time so that they have time to care for their children. Most women on welfare want employment. Part-time work outside the home should also be an option for them. Scholars and activists have made a variety of policy proposals that would give economic value to caretaking activities. These would benefit most children and their parents.

Economist Nancy Folbre advocates "public compensation for the value of family labor." These could be tax credits for family or community labor or some form of family allowances. Folbre proposes that "regardless of income level, or biological relationship, all those who devote time and energy to caring for children, the sick, or the elderly outside the market economy should receive some remuneration." Folbre supports her proposal by arguing that "children, like the environment, are a public good." She points out that parental decisions about child rearing and the resources they dedicate to it, although made individually, affect everyone economically. Many countries' social security programs are "based on transfers from the working to the retired population, which means that all the elderly depend on other people's children."[40]

Even when the elderly depend largely on private pensions and individual savings, Folbre contends that "the rate of return on savings and the prices of basic commodities...are strongly affected by the productivity of the working age generation." She points out that although it is appropriate to advocate a more equal sharing of responsibilities for child care and domestic labor between female and male kin, these efforts will not be sufficient given changing family and household structures. Given the potential benefit that older generations will receive from younger generations, shared responsibility for children is arguably in the best interest of all.

In our advocacy for the well-being of children, we must be careful not to limit women's role to that of mothering or to limit "mothering" to women. In her discussion of gender and social citizenship, Anna Shola Orloff criticizes paternalistic welfare policies that keep women subordinate and dependent. She offers criteria for evaluating the extent of paternalism in a welfare state: (1) "the extent to which the state has taken over the provision of welfare services," as it is more democratic and egalitarian than the market or the family; (2) "the relative treatment of paid and unpaid workers"; (3) "the bases of people's claims to social citizenship rights," which should be as citizens rather than as workers; (4) "women's access to paid work"; and (5) "women's capacities to form and maintain autonomous households," which are necessary to women's freedom from compulsion to enter or stay in marriages in order to obtain economic support.[41] These criteria are useful guidelines for a progressive vision of a common good in which women matter, too.

Progressives advocate translating justified basic-needs claims such as child care, health care, housing, education, income, and employment, into social or economic rights. This moves toward a proactive rather than reactive state, which recognizes not only civil and political rights and citizenship but also social and economic rights—social citizenship. This is a progressive vision of the general welfare, a common good which takes into account children's need for care and does not assume that a woman's life is necessarily like that of a man. I disagree with those communitarian and feminist critics who charge that rights-talk is inherently individualistic and androcentric. Rather, as Elizabeth M. Schneider contends, striving for rights can be both political process and an assertion of our identity and vision.[42] These are visionary goals, not currently on the political agenda. In fact, the recent welfare reform (PRWORA) was a significant move away from such a vision. Welfare benefits (meager as they were) are no longer an entitlement for people who fall into poverty, nor were they replaced with any universal social or economic rights. However, our task is, as ethicist Gary Dorrien says, "to uphold a long-term vision of the common good while working to achieve attainable goals toward that end."[43] Progressive religious and secular people can form alliances around such a vision.

As the damaging effects of welfare reform become better known, possible attainable goals toward this end are alternative income support programs through restructuring of unemployment insurance. The Institute for Women's Policy Research has proposed to decrease the work experience and earnings requirement, limit disqualifications for job-leaving that results from caregiving activities (childbirth or illness), and provide transitional unemployment benefits for those entering or returning to work.[44] These changes would make many more poor women eligible to receive unemployment insurance. Changes in unemployment insurance and temporary disability leave could gain support in the current political climate, as they are linked to direct contributions and thus may be more acceptable.

Scholar and activist Gwendolyn Mink advocates "reuniting all single and/or unemployed parents in a unitary program for social provision along the model of the survivors' insurance system."[45] This would be an expansion of current Social Security payments to dependent children of a deceased parent. Activist Theresa Funiciello supports this proposal, as it makes no distinction among children on the basis of their parents' status. Current congressional proposals to expand Medicare to provide health insurance for uninsured children are a model of an expansion of accepted social provision programs to include new beneficiaries. If a majority of voters become persuaded that children are indeed a "public good," expansion of social provision programs is possible.

Funiciello also supports providing a guaranteed annual income as another alternative.[46] One form this might take is a negative income tax. Economist Herman Daly and theologian John Cobb argue for this in their book *For the Common Good.* They note that the current system of social provision is inequitable, inefficient, and demeaning. "A preferred system should: (1) require that the truly basic needs of all be met, (2) be simple and inexpensive to implement, (3) require a minimum of information from recipients and impose a minimum of special conditions upon them, and (4) provide a strong incentive to work. One approach that meets all these requirements is the negative income tax."[47] Daly and Cobb note that no one claims that the market fairly distributes income or prevents poverty. Governmental action is necessary if the basic needs of all are to be met.

Although the idea of a guaranteed annual income seems unrealistic in the current political climate, continuing high levels of unemployment may lead to new ways of thinking about the connection between income and work. The current obsession with putting welfare mothers into the paid work force is inconsistent with our evolving technological society, in which there is and will continue to be a decreasing need for wage workers. Our future will necessarily focus less on how to put everyone to work and more on how to find work for all who need it. In this context, policies that recognize the economic and social value of nonmarket child care and other useful community labor are especially timely.

Conclusion

The well-being of many vulnerable children and their families is at stake in the ongoing experiments with welfare reform. Policy guidelines and proposals must move beyond punitive welfare reform toward social citizenship with effective programs to reduce poverty, share responsibility for children, and give economic value to caregiving, so that children in different kinds of families may flourish. Theresa Funiciello, once a homeless welfare mother, now an organizer, advocate, author, and policymaker, charges: "Justice requires us to be critical of the balance in our everyday lives. It requires us to reconcile what we do with what we ought to be. There will be justice only when the uninjured parties are as indignant as the injured parties."[48] Our theological ethic calls us to compassion and solidarity with the poor and oppressed. Progressive religious communities should advocate for justice with the injured parties. Let us struggle together for a common good that encompasses the welfare of all children and their families.

Notes

1. Leatha Lamison-White, "Poverty in the United States: 1996," *Current Population Reports,* Series P60-198, U.S. Department of Commerce, Bureau of the Census (Washington, D.C.: Government Printing Office, 1997), 7–8; "Poverty in the United States: 1992," *Current Population Reports,* Series P60-185, U.S. Department of Commerce, Bureau of the Census (Washington, D.C.: Government Printing Office, Sept. 1993), x.

2. According to an Urban Institute study, the legislation that was adopted could throw an additional 1.1 million children into poverty—a 10-percent increase in the number of children living below the poverty line. The Center on Budget and Policy Priorities reached similar conclusions. See Elizabeth Shogren, "Study Warns of Welfare Reform Impact," *Los Angeles Times,* July 26, 1996, A16. A prior study by the Department of Health and Human Services, which was suppressed by the administration, reached similar conclusions. See Ruth Sidel, *Keeping Women and Children Last: America's War on the Poor* (New York: Penguin Books, 1996), 103–4.

3. Elizabeth Shogren, "Historical Overhaul of Welfare," *Los Angeles Times,* Aug. 23, 1996, A1 ff., and Randy Albedla, "Farewell to Welfare, but Not to Poverty," *Dollars and Sense,* November–December 1996, 16–19.

4. For presentation of the conservative charges, see Robert Rector, "Welfare Reform, Dependency Reduction, and Labor Market Entry," *Journal of Labor Research* (1993): 283–97. For refutation of these claims, see, among others, Sanford M. Dornbusch and Kathryn D. Gray, "Single Parent Families," in *Feminism, Children, and the New Families,* ed. Sanford M. Dornbusch and Myra H. Strober (New York: Guilford, 1988), 274–96; Laurie J. Bassie, "Employment and Welfare Participation among Women," *Economic Inquiry* (1990): 222–38; Steven K. Wisensale, "A Commentary on 'The Welfare State and Family Breakup: The Mythical Connection,'" *Family Relations* (1991): 151–52; Richard K. Caputo, "Family Poverty, Unemployment Rates, and AFDC Payments," *Families in Society* (1993): 515–26; Mimi

Abramovitz, "Challenging the Myths of Welfare Reform from a Woman's Perspective," *Social Justice* (spring 1994): 17–21; and Gwendolyn Mink, "Welfare Reform in Historical Perspective," *Social Justice* (spring 1994): 114–31.

5. W. Norton Grubb and Marvin Lazerson, *Broken Promises: How Americans Fail Their Children* (New York: Basic Books, 1982), 78–79.

6. "Money Income in the United States: 1995," *Current Population Reports,* Series P60-193, U.S. Department of Commerce, Bureau of the Census (Washington, D.C.: Government Printing Office, 1996), vii; Faye Fiore and Ronald Brownstein, "Most in the U.S. Got Richer, Poor Got Poorer in 1996," *Los Angeles Times,* Sept. 30, 1997, A1, A14; Lawrence Mishel and Jared Berstein, *The State of Working America* (Washington, D.C.: Economic Policy Institute, 1994).

7. Lynn Smith, "Politics Aside, People Want What's Best for Children," *Los Angeles Times,* February 9, 1997, E2.

8. Ada María Isasi-Díaz, "Solidarity: Love of Neighbor in the 21st Century," in *Mujerista Theology* (Maryknoll, N.Y.: Orbis Books, 1996), 86–104.

9. Delores Williams, *Sisters in the Wilderness: The Challenge of Womanist God-Talk* (Maryknoll, N.Y.: Orbis Books, 1993), 201.

10. Isasi-Díaz, *Mujerista Theology,* 89, 103.

11. Laurel Schneider, quoted in Elisabeth Schüssler Fiorenza, *But She Said: Feminist Practices of Biblical Interpretation* (Boston: Beacon, 1992), 163.

12. Nancy Fraser and Linda Gordon, "'Dependency' Demystified: Inscriptions of Power in a Keyword of the Welfare State," *Social Politics* (1994): 21.

13. Ibid., 22.

14. Diana Pearce, "Welfare Is Not *for* Women: Why the War on Poverty Cannot Conquer the Feminization of Poverty," in *Women, the State and Welfare,* ed. Linda Gordon (Madison: University of Wisconsin Press, 1990), 275.

15. Fraser and Gordon, "'Dependency' Demystified," 23–25.

16. Hilda Scott, *Working Your Way to the Bottom: The Feminization of Poverty* (London: Pandora, 1984). Marilyn Waring, *If Women Counted: A New Feminist Economics* (New York: Harper & Row, 1988). Chapter 12 of Waring's book suggests a useful model for incorporating unpaid work into national economic statistics.

17. See Pamela Brubaker, *Women Don't Count: The Challenge of Women's Poverty to Christian Ethics* (Atlanta: Scholars Press, 1994), 34–42, for a discussion of studies of this issue and attempts to redress it at the international level.

18. Julie A. Nelson, "The Study of Choice or the Study of Provisioning? Gender and the Definition of Economics," *Beyond Economic Man: Feminist Theory and Economics,* ed. Marianne A. Ferber and Julie A. Nelson (Chicago: University of Chicago Press, 1993), 36. For my critique of neoclassical economics, see "Economic Justice for Whom: Women Enter the Dialogue" in *Reli-*

gion and Economic Justice, ed. Michael Zweig (Philadelphia: Temple University Press, 1991), 108–10.

19. Diana Strassmann, "Not a Free Market: The Rhetoric of Disciplinary Authority in Economics," in *Beyond Economic Man,* ed. Ferber and Nelson, 55, 63. See also Amartya Sen, *Resources, Values and Development* (Cambridge: Harvard University Press, 1984).

20. Pamela Couture, *Blessed Are the Poor? Women's Poverty, Family Policy, and Practical Theology* (Nashville: Abingdon, in cooperation with the Churches' Center for Theology and Public Policy, 1991), 169, 173. Couture draws on the ethics of Martin Luther and John Wesley to develop her own ethic of care and shared responsibility.

21. Gosta Esping-Anderson, *The Three Worlds of Welfare Capitalism* (Princeton, N.J.: Princeton University Press, 1990), 26–27.

22. Fraser and Gordon, "'Dependency' Demystified," 13. See also Virginia Sapiro, "The Gender Basis of American Social Policy," in *Women, the State, and Welfare,* ed. Gordon, 36–54.

23. See, for instance, Teresa L. Amott, "Black Women and AFDC: Making Entitlement Out of Necessity," in *Women, the State, and Welfare,* ed. Gordon, 280–98; and Frances Fox Piven, "Ideology and the State: Women, Power, and the Welfare State," in *Women, the State, and Welfare,* ed. Gordon, 250–64.

24. Virginia Ellis, "State Democrats Set Stage for Welfare Battle with Wilson," *Los Angeles Times,* May 8, 1997, A1, A40.

25. Joel F. Handler and Yeheskel Hasenfeld, *The Moral Construction of Poverty: Welfare Reform in America* (Newbury Park, Calif.: Sage, 1991), 164–65.

26. Nancy Fraser, "Women, Welfare, and the Politics of Needs Interpretation," in *Unruly Practices: Power, Discourse and Gender in Contemporary Social Theory* (Minneapolis: University of Minnesota Press, 1989), 168. For a lucid exploration of significant moral questions in regard to the "traditional family," see Susan Moller Okin, *Justice, Gender, and the Family* (New York: Basic Books, 1989).

27. A useful source for understanding the limits of the market in redressing poverty is Walter L. Owensby, *Economics for Prophets: A Primer on Concepts, Realities, and Values in Our Economic System* (Grand Rapids, Mich.: Eerdmans, 1988).

28. Jeff Leeds, "Study Fuels Debate over Welfare Reform," *Los Angeles Times,* June 3, 1996, B12.

29. "Even in families with two wage earners, a fifth remain poor" (Joel F. Handler, *The Poverty of Welfare Reform* [New Haven, Conn.: Yale University Press, 1995], 36).

30. Donald J. Hernandez, *America's Children: Resources from Family, Governments, and the Economy* (New York: Russell Sage Foundation, 1993), 435, 414, emphasis added.

31. Gina Adams, Karen Pittman, and Raymond O'Brien, "Adolescent and Young Adult Fathers: Problems and Solutions," in *The Politics of Pregnancy: Adolescent Sexuality and Public Policy,* ed. Annette Lawson and Deborah L. Rhode (New Haven, Conn.: Yale University Press, 1993), 216–37.

32. Laurie Goodstein, "Churches Can't Feed Many More Hungry," *Tampa Tribune,* February 26, 1995, A1.

33. Handler and Hasenfeld, *Moral Construction of Poverty,* 29.

34. Ellis, "State Democrats Set Stage," A40. The plan adopted by the legislature and signed by the governor was a compromise between the governor's and the Democrats' proposals. Wilson's two-year limit was adopted for current recipients, with only eighteen months for new ones. However, counties can extend this limit another six months. Able-bodied adult recipients must engage in work *or training* for twenty hours a week, thirty-two hours a week after Jan. 1, 2000. Mothers of newborns will be exempted from these requirements for six months, with counties having the option to reduce this to three months (Wilson's proposal) or extend it to a year (Virginia Ellis and Max Vanzi, "Legislature OKs Major Revamping of Welfare System," *Los Angeles Times,* August 5, 1997, A1, 14).

35. Teresa Amott, "Reforming Welfare or Reforming the Labor Market: Lessons from the Massachusetts Employment Training Experience," *Social Justice* (1994): 33–37. Participants in such a program at Cleveland State University, where I taught from 1990 to 1994, gave it high marks. They see it as a way to make a real difference in their own and their children's lives. Critical to the program's success, which has been documented by administrators and funders, are child-care provisions and a mentoring program.

36. Roberta Spalter-Roth and Heidi Hartmann, "AFDC Recipients as Caregivers and Workers: A Feminist Approach to Income Security Policy for American Women," *Social Politics* (summer 1994): 190–210.

37. Roberta Spalter-Roth, "The Real Employment Opportunities of Women Participating in AFDC: What the Market Can Provide," *Social Justice* (1994): 60–70.

38. Esping-Anderson, *Three Worlds,* 27–28. He also identifies another variation of the "institutional state" form of welfare capitalism, described as "conservative-corporatist regimes which preserve status and class differentials," as found in Italy, France, and Germany. This type resonates with organic conceptions of the common good in traditional Roman Catholic social teaching. Needless to say, the social-democratic form is found in the Nordic countries, but Esping-Anderson notes no single pure case.

39. U.S. Conference of Catholic Bishops, *Economic Justice for All: Catholic Social Teaching and the U.S. Economy* (Washington, D.C.: U.S. Catholic Conference, 1986). For a critical assessment of Roman Catholic social teaching in relation to women's reality, including this pastoral, see Brubaker, *Women Don't Count,* 59–99.

40. Nancy Folbre, *Who Pays for the Kids? Gender and the Structures of Constraint* (New York: Routledge, 1994), 258, 254.

41. Ibid., 258–59. Anna Shola Orloff, "Gender and the Social Rights of Citizenship," *American Sociological Review* 58 (June 1993): 323. Also see Barbara Hobson, "No Exit, No Voice: Women's Economic Dependency and the Welfare State," *Acta Sociologica* (1990): 235–50.

42. Fraser, *Unruly Practices,* 183. Schneider, "The Dialectic of Rights and Politics: Perspectives from the Women's Movement," in *Women, the State, and Welfare,* ed. Gordon, 226–49.

43. Gary J. Dorrien, *Reconstructing the Common Good: Theology and the Social Order* (Maryknoll, N.Y.: Orbis Books, 1990), 175.

44. Roberta M. Spalter-Roth and Heidi I. Hartmann, "AFDC Recipients as Care-givers," 190–210.

45. Mink, "Welfare Reform in Historical Perspective," 127.

46. *Tyranny of Kindness: Dismantling the Welfare System to End Poverty in America* (New York: Atlantic Monthly Press, 1993).

47. John Cobb and Herman Daly, *For the Common Good: Redirecting the Economy toward Community, the Environment, and a Sustainable Future,* rev. ed. (Boston: Beacon, 1994), 316. Their chapter "Income Policies and Taxes" (315–31) discusses the strengths and weaknesses of this proposal and other proposed tax changes. Christian ethicist Warren Copeland also supports a negative income tax. See his *And the Poor Get Welfare: The Ethics of Poverty in the United States* (Nashville: Abingdon, 1994), 183.

48. Theresa Funiciello, "The Fifth Estate: How and Why the Poverty Industry Distorts Welfare Issues and Displaces the Interests of People on Welfare," *Social Justice* (1994): 97.

[2]

Liberation from the Welfare Trap?

Ellen Ott Marshall

FOR THE FIRST TIME SINCE the creation of Aid to Families with Dependent Children in 1935, poor women and children are no longer guaranteed financial assistance from the federal government. Congress discontinued this entitlement on October 1, 1996, five weeks after the "Personal Responsibility and Work Opportunity Reconciliation Act" became law. One year later, two million fewer individuals received cash assistance.[1] For many, this statistic reflects the liberation of poor Americans from the welfare trap. But there is also an increase in the number of visitors to food pantries, emergency shelters, and soup kitchens, compounded by a shortage of available, low-skill jobs in many urban areas.[2] In one of the most promising states, only 29 percent of the cases closed in the first year were closed because the principal recipient secured employment. And, among this successful 29 percent, the average hourly wage was $5.82.[3] Even these few statistics prompt the question: Has the move from welfare to work been a liberating experience?

Proponents of the Personal Responsibility and Work Opportunity Reconciliation Act describe it as the path to liberation from the welfare trap because it emphasizes the "creation of opportunity" rather than the "distribution of benefits."[4] In other words, one of the fundamental assumptions underlying this approach is that providing the "means to achieve" is equivalent to providing freedom and opportunity. The most tangible vehicle for this provision of means is the Individual Responsibility Plan (IRP) in its various state forms.[5] In order to continue to receive cash assistance in Tennessee, for example, welfare applicants must sign an IRP which details an employment strategy, sets forth obligations for the individual, and describes services to be provided by the state. Depending on the participant's age and background, the employment strategy may include further education, job training, or immediate job placement which the recipient must pursue forty hours per week.[6] The package of services made available to each participant may include various amounts of cash assistance, food stamps, transportation assistance, child care, and Medicaid.[7] At their best, therefore, IRPs are intended to provide participants with the means to achieve self-sufficiency.

As we shall see, however, the average long-term welfare recipient lives in a socioeconomic environment which inhibits her *freedom* to achieve.[8] In this environment, characterized by William Julius Wilson as "social isolation," the opportunities offered by a welfare-to-work plan are not real opportunities. Because IRPs do not take social isolation into account, they provide the means to achieve without addressing the web of factors which stifle an individual's freedom to achieve. Thus, there is a gap between the expectations of the program and the socioeconomic realities of its participants. The program assumes a context in which the opportunities it offers are real opportunities. In such a context, exiting the welfare rolls would truly signify economic independence. But for those participants circumscribed by social isolation, liberation from the welfare trap means destitution rather than freedom. Moreover, because this path to economic independence is laden with the language of personal responsibility, the woman who remains impoverished is held accountable for the failure of the program.

These are clearly public policy issues. But my concern is a moral one, rooted in two fundamental convictions. The first is the Christian mandate to care for the most vulnerable members of society. As followers of one who ministered to the marginalized, Christians have a responsibility to stand with and serve those in need. The second conviction is the theological claim that all individuals are created for freedom. Based on this claim, we are obligated to dismantle structures which suppress flourishing, such as social isolation. As Christians and as citizens, therefore, we have a responsibility to ensure that all individuals can flourish in our society, that all individuals have the chance to realize their full potential. To fulfill these mandates, we must not only open our hearts and behave charitably, but also educate ourselves so that we can make informed assessments of public policies and work to change them when they violate moral requirements. Thus, our first step as Christians, moral agents, and responsible citizens is to ask H. Richard Niebuhr's question: What's going on? My aim in this chapter is to provide an accurate description of one welfare initiative and its impact on women and children and to suggest an appropriate response. As summarized above, Individual Responsibility Plans do not take into account social isolation and therefore place women and their children in an increasingly vulnerable position. It is our responsibility, therefore, not only to work steadily to dismantle the structures which suppress flourishing, but also to ensure legislative and community-based supports as long as those structures persist.

One of the first things to clarify about this legislation is that, contrary to mainstream discourse, there is no crisis of expenditure and dependency. In 1992, AFDC expenditures amounted to a smaller proportion of the federal budget than they did in 1975.[9] In the 1990s, AFDC has consistently amounted to less than 1 percent of the federal budget.[10] Similarly, statistics about actual usage of public assistance reveal the concern over dependency to be unwarranted. Fifty percent of recipients exit AFDC in the first year, and 75 percent exit in the first two years. This means, for example, that although 5 percent of the U.S. population received cash assistance in 1995, only 2–3 percent are long-term welfare recipients.[11] A second point that contradicts mainstream assumptions is that there is no conclusive, promising evidence regarding welfare-to-work initiatives and job prospects for AFDC recipients. Despite nearly thirty years of welfare-to-work initiatives (since workfare was first legislated in 1967) and countless studies at the national and local levels, "no one program or course of action has been demonstrated as clearly better than another."[12] Moreover, as will be discussed later, there is little assurance that the average long-term welfare recipient (a single mother with small children, little education or work experience) will be able to secure a good job.

Given all of these factors—with a small percentage of federal dollars devoted to cash assistance, a relatively small percentage of the population impacted by this program, and with so little certainty as to how one might truly enable self-sufficiency—why reform now? Perhaps, as many observers suggest, welfare reform is prompted by what AFDC represents rather than by what it does.[13] In other words, this public assistance program is the target of so much attention because of the symbols, values, and stereotypes entwined with it rather than because of the actual administration, fiscal detail, and statistical impact of the programs. Some of these symbols appear in the following excerpt from President Clinton's speech announcing his decision to sign the bill.

> Today the Congress will vote on legislation that gives us a chance...to transform a broken system that traps too many people in a cycle of dependence to one that emphasizes work and independence, to give people on welfare a chance to draw a paycheck, not a welfare check. It gives us a better chance to give those on welfare what we want for all families in America, the opportunity to succeed at home and at work.[14]

Clinton draws on old, familiar symbols, the traditional family and the work ethic, and on a relatively new symbol, namely the welfare trap. The latter symbol has tremendous bipartisan appeal because it allows conservatives to denounce a program that has, in their opinion, outlived its purpose and allows liberals to acknowledge the problem without blaming the victim. Dismantling welfare becomes a venue for promoting the work ethic and other mainstream values. It is welfare that destroys initiative, motivation, and competitive impulses and therefore stands in the way of individual achievement and of market forces. Thus, both parties find common ground in the assertion that the current welfare system should be replaced with a program that gives individuals opportunities to live more responsibly, to hold together a marriage and family, to receive an education, and to work. And the Individual Responsibility Plans, ostensibly, provide the means for this more responsible and productive lifestyle to be realized. Or, more accurately, the IRPs move individuals off of welfare and into the free market where they can join the competitive race for a livelihood.

At their best, the Individual Responsibility Plans, in their various state forms, prepare an individual for economic independence, give her the education and training she needs to get a job, and provide for her in the transition period. The recipient's caseworker guides her through a comprehensive plan of action to which the recipient agrees. The state provides cash assistance, education, job training, and even transportation and child care when the individual becomes employed. The state also provides transitional assistance, food stamps and housing assistance if necessary.[15] In sum, the ideal Individual Responsibility Plan would offer a perfect balance of benefits and burdens, giving the individual what she needs to move toward economic independence.

Even in this best-case scenario, however, there is a federally legislated five-year lifetime maximum for receiving public assistance, a fixed block grant for the state's welfare budget, federally established percentage goals for work participation, and a reduction of $54 billion in spending for public assistance by 2002. My concern is that, even in this best-case scenario, the program assumes a certain social and economic context in which all of the opportunities afforded by IRPs are real opportunities. In such a context, the federally established time limits and budget constraints would not impinge upon the recipient's ability to acquire all of the services she needs. In other words, the Individual Responsibility Plans place tremendous faith in the symbol of individual success in the marketplace. Is this faith justified, or is the symbol of individual success in the marketplace in tension with the socioeconomic realities surrounding welfare recipients?

In his 1987 book *The Truly Disadvantaged*, William Julius Wilson defines social isolation as "the lack of contact or of sustained interaction with individuals and institutions that represent mainstream society."[16] Throughout his writing over the last ten years, Wilson describes neighborhoods of concentrated poverty, characterized by limited economic opportunities and multiple social restraints, ranging from the practice of redlining to weak school systems.[17] Expanding on the multiple constraints found in poverty settings, the authors of a recent book of essays, *The Work Alternative* (1995), explore the implications of social isolation on employment prospects for welfare recipients. The authors do not use Wilson's language, but they do describe a labor market in which the average AFDC recipient lacks the freedom to achieve and may well be trapped by social isolation. The authors agree that low-wage, low-skilled jobs are available, but argue consistently that these jobs will not move former welfare recipients toward economic independence even if they are able to work full time, year round. Gary Burtless, a senior fellow at the Brookings Institution, sums up this shared position by concluding that the research does "not show that job finding is impossible for women who receive AFDC. [But it does] show that many women who eventually find jobs will earn too little to support themselves and their children with any degree of comfort."[18] Moreover, as more low-skilled workers leave the welfare rolls and flood the market, wages and other job attributes will be driven down so that job seekers will continue to "face a labor market with low earnings and few advancement opportunities."[19]

The real opportunities for achievement are further diminished for women dealing with substance abuse or domestic violence, or who have little education and job experience, learning disabilities, or children with emotional or physical problems. Rebecca Blank, an economics professor at Northwestern and researcher in the university's Urban Policy Studies program, discusses these multiple burdens and criticizes the current legislation for not adopting the long-term approach these women need to move successfully from welfare to work. She writes, "given the limited funds and the very short time frame for public assistance, it may be impossible under this legislation to deal adequately with women who face multiple environmental and personal problems."[20] For women living in either isolated rural areas or urban areas of concentrated poverty, their own financial straits may be compounded by the impact of welfare cuts on the neighborhood. The journal of the Brookings Institution, *The Brookings Review,* devoted a recent issue to urban concerns, and several authors described the relationship between public assistance and social isolation. In her essay "Is Anybody Listening?" Margaret Weir, another Brookings research fellow in economics, makes a strong case for the extra burden placed on urban areas by this recent welfare legislation.

Big cities contain areas of concentrated poverty where cuts in welfare will have ripple effects likely to harm entire neighborhoods. As cuts endanger the ability of welfare recipients to pay rent and to patronize local businesses, whole neighborhoods face new instability. Abandoned housing and empty stores not only invite crime, but also pose a direct threat to the progress that neighborhood groups have made in recreating the social fabric of many poor neighborhoods once left for dead.[21]

The overarching theme in all of these economic and sociological assessments is that moving off of welfare is not solely a matter of personal responsibility. In other words, an individual's ability to become self-sufficient depends on a whole range of factors from personal health and well-being to a community's commitment and capacity to provide good jobs. Considering factors of social isolation that inhibit women and their families from joining mainstream society supports the claim that the symbolic goal of economic self-sufficiency in the free market is most definitely in tension with the socioeconomic realities of welfare recipients.

Like Wilson's concept of social isolation, Amartya Sen's notion of "capability to function" also helps us assess the adequacy of IRPs. In his 1992 book, *Inequality Reexamined,* Sen emphasizes the thoroughness of human diversity. We differ not only according to personal characteristics, but also by external situation.[22] Any measurement of inequality, then, must take all of these aspects into account: the individual, her resources, and her context. To that end, Sen suggests that inequality be measured not only in terms of goods and resources, but also in terms of capability to function.[23] Capability to function is a sweeping concept that includes the multiple aspects of a person's life which shape his or her real opportunities—personal *and* external characteristics, biographical sketch *and* socioeconomic context. Sen thus broadens the scope of his economic analysis to consider not just provision of means, but also the context in which the goods are received. Without this broad scope of consideration, we measure goods, but not freedom.

Sen understands freedom as the real choices an individual has. For example, is she free to choose one course of action, one way of living, one possible vocation over another?[24] In order to answer this, we have to evaluate the individual-in-society rather than just the individual. We must take into consideration the socioeconomic context in which she lives as well as her level of education, amount of work experience, and family responsibilities. Applying Sen's language to the issue at hand, we can say that a welfare recipient's capability to function is not determined solely by the skills she learns in a job-training session, but also by the real opportunities she has to secure and keep a job while caring for her family. In other words, her *real* opportunities are determined not by her IRP, but by the socioeconomic context in which she lives. And, as the research cited earlier shows, myriad forces inhibit an individual's freedom to achieve despite the various services provided to her. Sen's economic analysis, coupled with Wilson's sociological description, thus undermine a fundamental assumption behind IRPs, namely that providing the means to achieve is equivalent to providing freedom and opportunity.

Given these realities, Individual Responsibility Plans cannot ensure the freedom to achieve. As time limits approach, this fact takes on grave moral implications not only because many needy women and children will be denied further assistance, but also because these same women will be held personally responsible for remaining poor despite the state's best efforts. This situation demands a thoughtful and heartfelt moral response, as well as sociological and economic analysis. Because all persons deserve to realize their full potential, social welfare policy should aim to ensure conditions necessary to human flourishing. As we have seen, these conditions do not exist for many poor families, and the current welfare program, with its emphasis on individual responsibility, will make it very difficult for these families to prove themselves deserving of public assistance.[25] Those of us who are financially stable have a moral responsibility to care for these families, and we can begin to do this by advocating for fair appeals procedures and by creating supportive networks within the community. For example, MANNA, a local hunger relief organization in Nashville, Tennessee, hosts regular meetings to educate the community about the effects of welfare reform. Other nonprofit organizations and individuals have joined coalitions, such as the REAL Coalition for Welfare Reform and the Tennessee Commission on Social Welfare (TCSW), to increase their presence in state legislative committees. Indeed TCSW was instrumental in crafting and ensuring the inclusion of several important amendments to the Families First bill. And, as will be discussed shortly, many churches have partnered with a micro-lending organization to help welfare recipients build a savings account and acquire assets.

One of the most immediate concerns, however, is ensuring a fair appeals process. Each state is required by the federal government to "provide opportunities for recipients who have been adversely affected to be heard in a State administrative or appeal process."[26] The federal law also stipulates that the family of an individual who has been subject to physical, sexual, or mental abuse may continue to receive assistance for more than five years.[27] In addition to this "hardship exemption," states are to define "good cause exemptions" by which an individual may be excused from participating in work requirements or continue to receive assistance after a time limit has passed.[28] For example, in Tennessee, the caseworker may grant a good cause exemption if the recipient has complied with the Personal Responsibility Plan, has neither refused nor voluntarily quit a job (without good cause), earns less than the maximum grant for her family size, and would continue to receive support were it not for time limits. Regarding the work requirements, an individual will not be sanctioned for noncompliance if the work or the necessary services (child care and transportation) are no longer available, if she can prove that she is sick or caring for a sick relative, or if there is a temporary emergency. In Tennessee, the caseworker uses state guidelines to make these determinations but may also grant exemption for other reasons deemed appropriate.[29] In light of these provisions, we must acknowledge that recipients whose benefits are discontinued do have recourse to an appeals process and legislative stipulations which may serve as footholds for requesting further assistance.

Other aspects of these processes and their application, however, may prompt a less sanguine response. First, because state procedures vary, it will be extremely difficult to monitor the fairness of the appeals process. Thus far, states have made statistics about the decreasing welfare rolls much more readily available than statistics detailing the number of appeals and their outcomes.[30] Moreover, as of this writing, the appeals process has yet to be tested by those who reach their time limits and continue to need assistance. In Tennessee, the case managers will review each case before the eighteen-month or five-year time limit to determine whether good cause exists for extending the benefits. While a case manager may have the best intentions, she will probably not have the time to thoroughly review the situation for each of her eighty clients.[31] Moreover, if an individual appeals her case within ten days, she may continue to receive benefits until the judge makes a final determination. However, if the judge denies her appeal, she must repay "the excess benefits."[32]

One further reason for caution is that the political goal for welfare reform is to *reduce* the welfare rolls. It would be naive to think that the evaluation of appeals and the determination of good cause are immune to this goal and the rhetoric surrounding it. For instance, according to federal guidelines, a state is not allowed to provide hardship exemptions to more than 20 percent of its caseload.[33] However, studies on domestic violence, which is just one such good cause exemption, consistently reveal that 60 percent of welfare recipients suffer abuse.[34] Clearly, the political agenda of roll reduction rather than statistics like this established the 20 percent ceiling and will similarly impact the appeals process. Such examples highlight the tremendous imbalance of power that marks the agreement between the state and the welfare recipient. Indeed, for twenty-five years, the well-known social welfare historians Francis Fox Piven and Richard Cloward have pointed to this imbalance of power as the gateway to manipulative welfare legislation. In their words, "any institution that distributes the resources men and women depend upon for survival can readily exert control over them."[35] We must remember that any allowances by the state for an appeals process remain under the shadow of this fact: the state's primary interest is to reduce the welfare rolls. In other words, the case manager's decisions about her client's well-being are, unfortunately, not made in a neutral environment. Weighing in on each decision is the political goal to decrease spending for public assistance. And that fact necessarily calls into question the fairness of any appeals process or bureaucratic decision affecting the life of a poor woman and her children.

These larger political concerns, joined with the reality of social isolation and the legislative footholds for advocacy described above, set the agenda for those concerned about the plight of welfare recipients under this legislation. As citizens in a political process, we must advocate for a fair appeals procedure and monitor this procedure to ensure that the good cause and hardship exemptions are truly granted as needed. Without these legislative supports functioning truly and fairly, there will be no support for those "liberated" welfare recipients who remain destitute. Because IRPs do not address social isolation and fail to ensure the freedom to achieve, real and true back-up measures must be in place and functioning with the interests of poor women and children in mind.

In addition to advocating for a fair appeals process, we have a responsibility to create structures within the community to support those who cannot meet the expectations and time limits of the IRP. Across the country, civic and church organizations work either in conjunction with or in lieu of state programs to meet the needs of welfare recipients in their communities. Certainly, the burden for these efforts falls most heavily on those churches and organizations already serving the poor because of commitments which long precede this welfare legislation. And it is unfair and unrealistic to expect these same committed people to pick up the slack for an insufficient social welfare policy and for an unsympathetic majority. It is important, then, to stress that these efforts are examples to be followed rather than examples offered to quell concern. For instance, the Tennessee Network for Community Economic Development (or TNCED) organizes peer lending groups across the state for low-to-moderate income earners. The aim is to build assets which make the move off of welfare more feasible and long-lasting. Participants make deposits into an Individual Development Account (IDA), and a civic or church group contributes a two-to-one match to the savings account. The involvement of the church or civic group may be limited to this financial contribution or be expanded to host a peer lending group in which IDA savers participate in financial literacy training. Some Nashville area churches have further expanded their role to act as a sponsor for individual families.[36]

These community responses may not dismantle social isolation, but they do provide supportive structures so that welfare recipients are not further harmed by the unrealistic expectations of this public policy. Individual Responsibility Plans expect that participants will outgrow the need for public assistance if they engage their welfare-to-work program with diligence and commitment. But, as we have seen, the average long-term welfare recipient lives in a context which limits her real opportunities regardless of the effort she puts into her IRP. For these women and their families, these programs do not promise liberation, but threaten greater poverty and stigma. The gap between the program's expectation and its participants' real opportunities makes the need for a fair appeals process and community support even greater. These responses rest on a radically different assertion than that which undergirds IRPs, namely that economic independence is not solely a matter of personal responsibility. Rather, socioeconomic circumstances shape an individual's freedom to achieve. Therefore, it is up to the community to harness all of its resources, governmental and non-governmental, to create spaces in which every person may realize her full potential. It may be beyond the scope of this particular legislation to dismantle social isolation, but it is within its scope to jettison its participants into the labor market with or without support. Given the tenuous circumstances and multiple burdens of many poor women, social welfare programs must not only equip them to compete, but also support them if they (and their children) lose this competitive race.

Notes

1. Dept. of Health and Human Services Administration for Children and Families, Office of Public Affairs, "Change in Welfare Caseloads Since August 1996" (Washington, D.C., 1997); available from http://www.acf.dhhs.gov/news. As of July 1997, the number of recipients for cash assistance dropped to 10.2 million from 12.2 million in August 1996.

2. Paul Shepard, "Cities Survey Hints at Job Shortage," Associated Press, Nov. 21, 1997; available from http://www.washingtonpost.com. Thirty-four cities responded to a survey conducted by the National Conference of Mayors in which they were asked about job availability and social service usage since the implementation of the welfare law. Thirteen cities forecast tremendous job shortages ranging from 6,734 in St. Louis to 75,303 in Detroit. They also noted a sharp increase in requests for emergency food assistance from those who no longer qualify for food stamps.

3. Office of [Tennessee] Governor Don Sundquist, "Families First Is Working: Governor Cites University of Memphis Report as Program Celebrates First Anniversary," Sept. 2, 1997 (press release); Linda Rudolph, commissioner of the Dept. of Human Services in Tennessee, "Remarks of Commissioner Linda Rudolph: Open Cabinet Meeting" (Nashville, 1997). Regarding the remaining case closings: 18 percent were closed because the caretaker refused to sign the Personal Responsibility Plan; 21 percent were closed because the caretaker failed to comply with work requirements; the remaining 30 percent requested that their cases be closed "usually because they found jobs on their

own, they began receiving child support or they had some resources from family or friends," according to Commissioner Rudolph.

4. Tennessee Dept. of Human Services, "Families First: Summary Statement" (Nashville: TDHS, 1996), 1.

5. Personal Responsibility and Work Opportunity Reconciliation Act of 1996, H.R. 3734, section 408.b; available from http://thomas.loc.gov.

6. Tennessee Dept. of Human Services, "Variances between the Federal Law and the Tennessee State Plan" (Nashville: TDHS, 1996); Tennessee Dept. of Human Services, "Work Requirement" (Nashville: TDHS, 1996). In Tennessee, a participant may be exempt from the work requirement if s/he has a "medically verified disability," "is determined to be incapacitated," "proves that he/she is needed in the home full-time to care for a related disabled child or adult relative who lives in the home," "is age sixty (60) or older," or is "under 18 [and has] a child under 12 weeks old."

7. H.R. 3734, section 408.b.2.

8. The distinction between means and freedom to achieve is developed by Amartya Sen in his book *Inequality Reexamined* (New York: Russell Sage Foundation, 1992), which will be discussed later. Sen received the Nobel Prize for Economics in 1998.

9. Nathan Glazer, "Making Work Work," in *The Work Alternative,* ed. Deborah Smith Nightingale and Robert H. Haveman (Washington, D.C.: Urban Institute Press, 1995), 20. According to historical data from the Office of Management and Budget, the federal outlay for 1975 was roughly $332 billion. Glazer records AFDC expenditures that year as $5 billion, constituting 1.5 percent of the federal budget. (The 1996 legislation changed the name AFDC to Temporary Assistance for Needy Families (TANF). However, I intentionally refer to AFDC here because these comments describe statistics and sentiments that predate TANF).

10. Dept. of Health and Human Services, Administration for Children and Families, Office of Public Affairs, "Estimated FY 1997 State Family Assistance Grants Under P.L. 104-193" (Washington, D.C., 1997), available from http://www.acf.dhhs.gov/news; Office of Management and Budget, "Budget of the U.S. Government Fiscal Year 1997" (Washington, D.C., 1997), available from http://www.cher.eda.doc.gov/BudgetFY1997. According to the Department of Health and Human Services, the expected allotment for FY 1997 State Family Assistance Grants is $16.5 billion, still less than 1 percent of our federal budget. Moreover, this spending pales next to the amounts spent on Social Security ($368 billion) and national defense ($259 billion).

11. Joel Handler and Yeheskel Hasenfeld, "Introduction to Welfare" (New York: Twentieth Century Fund, 1996), available from http://www.epn.org/tcf/welfintro.html#q17; Dept. of Health and Human Services, Administration for Children and Families, Office of Public Affairs, "Percentage of the US

Population on Welfare since 1960" (Washington, D.C., 1997), available from http://www.acf.dhhs.gov/news.

12. Glazer, "Making Work Work," 30.

13. Ibid., 21. For further discussion of the symbols and ideology surrounding welfare reform historically, see Linda Gordon, *Pitied but Not Entitled: Single Mothers and the History of Welfare* (Cambridge: Harvard University Press, 1994); Joel F. Handler and Yeheskel Hasenfeld, *The Moral Construction of Poverty: Welfare Reform in America* (London: Sage, 1991); Michael B. Katz, *The Undeserving Poor: From the War on Poverty to the War on Welfare* (New York: Pantheon, 1989).

14. William J. Clinton, "Text of President Clinton's Announcement on Welfare Legislation," *New York Times,* August 1, 1996, A10.

15. These are all options for the state, described either in H.R. 3734 or in Tennessee's Families First summary.

16. William Julius Wilson, *The Truly Disadvantaged: The Inner City, the Underclass, and Public Policy* (Chicago: University of Chicago Press, 1987), 60.

17. For an overview of Wilson's sociological assessment and public policy recommendations for welfare reform, see chapter 8 of *When Work Disappears: The World of the New Urban Poor* (New York: Alfred A. Knopf, 1996).

18. Gary Burtless, "Employment Prospects of Welfare Recipients," in *The Work Alternative,* ed. Nightingale and Haveman, 86.

19. Rebecca M. Blank, "Outlook for the U.S. Labor Market and Prospects for Low-Wage Entry Jobs," in *The Work Alternative,* ed. Nightingale and Haveman, 33.

20. Rebecca M. Blank, "Policy Watch: The 1996 Welfare Reform," *Journal of Economic Perspectives* (winter 1997): 173.

21. Margaret Weir, "Is Anybody Listening?" *The Brookings Review* (winter 1997): 31.

22. Sen, *Inequality Reexamined,* 1–2.

23. I should note at the outset that I use Sen's capability approach differently with regards to welfare and poverty. In his chapters on these topics (6 and 7), he offers the capability approach as a measure of poverty. I use it here in order to assess a policy.

24. Sen, *Inequality Reexamined,* 39–40.

25. For further discussion of shifting definitions of the "deserving poor" through history, see Handler and Hasenfeld, *The Moral Construction of Poverty;* Katz, *The Undeserving Poor.*

26. H.R. 3734, section 402.1.A.i; section 402.1.B.iii.

27. H.R. 3734, section 408.7.C.i–iii.

28. H.R. 3734, section 408.10.B.

29. Tennessee Dept. of Human Services, *Case Managers' Families First Handbook* (Nashville: TDHS, 1996), 204, 234–35.

30. At the time of this writing, I have been unable to locate any statistics regarding appeals and outcomes for any state, including my own.

31. Tennessee caseworkers have an average of eighty Families First clients, but this number grows to three hundred when food-stamp clients are included.

32. Tennessee Dept. of Human Services, *Case Managers' Families First Handbook*, 268.

33. H.R. 3734, section 408.7.C.ii.

34. Jessica Pearson, Nancy Thoennes, and Esther Ann Griswold, "Colorado Model Project: Child Support and Domestic Violence: The Victims Speak Out" (Denver: Center for Policy Research, 1998). The authors of this study examine the gap between the percentage of welfare recipients who suffer domestic violence and the percentage who apply for a good cause exemption. It provides a helpful overview of the literature about domestic violence and welfare reform and reviews the current debate between advocates for victims of abuse and proponents of this welfare legislation. A copy of this report is available from the Web site of the Administration for Children and Families of the U.S. Department of Health and Human Services (http://www.acf.dhhs.gov/programs/cse/rpt/mofc/4victims.htm).

35. Frances Fox Piven and Richard A. Cloward, *Regulating the Poor: The Function of Public Welfare,* 2d ed. (New York: Pantheon, 1993), 22.

36. Tennessee Network for Community Economic Development, "Peer Lending Summary" (Nashville: TNCED, 1997); Gene TeSelle, "Responding to 'Welfare Reform' at the Community Level," *Southern Communities* (Oct. 1996): 1–2. TNCED bases its approach, in large part, on the work of Michael Sherraden; see *Assets and the Poor: A New American Welfare Policy* (Armonk, N.Y.: M. E. Sharpe, 1991).

[3]

Decentering Poverty

Ruth L. Smith

My APPROACH TO CURRENT DEBATES about welfare reform is less direct than others in this volume but is equally concerned with the limitations of the terms of that debate and the serious consequences for those most immediately affected by it as well as for the larger society. I address my concern through examining the discourse of poverty in its relations with Christian beliefs and practices of salvation. Such an approach may appear far afield from public policy, but the discourse of poverty—that is, the habits of speech we use to identify, analyze, and describe poverty—constructs what we think poverty to be. In Christian traditions, the ethical-theological logics that link poverty with salvation decisively contribute to shaping experiences, relations, and ideals of poverty. It is tempting to consider that in this connection, the poor are the ones in need of the concerned Christian, but the Christian is also in need of the poor inasmuch as concern for the poor is believed to be the medium of salvation. I argue that in this complex relationship there is not only a demand for the alleviation of poverty but also a demand for the perpetuation of poverty.

The calls for voluntary agencies in the United States to increase their services as government agencies decrease theirs make this an opportune moment to consider religious assumptions about poverty which inform cultural and policy formulations of giving and receiving assistance. Societal notions of poverty still draw on these assumptions, despite the largely secular character of public life. Karl Marx makes the argument that Christianity legitimates existing social conditions to support the interests of the ruling classes, in part by spiritualizing poverty as a state of holiness and as a condition to be alleviated only in the next world.[1] I pursue a different angle by arguing that the ideals of voluntary poverty contribute to the assumption that involuntary poverty is a condition society cannot do without. While the configurations vary historically and with regard to class, gender, and race, they consistently reproduce narratives that connect goodness, poverty, and the ultimate fate of one's soul in religious and secular narratives about salvation and its consequences for individuals and societies.

To develop my argument and perspective, I identify the Christian idealizations of voluntary and involuntary poverty. Then follows an analysis of poverty in the medieval Roman Catholic Church which explicitly connects voluntary and involuntary poverty in a well-developed theological dynamic of renunciation, charity, and salvation. I then consider theoretical and theological arguments of the last two centuries that are critical of certain aspects of the Christian view of poverty and salvation but retain some of these same assumptions in their proposed notions of salvation. Finally, I consider associations of poverty, asceticism, and salvation in practices of authority. The discourse linking poverty, asceticism, and salvation bears the awkwardness of multiple perspectives, not all taking the same route but often loosely sharing the legacies of Christian referents. For that reason, it is important to outline the two primary Christian idealizations.

Idealizations of Poverty in Christianity

Christian traditions identify two clusters of moral/spiritual ideals about poverty. One is that of voluntary poverty, which in contemporary discussions of virtue can be identified as the attitude that goods should be fairly distributed or as the act of dispossessing oneself by goods by choice.[2] Voluntary poverty in this chapter refers to the ascetic tradition in which persons choose to sacrifice worldly goods for the sake of spiritual purification, union with God, and compassion for those who are suffering. The goods of food, clothing, and shelter, except for minimal requirements, are just the beginning of what is left behind in the turn from the world; voluntary poverty also traditionally involves relinquishing the worldly goods of security, power, and the ego-self. The other spiritual/moral ideal ensues from involuntary poverty, in which persons are poor because of political/economic circumstances. While these circumstances are worldly, the suffering they cause is understood to invite heightened divine concern for and heightened divine presence in the human being who so suffers. In this nexus of suffering and divinity, the involuntarily poor are often the special concern of the voluntarily poor, evident in monastic and other organized religious assistance. Christians who are not poor, by choice or circumstance, have historically venerated the voluntarily poor for their goodness and good works and attributed humility and innocence to the involuntarily poor on the basis of their vulnerability and need. In the history of these ideals in Christianity, poverty and eternity coalesce, in that to give to the poor in either position is to give toward one's own salvation.

In Christianity, the practices of voluntary asceticism are considered necessary to seek and express a more purely spiritual life than is available within what the ascetically oriented believe to be the compromised terms of ordinary morality. Voluntary poverty in Roman Catholic monastic discipline refers to one of the three vows, along with chastity and obedience, that men and women take as part of membership in religious orders. In Protestantism, voluntary poverty most distinctly takes the form of the "inner-worldly asceticism" of Calvinism (to use Max Weber's phrase), which entails disciplines of frugality and rejection of material display chosen in the context of engagement with the world instead of the monastery. Related versions of asceticism are evident in Lutheranism, Methodism, and other Protestant groups that initially define themselves in terms of the Reformation's idealization of the early church, including its mission to the poor, and are also part of Christian teachings of self-sacrifice and selfless compassion.

By contrast, involuntary poverty conventionally refers to those who are without sufficient economic means to provide food, clothing, and shelter for themselves and their households for reasons not of their own choosing or control. The factor of choice is complex, but for this argument it indicates the difference between those who willingly choose an ascetic life and those who do not. Christianity relies on both expressions of poverty to provide markers of spiritual hierarchy articulated in notions of innocence, humility, renunciation, sacrifice, charity, reward, and transcendence.

Renunciation, Charity, and Salvation

The development of Christian monastic orders encourages more-communal, less individualistic heroic models of renunciation than had been prevalent in earlier Eastern ascetic Christianity but continues the rejection of wealth as part of their ascetic practice. The orders are under the double injunction to live in poverty and to give to the poor; they especially are invested in poverty and giving as part of the sacrifice of self, exercise of spiritual discipline, and journey of spiritual development.

In emphasizing the two ideals of poverty, ascetics look to the life of Jesus, for whom poverty is one of several markers of the renunciation of this world and at the same time of concern for and identification with those considered societally outcast. Even monastic orders not founded exclusively for service, such as the Benedictines, are enjoined in numbers fourteen and fifteen of the seventy-two "Instruments of Good Works" in *The Rule of St. Benedict* to "comfort the poor" and to "clothe the Naked."[3] And throughout the Middle Ages, renewed vows of poverty and giving to the poor are common ways by which wayward orders attempt to relegitimate themselves after falling into corruption and disrepute.

Jesus' commandments first to love God and then to love one's neighbor— numbers one and two in the Benedictines' "Instruments"—have been taken to place love at the heart of Christianity. The interpretation of this love in a religion which looks both toward this world and away from it has been described as agape, or selfless love toward the other, which includes ascetic practices that combine self-sacrifice and pastoral-moral concern.[4] The qualities of love are also translated as "charity," the love which Paul recommends above all in the thirteenth chapter of 1 Corinthians. The extension of charity or love or agape toward the poor is often described as simple, associated with the adjectives "humble" and "innocent" as though this giving were a kind of natural, unmediated practice that erases itself of all social relations and their consequences. Yet giving is a social/religious relation of the exchange of need, the need for goods with the need for salvation: the ascetic needs the poor for his or her salvation, and the poor person needs the ascetic for his or her bread.

In giving to the poor, the great commandments to love and the great need for salvation come into spiritual alignment for the giver, yet the relationship between the voluntarily and involuntarily poor is not a reciprocity of equals. Christians make distinctions between the spiritual status of the two kinds of poverty by emphasizing the choice and selflessness through which the ascetic is more pure. Giving to the poor who are in need is an obligation the poor cannot meet, and the humility of these poor persons is assigned lower status than the humility of those voluntarily seeking poverty.

Problems between reciprocity and hierarchy are not only present in Christianity but also appear in other traditions that connect salvation with suffering. In the monastic practices of Buddhism, the poor are a consistent concern in injunctions and stories in popular and scholarly texts.[5] Historically, attention to the poor is not, however, as consistently a part of Buddhist ascetic practice, with its strong teaching of enlightenment through wisdom. In this case, the superiority that undercuts reciprocity is more likely to be that of wisdom over poverty. To an extent this also pertains to some Christian monastic orders, but Christian reciprocity is more likely to be undercut by the distinction between giver and recipient in charity. Awareness of this difference helps clarify the reliance of Christian notions of renunciation on giving to people in need and the intensity of the moral/spiritual tensions between voluntary and involuntary poverty.

The Christian focus on agency insists on a line between the activity of willing (that is to say, giving) and the passivity of not-willing (that is to say, receiving) that pervades even the ascetic's relinquishment of self in charity. Augustine's writings on charity and alms-giving became one of the central referents for Christian monastics and other believers of the Middle Ages.[6] In considering the qualities that should motivate giving to the needy, Augustine classifies ministering to hunger and thirst as a kind of "medicine"—medicine being those things that pertain to the body, in distinction from ministering to the soul, which is classified as "discipline." Augustine expresses two specific concerns as he struggles to formulate theological and administrative issues that poverty raises for himself and the church. One is that compassion be expressed from the motive of pure benevolence, not from the motive of empathy with those suffering, which would involve one's own interests and emotions. The other specific concern is that giving for bodily needs be accompanied by giving for the needs of the soul, because the soul is higher and, through discipline, should control all aspects of medicine.[7] The first identifies the notion of selflessness requisite for spiritual giving and the second identifies the tensions of body and soul with which all believers imputedly struggle and by implications identifies the poor as the vehicle with which to address this tension.

Because the health of the body is nothing without the health of the soul, Augustine counsels that the body not be ministered to as an end in itself. "[One], then, who loves his [or her] neighbor endeavors all he [or she] can to procure...safety in body and in soul, making the health of the mind the standard in...treatment of the body."[8] Augustine's worry, however, that the body as a body might be given too much attention is not first about hunger but about sex. In Augustine's view, it is sex that is the primary danger in the sensuality of the appetites and that pervades all other needs, despite the created goodness of the body. During the years following Augustine, church documents and visual arts translate bodily reference into sexuality to such an extent that any physical need is represented as at least implicitly erotic and therefore sinful. Everyone is a child of Adam and Eve, and everyone's clothing testifies to being caught consorting with the snake and picking the apple; every human body presents to others the knowledge that it is about sex covered up.[9]

While Christians, to varying extents, associate the body with the sinfulness of this world, they also develop traditions of caring for the body through hospitals and programs for food and clothing, at times in the most extreme circumstances of need, suffering, and danger. This care expresses, however, not the resolution but the tension between Christian activity in this world and its negation of this world, encapsulated in the body, which it would be dangerous to love. Historian Carter Lindberg finds that in the Middle Ages, Roman Catholics continued to emphasize the superiority of spiritual to merely corporal charity. This hierarchy is practiced by subordinating the value of physical care for the poor to the value of the self-mortification for the giver who touches the poor and to the value of converting the soul of the poor for God.[10] In the dichotomy and hierarchy of body and spirit, the involuntarily poor represent the body, and the voluntarily poor represent the spirit. This indicates that the state of the soul of the poor is negotiable according to the need of the ascetic practitioner, who from one stance needs contact with the humility of the poor whose spirit is already closer to heaven and from another stance needs contact with the impurity of the poor to express the ascetic's spiritual need for the physical punishment of self-sacrifice.

Nonetheless, to love the poor is safer than to love other persons or aspects of this world, because the poor are symbolically construed to be less of this world. The poor, then, are the privileged site of this-world denial and also the persons presumably in greatest need of worldly goods. This tension is resolved for the poor through the ascetic belief that, from a spiritual perspective, poverty is superior to wealth. The tension is resolved for those with wealth through the interpretation of poverty as poverty of the spirit only, and wealth as the means by which to finance ministry to the poor. In turn, religious institutions need the poor to attract the monetary gifts of the wealthy, as Lindberg observes in his analysis.[11] In the overall spiritual economy of poverty of the Middle Ages, the poor are counseled patience for well-founded hope for their souls in the next life, and the rich are counseled alms-giving for probable hope for theirs. "Poverty was good for everyone: the poor person was theoretically in an ideal state for salvation, and the rich person could secure the future by serving the poor."[12]

These theological arrangements articulate the static hierarchies of feudal society, and they also articulate the fluidities necessary to sustain the hierarchies. In a society in which people believe that salvation is theological, the poor are a means of securing everyone else's needs for salvation; poverty can be theologically elaborated according to whatever these needs are. For ascetics, the poor, as humble recipients of gifts, express the spiritual purity of the heavenly realm and express the impurity of the social/earthly realm as the suffering of bodily life, serving as a vehicle with which to separate the two realms. For the church and the wealthy, the poor mediate the heavenly and earthly realms by making it possible for wealth and power to coexist with salvation through giving to those whose bodies are in need. In this instance, hungry bodies are the route instead of the obstacle to spirit. Poverty is constructed in both cases to take whatever shape spiritual coherence requires, and this need overrides any problem of inconsistency in notions of poverty. What is consistent is that the poor are never theologically or politically equal to others, but always higher or lower.

Lindberg argues that the theological reading of poverty that persisted amidst the massive social upheaval of the shift from agrarian to urban societies in eleventh-century Europe prevented development of social policies to deal with major social and economic change. Thinking about poverty continued to find its reasoning from the older theological discourse, despite the gradual development of governmental and citizen-sponsored institutions for the poor. While there was a lack of political and economic discourse about poverty, in the face of changes and their anxieties (including the plague), religiosity increased and the theological interpretations of poverty shifted somewhat. The church sharpened the distinction between the voluntarily and the involuntarily poor—a distinction accompanied with greater hostility toward the involuntarily poor, who were as likely then to become beggars as to be ministered to through religious organizations. Chosen poverty increasingly was singled out as an ascetic virtue, embodied in the Franciscan and Dominican orders, while at the same time begging monks were often no longer accepted within city walls.[13] The church seemed to be indisputably in control of the older discourse of poverty and yet was struggling to adapt it to fit an urban, monetary political economy. In these shifts the voluntary and involuntary poor increase and overlap in new ways, and in the process poverty becomes simultaneously more problematic and more idealized in European societies.

Protestant reformers in the sixteenth century introduced new approaches to alleviate poverty, in part to enforce injunctions against religious and nonreligious begging (now read as disorderly) and in part to exercise new ideas of salvation as the given precondition of life instead of the goal to be hoped for only at the end of life. If only God gives salvation and if salvation is given as a presupposition of life and not its end reward, then, by Luther's argument, the theological economy of poverty and salvation crumbles because there are no requirements for salvation. Salvation lies in God's acceptance of the person just as the person is as a human being.[14] New ordinances and programs emphasizing public responsibility for the poor appear at this time, based not on poverty as an exalted spiritual condition but on notions of shared human dignity.[15] Luther's thinking about poverty itself narrows in scope as it becomes more embedded in his own hierarchical divisions, even as a Lutheran ethic of service emerges based on Christian concern for relations in this world instead of sacrifice and salvation.

Yet the association of the poor with salvation persisted, as did inattention to the causes of poverty and to the poor themselves on any extended basis. While giving to the poor had been central to the salvation narratives and practices of

Christianity, missing from the history of Christianity was a developed recognition of the agency of the poor themselves as givers. Further, the qualities of the souls of the involuntarily poor were constrained by a religious ideology not only about the problematic character of the body and bodily need but also about the superiority of the nonpoor giver who through a reversal could be understood to be the one who provided access to salvation with expressions of charity. The nonpoor represented the agency of the poor by determining how the poor were supposed to respond to being given to: with humility and gratitude. During the nineteenth century, this dynamic developed in philanthropic and mission movements—especially, though not exclusively, on the part of middle-class women who extended their own domestic ideals of self-sacrifice into ordering principles for those who were poor; this charity often entailed notions of religious and moral conversion.[16] Among such religious missions, concern for the salvation of the poor again expressed the need among the middle classes to save the poor in order to save themselves.

While the poor are still associated with salvation, they are also increasingly associated with sin and with resistance to the moral possibilities of the religious (as well as the political-economic) conversion opportunities offered by middle and even working classes. Nineteenth-century divisions between the deserving and the undeserving poor shift inconsistently in the ways institutions articulate the moral and economic conditions of the poor, elaborate their social significance, and design and implement policy.[17] There is no one way in which the terms deserving and undeserving are deployed. Nonetheless, amid their variations, the middle classes drive inequality into the poor themselves, so that neither the "deserving" nor the "undeserving" poor are considered equal to the citizen or even the proletariat. Referents such as "responsible" and "irresponsible," "hard-working" and "lazy," "chaste" and "promiscuous" are used increasingly to distinguish not only the nonpoor from the poor but also the working from the nonworking poor, and eventually the "good" poor from the "bad."[18] As with the eleventh century, it seems to be the case that the older ascetic language about poverty retains its authority as the terms of salvation, sacrifice, humility, and renunciation blend with new notions of society, individuality, and progress to help establish the moral spaces of the new bourgeois and the marginalization of the poor.

Social Transformation and the Idealizations of Poverty

Readers may argue that the problem I am wrestling with has already been resolved by social theorists and critical theologians over the last two centuries who have analyzed asceticism and poverty in Christianity. These thinkers identify poverty in relation to bourgeois authority structures in religion and political economy and call for change in these structures on behalf of those outside the bourgeois classes. At the same time, these analyses (even when arguing for the priority of the poor or the revolution of the oppressed) do not resolve the problem of the discourse of poverty that I am arguing—that of relying on poverty, asceticism, or a nonbourgeois class to mediate some kind of salvation. A look at the ambiguities these thinkers introduce in their imputed resolutions brings forward the gaps between the discourses of social change and the problems of poverty.

Karl Marx critically connected poverty and religion through his argument that religion is an aspect of class rule which gains its particular character from its claims beyond worldly to ultimate authority. Through religious claims (and Marx was thinking primarily of Christianity), the class which owns the means of economic production legitimates its cultural rule over the working class, in part by using Christianity to articulate a religious narrative of this world as a "veil of tears." This narrative renders action on the part of the working classes futile by encouraging suffering and acceptance in this world, with hopes for salvation postponed to the world to come. It is in this sense that religion is "the opium of the people."[19] The worship of God entails the worship of poverty, which masks and sustains the authority of the owner classes over the poor. From one perspective, Marx was transferring the logic of heaven to the logic of earth in order to make poverty a political and economic question. Drawing on his economic critique as well as his Jewish heritage, Marx argued that salvation is not a matter for the next world but for this one, and the poor need to benefit from it in the here and now if salvation is to have any appropriate authority. By connecting the proletariat with salvation, Marx in effect established the authority of the process of class struggle and reinforced the proletariat's dual social/economic role. As industrial workers, they were in a position to end their own oppression because they had a basis on which to organize against the control of the bourgeois and eventually to bring about the conditions for the freedom of all human beings.[20]

By the poor, however, Marx did not mean all poor people but only those "artificially impoverished," whom he identified as the proletariat. This group was impoverished by its place in the relations of capitalist production, in contrast with the "naturally arising poor" who may eventually come into the industrial working class.[21] For the most part, though, Marx and Engels associated the poor with nature and mechanical action, having no inner or outer potential for revolution in their constitution and position outside the entirety of class relations; this stood in contrast to the proletariat, whose organization and revolution were eventually to liberate all of humanity.[22] Two familiar, complementary logics of poverty are at work here: the elevated poor, whose suffering gives them special spiritual status, and the degraded poor, whose bodily condition renders their spirits intransigent to salvation. And in aligning the proletariat with the redemption of society, Marx, too, was reliant on one group of the poor to mediate salvation. The point is not to have caught Marx in a self-contradiction with his criticism of religion but to observe the persistence of the idealizations of poverty and their roles in salvation.

The earlier social gospel movements and contemporary liberation theologies have attempted to disconnect poverty from traditional theological discourse and connect poverty to a progressive democratic theological discourse. Both developments address poverty within a critical view of capitalism, with its economic classes, and of Christianity, with its hierarchical notions of sin and salvation. In defining the "Christian social order," Walter Rauschenbusch states that: "Modern humanity can never be saved until the working class is saved."[23] He argues that identification with the suffering of this class would help in the "rise" of this class from its difficult working and living conditions and would sensitize the rest of society about the contributions of the working class to the economy and general societal life.[24] This view is part of Rauschenbusch's reform-oriented notion of social sin in contrast to the view that sin is only an individual, private matter not subject to the scrutiny of other human beings.[25] The working class is the key both to understanding the injustices that make social sin a reality and to the kind of salvation that would bring justice and that merits hope. From this social gospel perspective, there is no salvation without economic and political justice goals, to be achieved through major economic and religious reform.

Gustavo Gutierrez and other liberation theologians of the later twentieth century have argued for a view of salvation much more aligned with the voices of the poor themselves—of those, largely Latin Americans, who fall outside of the working classes and therefore of traditional notions of revolution. The orientation is one of identification not with middle-class philanthropy and reform but with the actual lives and struggles of people in their communities. Such identification entails reciprocal relations, in contrast to the dominating, hierarchical relations that often characterize Christian traditions of charity. Faith is defined by one's solidarity with the poor, expressed most concretely by interacting in relations which presume that poor people are the authorities on formulating the terms of their life conditions, and by participating in their religious expressions of resistance, acceptance, and sanctification. The primary divide in this experience is between oppressed and oppressor, and faith requires the continuous process of separating oneself from the dominator.[26] Salvation is mediated through the ongoing struggle for liberation, a struggle which cannot be defined apart from its historical processes in this world.[27] There is no salvation without the liberation of the oppressed, which requires radical economic and religious change.

Despite significant differences between Rauschenbusch and Gutierrez, these two important critical notions of salvation are linked and tempered by claims that continue discursive practices of tying the salvation of everyone else to the poor and of making poverty the central interpretive image for theology, ethics, and economy. The concern for poverty could be affirmed as an achievement on behalf of the working classes and the poor that results in supporting social movements, addressing oppressive conditions, and shifting the consciousness and practice of some middle-class people. The association of the poor with salvation, however, is part of an older tradition that implicitly requires that the poor alleviate the moral and religious anguish of the privileged classes. Further, the notion of consciousness reproduces the dualistic/monistic assumption that one is either faithful or unfaithful, with the poor or against them, even though Gutierrez argues against the European metaphysical dualism of the two realities of a political world and a spiritual world, a difficulty Kathleen Sands discusses in her analysis of liberation theology.[28] As a consequence, dualisms of good and evil, power and powerlessness, social and natural, salvation and wealth, in which each term opposes and presupposes the other, reinstantiate the requirement of poverty in the terms of salvation.

These dualisms also emerge within asceticized notions of "social sin" in current liberation thinking inasmuch as it reproduces the emphasis on bodily self-renunciation. While "social sin" indicates a less personalized and more historicized notion of guilt and responsibility, it can remain oppressive in sanctions of suffering, self-sacrifice, and the rejection of all desire as a threat to spiritual worth. Delores Williams addresses this issue in her womanist theology of "social sin" and the African American community. Williams argues in disagreement with African American theologian of liberation James Cone and with spiritual songs and slave narratives that emphasize the denial of self in response to suffering and that devalue bodily experience in relation to spiritual experience.[29] For Williams, these views also place sin outside the African American community, implying that this community is without sin. A womanist perspective affirms the significance of bodily and sexual experience and therefore includes their abuse as part of social sin inside as well as outside of the African American community. Most significant in Williams's judgment is the need for a notion of "social sin" to face the abuse of black women's self-esteem as a result of oppression. "In the construction of a womanist notion of sin informed by the Black community's and Black theology's belief in social sin, it is quite legitimate to identify devaluation of Black women's humanity and the 'defilement' of their bodies as the social sin American patriarchy and demonarchy have committed against Black women and their children."[30]

In her analysis of liberation thinking, Williams locates another aspect of the requirement for emblems of self-sacrifice in salvation-liberation projects. Further, she describes social sins which cannot be named within the ascetic logic for which the body, on its own or in conjunction with the mind and soul, is a predetermined site of impurity. If the body is an emblem of sin, then the best it can do is become an emblem of self-sacrifice, and, as such, there is something right about a body that is hungry or otherwise abused. The problems of poverty cannot be addressed apart from the desires for health, identity, and well-being. But these aspects cannot be taken into account by simply adding them into older models of social change, such as those that may exhort adherents to freedom while retaining the authority patterns of ascetic ideals that sanction suffering, especially the bodily suffering of those whose spiritual representations vacillate between the ideal and the degraded—women and those who are poor. The gaps between these models and the issues of poverty indicate that the association of ascetic ideals with involuntary poverty is not a matter of ideals misapplied but of the construction of the ideal itself.

Authority Practices and Ascetic Requirements

Christianity is not the only tradition whose ascetic ideals rely on the poor as well as women for categories of impurity. For example, in the Hindu *Samnyasa Upanishads,* the impurity of the body is codified as the woman's body, which in turn represents all that is cast off as part of the detritus of society.[31] In contemporary Southeast Asian Buddhism, the patterns of male domination contribute to the persistent popularity of the story of Prince Vessantara, who decides to give up everything, including his wife and children, to take up the ascetic life.[32] In these representations, women and the poor are categories that share differentially shifting and hierarchical ambiguities that communicate authority relations as part of ascetic practice itself. Among these different traditions of renunciation, Christianity is distinct in the strenuousness of its demands on the poor because of the extent to which it holds them to both the higher spiritual standard of voluntary poverty and idealized involuntary poverty and the lower standard of those considered to be most degraded by their bodily existence.

The authority practices of Christian asceticism and salvation controlled by renunciation and self-sacrifice have been critiqued from several perspectives. Womanist thinking has been particularly critical of the ideas of suffering and servanthood tied into the traditions of sacrifice and obedience. For example, Emilie Townes argues that "suffering, and any discussion that accepts suffering as good, is susceptible to being shaped into a tool of oppression."[33] Ecologists have criticized the dualisms of asceticism that entail the devaluation of this world and of life itself.

White feminists have criticized the dualisms that devalue women and women's activities as antithetical to spiritual expression, as in Nel Noddings's argument that the virtues of asceticism extol suffering and moral heroism. In *Women and Evil*, Noddings criticizes William James's claim that poverty is the cornerstone of sainthood. In Noddings's analysis, poverty is part of the agonistic striving that James accords to sainthood; its stringencies indicate the achievement of a heroic status by heroic means.[34] In the morality of heroic asceticism, poverty is attached to manliness, masking the fear of femininity entailed in heroic asceticism, as Noddings notes. And I would add, heroic asceticism masks fear of nonvoluntary poverty itself, which in James's terms is constructed as a feminizing condition in its imputedly non-agential qualities of innocence and humility. Noddings identifies in James the problem of defining religion as asceticism and opens the way to considering a notion of religion in which relations of suffering and sacrifice demand critical attention but lose their authority to articulate the traditional narratives of salvation.

Noddings criticizes the polarities of moral condemnation and elevation deployed when people valorize the virtues of poverty and at the same time blame those who are poor for not overcoming poverty. Nevertheless, she reproduces the duality and hierarchy of giving and receiving by associating care with those helping the poor and helplessness with poverty. This unexamined move prevents her from recognizing narratives and activities that are more complex than the dualities of agency and the negation of agency, care, and helplessness. For example, Noddings has no way to account for the African American woman who can get no other work than that of caring for white people's homes and children in order to support her own children, whom she must leave on their own and yet still mother. The problem can be seen in the stories Katie Cannon tells of her own mother, who cleaned white women's houses, kept many additional odd jobs going, ensured that her family was active at church, and taught her children to live in a world without protection.[35] Cannon would push Noddings not to add another story to her notion of care but to consider more critically the authority and power relations of its root in the ascetic-charity practices of Christian compassion, especially as they come to us from nineteenth-century middle-class notions of virtue.

Gustavo Gutierrez struggles with questions of authority in his notion of a dialogue with the poor, but in his dialogue the poor remain the untouchable authority that governs everything else. There is a moment of truth in recognizing the authority that each person has over her or his own experience. However, to extend this moment into a theory of absolute knowledge erases its social character and its subjectivity. When a particular form of knowledge is assumed to be total and not partial, and to be immune from all interests and values deemed undesirable, the result is an asocial and ahistorical finished consciousness that mirrors the bourgeois view of its own moral consciousness as total, complete, and impermeable.

Marianne Janack's analysis of the feminist claim to women's epistemic priority is helpful here. Janack argues that we should shift from claims of epistemic privilege to critical questions about ways epistemic authority is "conferred" in practices and institutions. The authority of epistemic privilege, according to Janack, entails an unmediated, unambiguous view of experience, a kind of private revelation not submitted to public exchange or scrutiny.[36] To attribute epistemological privilege to the poor leads to attributing and requiring unambiguous goodness of the poor, whose consciousness is then imputedly innocent because it is free of societal interaction, or because it is only the result of external social forces, with no agency of its own. Such an attribute of privilege can further imply that the poor are a unitary and permanent group marked off by mind and body from everybody else. This perspective ignores the multiple kinds and experiences of poverty and the ease with which any person in this society can become poor. It also articulates a familiar claim that the poor are the vehicle of morality for everyone else and as such can represent only good or evil.

As a consequence, in Christianity the agencies of involuntary poverty are articulated as various alignments and valuations of lack and fullness.[37] In this cipher the voluntary and nonvoluntary are both merged and at odds: it is good to renounce material wealth, but it is bad not to participate in the freedom of the marketplace; it is good to be humble, and poor people should not make demands on society; the relinquishment of will is noble if pursued strenuously and is despicable if experienced out of powerlessness; it is worthy to give to the poor to entrust them with your soul, and the poor have nothing of spiritual worth to give; the poor are of value only if they can fulfill middle-class spiritual needs, and the middle classes are of value only if they can feel superior. The high demands on the discourse of poverty and on the poor themselves perpetuate all kinds of insidious superiorities and inferiorities whereby other people produce and reproduce their moral and spiritual status, preserving above all the authority of choice.

Without some notion of choice, voluntary poverty in Christianity would lose its spiritual authority. Granted, such choice is rarified since one is seen as succumbing to palpable spiritual pressure through practices leading to the ultimate surrender of one's will or ego. But this association of choice with ascetic practice is overridden in the case of the nonvoluntary poor. At the same time that people who are poor practice self-denial, the power of virtue is withdrawn from the poor so that their virtue, even if in compliance with these requirements, does not have the ultimate status of the virtues of chosen poverty. The virtues of the poor, inasmuch as the poor are seen to have them, are considered natural and therefore not an act of will. Yet the poor are also considered to be fully endowed with will, a reverse assumption evident in claims that everyone is an autonomous agent so that people are poor only because they choose to be. And one more perspective comes from Foucault's argument at its most strict, that all people in industrial societies submit to control from capitalism and from the legacy of Christian ascetic practices. The poor, like everyone else, only reinforce authority and order in their seemingly autonomous actions.[38]

The duality and hierarchy in Christian notions of renunciation do not simply express distinctions between body and soul, female and male, and receiver and giver. These distinctions articulate authority patterns in which the struggle for dominance entails the search for salvation and the search for salvation entails the struggle for dominance.

The blind alleys, double-binds, and circuitous routes produced in welfare policies are legion, with women and children often bearing the brunt of their worst consequences. Welfare policies are characterized by intractable contradictions: whether mixing prejudicial judgments of human behavior with rules about food stamps, or requiring that mothers on welfare find reasonably paying jobs while making it impossible for them to be educated for those jobs, or eliminating health care benefits while emphasizing women's responsibility for the well-being of themselves and their children.

Debates about welfare readily deploy notions of body and spirit in their regulations regarding food, work, and health care to articulate contemporary distinctions between the poor and the nonpoor and the deserving and the undeserving poor. As a society we rely on these markets of identity for economic and moral negotiation regarding who can be economically and morally saved. It is tempting to argue that the fraught character of the discourse of poverty simply indicates the desire to avoid confronting the conflicts of class. However, the continued presence of salvation stories, told in part and fragment here, with their referents of discipline, sacrifice, and bodily ambivalence, shows how such stories are required in order for our society to think morally as well as economically about goodness and evil, conflicts and their resolutions. To rely on poverty in these ways is to place it at the center of moral authority, a seemingly laudable move. However, to decenter poverty does not remove it from moral concern but fractures patterns of thinking and practice that require and reproduce poverty.

Notes

1. Karl Marx, "Introduction to a Contribution to the Critique of Hegel's 'Philosophy of Right,'" in *A Critique of Hegel's Philosophy of Right* (1844; Cambridge: Cambridge University Press, 1978), 131–42.

2. See John P. Reeder Jr., "Benevolence, Special Relations, and Voluntary Poverty: An Introduction," *Journal of Religious Ethics* 26, no. 1 (spring 1998): 5.

3. *The Rule of St. Benedict,* trans. and ed. Anthony C. Meisel and M. L. Del Mastro (Garden City, N.Y.: Doubleday, 1975), 52.

4. Gene Outka, "Universal Love and Impartiality," in *The Love Commandments,* ed. Edmund N. Santurri and William Werpehowski (Washington, D.C.: Georgetown University Press, 1992), 1–103.

5. Donald K. Swearer, "Buddhist Virtue, Voluntary Poverty, and Extensive Benevolence," *Journal of Religious Ethics* 26, no. 1 (spring 1998): 71–103.

6. Carter Lindberg, "Through a Glass Darkly: A History of the Church's Vision of the Poor and Poverty," *Ecumenical Review* 33 (Jan. 1991): 37–52, 39–40.

7. Augustine, "Of the Morals of the Catholic Church," in *The Basic Writings of St. Augustine, vol. 1,* ed. Whitney J. Oates (New York: Random House, 1948), see chaps. 26–28, pp. 342–46.

8. Ibid., 56.

9. Richard Leppert, *Art and the Committed Eye* (Boulder, Colo.: Westview Press, 1996), 216–23.

10. Lindberg, "Through a Glass Darkly," 48.

11. Ibid., 40–42.

12. Ibid., 41.

13. Ibid., 43–44.

14. Ibid., 46.

15. Pamela Couture, *Blessed Are the Poor?* (Nashville: Abingdon, 1991), 100–103.

16. Susan Thorne, "Suffer the Little Children: Victorian Evangelicals and Social Reform," paper presented at the Social Science History Association, New Orleans, October 11, 1996.

17. Karel Williams, *From Pauperism to Poverty* (London: Routledge & Kegan Paul, 1981), 95.

18. Michael B. Katz, *The Undeserving Poor* (New York: Pantheon, 1989), 14–15.

19. Marx, *Critique of Hegel's Philosophy,* 131.

20. Karl Marx and Fredrich Engels, "The Communist Manifesto," in *Essential Works of Marxism,* ed. Arthur P. Mendel (1848; New York: Bantam, 1971), 13–44.

21. Marx, *Critique of Hegel's Philosophy,* 142.

22. Ruth Smith and Deborah Valenze, "Mutuality and Marginality: Liberal Moral Theory and Working-Class Women in Nineteenth Century England," *Signs* 13 (winter 1988): 277–98.

23. Walter Rauschenbusch, *Christianizing the Social Order* (New York: Macmillan, 1912), 448.

24. Ibid., 450.

25. Walter Rauschenbusch, *A Theology for the Social Gospel* (New York: Macmillan, 1917).

26. Gustavo Gutierrez, *The Power of the Poor in History,* trans. Robert R. Barr (Maryknoll, N.Y.: Orbis, 1984), 90–94.

27. Ibid., 32–33.

28. Kathleen Sands, *Escape from Paradise: Evil and Tragedy in Feminist Theology* (Minneapolis: Fortress, 1994), 32.

29. Delores Williams, "A Womanist Perspective on Sin," in *A Troubling in My Soul: Womanist Perspectives on Evil and Suffering,* ed. Emilie Townes (Maryknoll, N.Y.: Orbis, 1993), 130–49, 138.

30. Ibid., 144.

31. Patrick Olivelle, *Samnyasa Upanishads: Hindu Scriptures on Asceticism and Renunciation* (New York: Oxford University Press, 1992), 76–77.

32. Margaret Cone and Richard Gombrich, *The Perfect Generosity of Prince Vessantara* (Oxford: Oxford University Press, 1977), xxi.

33. Emilie Townes, "Living in the New Jerusalem," in *Troubling in My Soul,* ed. Townes, 78–91, 85.

34. Nel Noddings, *Women and Evil* (Berkeley: University of California Press, 1989), 181–82.

35. Katie Cannon, *Katie's Canon* (New York: Continuum, 1995), 168–69.

36. Marianne Janack, "Standpoint Epistemology without the 'Standpoint'?: An Examination of Epistemic Privilege and Epistemic Authority," *Hypatia* 12 (spring 1997): 125–39, 133.

37. Ruth Smith, "Order and Disorder: The Naturalization of Poverty," *Cultural Critique* 14 (winter 1989–90): 209–29.

38. Michel Foucault, *Discipline and Punish,* trans. Alan Sheridan (New York: Vintage, 1979); and Michel Foucault, *The Use of Pleasure,* trans. Robert Hurley (New York: Vintage, 1990).

[4]

Rational Man and Feminist Economists on Welfare Reform

Carol S. Robb

WELFARE REFORM IS A WOMEN'S ISSUE, since women are the major clients of and jobholders in the welfare system. In each of the major means-tested programs in the United States, women and the children for whom they are responsible now comprise the overwhelming majority of clients.[1] Because women as a group are significantly poorer than men, and because women tend to live longer than men, significantly more women than men depend on the social welfare system as clients. Furthermore, women depend more on the social welfare system for jobs as paid human-service workers. When there are reductions in social spending, the jobs that are defunded are likely to be jobs that women have had.[2] So it is important that women have a voice about the shape of social welfare policies.

And yet it is very difficult to hear women's voices in the public debate about welfare reform. The loudest voices have been those of conservative males, who have argued that the AFDC program caused poverty by breeding dependency and promoting out-of-wedlock births.[3] While conservative white males have led the charge against public assistance programs, they are, I believe, simply using the reigning economic theory of what constitutes economic rationality. The main shape of "reform" has been to make public assistance grants smaller, attach more conditions and time limits to them, and thereby make them unattractive as a "choice" in the face of poverty. Beneath this reform are assumptions about what it means to act "rationally"; in economic language there is a "simplifying assumption" that human beings in the economic realm act as *Homo economicus,* or "economic man."

In this chapter I want to describe what I understand to be the neoclassical view of economic man and "his" rationality. Then I will look at the literature being generated by some feminist economists to see whether they question or challenge the neoclassical view of economic rationality. Third, I will ask whether a revised view of rationality would have any bearing on different models of public assistance. Finally, I will summarize my own view of what constitutes an appropriate policy direction for addressing poverty.

Rational Man in Neoclassical Theory

Key to neoclassical understanding of *Homo economicus,* or economic man, is a particular theory of rational choice: people are perceived to be persons independent from one another (the separative self), making decisions on three bases:

First, it is not possible to establish whether my enjoyment of social goods is greater or less than your enjoyment of the same or other goods (utilities are interpersonally incommensurable). This assumption means we cannot know which of two persons gained more from a given exchange because there is no unit of measure. Gain or advantage comes from the satisfaction of a person's subjective desires. But we do not know how to compare subjectivities.[4] It is therefore not theoretically legitimate to assert that you are worse off than I am, whether as an individual or as a group. Applied to groups, this assumption deprives programs for alleviating poverty of any economic rationale, particularly if they involve redistributing resources from one group to another.[5] Who is to say that my enjoyment of a second, vacation, home is less, or less important, than your enjoyment of an annual visit for basic health care? "Pareto optimality" is the main criterion of economic efficiency. It describes a state of economic distribution in which no one's utility can be raised without reducing the utility of someone else, even if that someone else is living in gross luxury.[6]

Second, preferences or tastes are unchanging and created outside the market, and hence are unaffected by interactions that occur within the market. The market is thus an arena for people to choose which utilities (goods that provide satisfactions, well-being) they will exchange, given their limited resources. It is a clearinghouse, taking in information about what consumers desire (as measured by willingness to purchase), influencing the production of goods and services. Interference with the market will therefore inevitably lead to distortions which will create greater problems than what the interference is designed to correct. This is another simplifying assumption that leaves out too much of human experience. It obscures several ways in which people who work together influence each other's tastes (people in the job market), people who live in the neighborhood influence tastes (people in the housing market), and the way gender inequality or racial discrimination is perpetuated through generations and thus affects how those discriminated against change their tastes in job options.[7]

Third, my satisfaction does not depend on your happiness or unhappiness. Agents are self-interested. Utilities are interpersonally independent. Only commodities consumed by an individual contribute to that individual's satisfaction. Consumption may include the giving of gifts and taking pleasure in someone else's happiness. But what is excluded from *Homo economicus* are concerns for other people's satisfactions or sufferings that do not express themselves as one's market activities. This "economic man" is indifferent to relative position in society.[8]

Here we have it: economic man springs up fully formed, fully active and self-contained; he has no childhood or old age, no dependence on anyone. The ability to choose is the normal state of being. The environment has no effect on him, except as the passive material, the constraints over which his rationality will make decisions.[9] I do not perceive this view of economic man as a model held up for us to emulate; rather, it is purported by economists to be the best standard method of actually analyzing market decisions.[10] Since women trying to raise children alone, and facing poverty, are not generally described in these terms, could the effort to create new welfare legislation based on this economic man possibly be legitimate? I consulted the newly developing literature coming from people identifying themselves as feminist economists, most of them women, asking whether they turn a critical eye to this view of rationality and "rational man." I read this literature with these questions: Are there different ways of depicting rationality? Would a different view of rationality have any bearing on legislative reform of laws governing public assistance?

Feminist Economists on Rationality

There are several themes that emerge in this literature. To begin with, there is general acceptance of the usefulness of simplifying assumptions, as all models use them.[11] Accepting the legitimacy of modeling, Julie Nelson proposes *enlarging the model* to recognize that persons are socially and materially situated. Rather than focus solely on exchange as the stuff of economics, why not view economics as centrally concerned with provisioning, providing the necessaries of life? Economics as attempting to provision persons would include making distinctions among goods and services as to whether they support survival and health or tend more toward luxury. There is a place for "needs" in economic (and, I would add, moral) theory. Perhaps we can acknowledge that needs are not always clearly distinguishable from wants, and nevertheless admit that our human bodies are dependent upon the physical environment.[12] "Without such an understanding of material connection, we have the scandal of professional economists working out endless theoretical yarns about preferences while a majority of people in the world live in a state of neediness apparent to any observer who has not lost her or his humanity."[13] Thus, the neoclassical model must be enlarged.

If provisioning (in addition to choice) becomes the core of the discipline, the sustenance of life becomes the focus, to be aided and abetted by any of these means: the market, household, government action, exchange, gifts, or even coercion. Choice, scarcity, and rationality are potentially useful tools, but not necessarily the central ones.[14] In effect, the whole purpose of economics shifts when the simplifying assumptions related to the person as agent are enriched with greater attention to social, and conceivably the environmental, sciences. And yet there remains a place for some form of rational choice when the purpose of economics shifts to provisioning.

Some feminist economists suggest the need to *deepen our understanding of rationality* by acknowledging that economic behavior is not only self-interested, but can also be motivated by duty, loyalty, and good will—or morality. The assumption that tastes are unchanging and external to the market will not prepare us to understand the cultural embeddedness in many women's decisions about whether to go into the paid labor force or to seek public assistance so they can focus on domestic labor. Simon Duncan and Rosalind Edwards found clear differences in the United Kingdom between groups of low-skilled white single mothers' and black single mothers' reasoning on this matter. It is not just preferences about paid and unpaid work that vary, but also the rationalities about motherhood and morality.[15] In Duncan and Edwards's study, white mothers tended to see motherhood and employment as incompatible, feeling that good mothers put family and home first. Hence they were less likely to be in the paid labor force. Black mothers were more able to integrate the identities of "motherhood" and "worker" so that to be a good mother meant being in full-time work. Hence they are more likely to be in full-time paid work, even though the labor market is racially and sexually discriminatory.

Duncan and Edwards conclude,

> People are indeed highly rational (given the imperfect information they hold) and they do weigh up the costs and benefits of alternative courses of action— but both what is rational, and what constitutes a cost or a benefit, are defined in

collective moral and social terms, not simply in individual utility terms (which in economic work is very often reduced to monetary terms). Collective moral and social mores are of course highly gendered.[16]

Hence, "gendered moral rationalities" are primary factors in explaining single mothers' decisions about whether to be in the paid labor force. This research challenges the too-simple notion that "preferences" or "tastes" determine rationality. These preferences and tastes, say Duncan and Edwards, change according to the social context, where they are collectively negotiated, sustained, modified, and changed.[17] But rationalities so differently located are not all equal in import; some people have more power than others and are able to impose their tastes on those less powerful. Conservative politicians in some sense know "culture" is significant in the welfare reform discussion. They not only want to cut state benefits but also wish to reinforce culturally traditional values. Ironically, Duncan and Edwards's research indicates that women with traditional values are least likely to seek paid labor.

Here is a third illustration of how rational choice continues to pervade the literature of feminist economists, while the meaning of this rationality is changed. In this instance, a feminist economist has *shifted the question*. One question for policy makers is whether public assistance makes it "rational" to be sexually immoral (measured by out-of-wedlock childbearing) and economically dependent. Rebecca Blank researched this question and found that, indeed, the overall *number* of out-of-wedlock births has been rising, but the birthrate for single women (the probability that a single woman will have a child) has not changed much at all. Between 1960 and 1990, the probability of single white women giving birth increased from 0.9 percent to 3.3 percent. The probability that single black women would give birth decreased from 9.8 to 9.0 percent. However, since fewer women are marrying than in previous decades, there are more single women, and hence more babies born to single women.[18] Blank also notes the declining fertility among married couples, such that if there were no increase at all in the number of out-of-wedlock births, the out-of-wedlock birthrate would still go up.[19]

Blank asks, Why are there more single women? The rise in births among unmarried mothers is not limited to those who rely on AFDC for support. Fewer teens are marrying today, but probably not because the structure of welfare programs encourages teens not to marry. The monthly support levels available from AFDC and food stamps fell steadily from 1960 to 1996–98, when "welfare as we know it" was undone. Cross-cultural comparisons reveal government support for single mothers is much lower in the United States than elsewhere, yet the United States has one of the higher rates of single motherhood, and the highest rate of teen pregnancy. Blank did not observe, but might have, that the rate of abortion is also higher in the United States than among other industrialized countries. The highest rate of teen pregnancy plus the high abortion rate point to a deep ambivalence about sexuality among American youth. They like it, but don't think they should, and thus don't prepare for it to prevent pregnancy. In this respect, teen pregnancies are not a result of choosing but of failing to choose.

Fewer teens, fewer women are marrying because women's ability to find jobs and support themselves (if insecurely in the low-wage labor market) has increased. At the same time men's ability to support a family (particularly men with few formal job skills) has declined, making them less attractive as marriage partners. For both high-school dropouts and graduates, wage rates adjusted for inflation have declined substantially since the late 1970s, by 5 to 15 percent, depending on skill level. And further, the social stigma associated with unwed motherhood has declined.[20]

One could infer from Rebecca Blank's research that teens who do not marry are rationally calculating that their life chances are better not marrying, even if that means they will be dependent on public assistance. She reflects the significance of the social knowing of poor pregnant teens, challenging again the second assumption comprising *Homo economicus:* that preferences or tastes are unchanging and created outside the market. These teens have been affected by poor educational systems, poor job prospects, and racism or sexism in the job market and are acting out of class and racial moral rationalities. They are not acting individually so much as in communities that have historically experienced exclusion from work plans remunerated enough to support family life. In effect, Blank is showing it will do little good to trim welfare programs, and in fact will do much harm, since jobs above poverty wage, with benefits, are necessary to make it possible for teens to marry, and welfare reform may do nothing to encourage job formation. Since the marriage market for many teens has broken down, the job market, and welfare if jobs fail, represent the more rational choice.

Feminist Economics and Welfare Policy

What have feminist economists suggested should be the proper focus for alternatives to AFDC? They have responded to the wider literature on women's poverty which includes three general policy directions: marriage-market proposals, labor-market proposals, and remuneration of reproductive work.

Marriage-market proposals tend to focus on ways to encourage women to marry before giving birth. They are based on the notion that family income is raised by fostering "traditional" family structures and by enforcing child support. If there are two parents in a family, there are potentially two incomes, rather than the one of a single-parent household. As the description of Rebecca Blank's research indicates, this direction is futile without a concerted effort to create above-poverty-wage jobs with sufficient benefits. Because of the absence of such an effort on the part of Congress, none of the authors represented in the literature developed by feminist economists have taken this approach.

Labor-market proposals have at least two emphases: preparing welfare recipients for the labor market, and reforming the labor market to adequately support women responsible for children. The Welfare Reform Act has taken the direction of encouraging women to move into the paid labor force, "encouraging" being a euphemism for time limits on eligibility for public assistance. Some feminist economists have made contributions to labor-market proposals, based on the premise that paid employment is the most significant factor in securing income for women above poverty levels. But they caution that, unfortunately, movement from welfare to the labor market will not necessarily move women out of poverty for structural reasons, particularly occupational segregation by gender and women's overrepresentation in the low-wage labor market. However, the Institute for Women's Policy Research (IWPR) has recommended *packaging* AFDC together with wage labor to support women's being in the paid labor force.[21]

In addition, feminist economists Barbara Bergmann and Heidi Hartmann have made proposals that would help both women receiving assistance and low-income two-parent families who would not have to go on welfare to qualify. Their "Help for Working Parents," or HWP, would guarantee health insurance to all currently uninsured families with children; provide child care for preschool children and after-school care for older children at no cost to families in the bottom 20 percent, at sliding-scale fees to middle-class families; provide more housing assistance to families with children, especially in high rent areas; convert support for single parents not in jobs from a mostly cash benefit into a benefit consisting mostly of vouchers (charge account at the supermarket, rent and utility vouchers, transportation vouchers, plus $100 cash per month).[22] Since the vouchers make recipients more visible as stigmatized "welfare queens," the voucher component of this proposal drew consistent criticism from other feminist economists. Otherwise, this program received significant support.

The HWP proposal is based on survey findings that 60 percent of women who received AFDC would rather have worked if they could have afforded to work, given costs of health care and child care. It increases the ability of all low-income parents to participate in educational and training opportunities, providing full-time child care to parents, whether they work in or outside the home or both. It would require $86 billion additional to AFDC costs, not including the training component which they believe should be budgeted as an educational rather than welfare program. The HWP again uses rational-choice theory, proposing programs that they perceive would make entering the labor market a rational choice for people who until now could not have made income above the poverty level if they had been in paid labor, particularly given the high cost of child care and health care.

Another labor-market proposal, by Teresa Amott, is actually labor-market *reform*. Amott claims the only successful welfare reform will be a reform that takes as its target the labor-market barriers of job segregation and the wage gap. Comparable-worth policies would result in dramatic improvement in the economic status of women employed in service occupations and industries. Raising the minimum wage would also have a significant effect, since about 60 percent of all minimum-wage workers are women. But it would take a 96-cent increase (in 1995) in the national minimum wage to have the same poverty-reduction effect for women workers as a comparable-worth policy that excludes small employers with fewer than twenty-five employees. In 1996 the minimum wage was raised from $4.25 to $5.15 per hour in two increments. Although this increase raised the income of many low-wage women workers, it did not bring the minimum wage to its value of twenty years ago.[23] Comparable worth would reduce the incidence of poverty-level wages among women in administrative-support (including clerical) jobs by 74 percent. It would also result in dramatic improvement in the economic status of women employed in service occupations and industries.[24]

These feminist economists emphasize participating, albeit on fairer grounds, in the paid labor force as an alternative to, or perhaps in conjunction with, something like AFDC. This choice of strategy is most likely seen by these economists to be a way of dealing with the perception that unpaid and paid work confer unequal power, which plagues women in every economic system except nonmarket communal ones.

There is, however, a third approach: *remunerating reproductive labor*. Building on the observations that large-scale unemployment is a permanent feature of industrialized economies, that many European countries do not view single mothers as a "problem," and that taking care of children and the elderly is good and important work, this approach puts greater value on caretaking and wants to provide decent remuneration for it. The pieces needed for this approach are universal health insurance, perhaps universal day care, a guaranteed annual income or at the very least a universal family allowance. These programs should be universal and not means-tested.[25] One author suggests paying for it by dismantling the paternalistic welfare bureaucracy altogether.[26]

This third approach is not well developed in the literature of feminist economists. An allowance to care for children is not viewed by most as the vision for welfare reform, probably because, as mentioned previously, these economists desire to avoid the two-tiered labor system of productive work (with status) and reproductive work (without status). The efforts to confer status with family allowances and other policies in several European countries were motivated in part by nationalist desires to increase fertility rates. In no country have family policies had this result, because none of them can adequately compensate women for the conflict between productive and reproductive work in industrialized countries. But I would argue that increasing fertility rates is an inappropriate goal, given our awareness of the rate at which human populations are destroying the habitat of other species as a global phenomenon. Among the feminist economists I have surveyed, I have seen no indication that the preference for wage-labor strategies to address women's poverty is rooted in a concern for the effects of human reproductivity on other species.

A Feminist Ethical Perspective

It is with great appreciation that I view the effort of feminist economists to name the gender assumptions of *Homo economicus*. It is a good corrective to be reminded of the dependence of all of us on the material world, as we are nature also, in addition to being culture-makers. We are dependent upon others in several stages of our lives, and some people are for unique reasons dependent throughout their lives. We are interdependent with others, human and non-human, throughout our lives in any case. In addition, most of us are also choosers with varying degrees of autonomy and constraints in these choices. We are affected by our social location and social ties, including experiences of solidarity, and in addition have values of our own that may be uncharacteristic of our social support networks. Thus we need to think about models that go beyond those based on the assumptions of "rational man."

What are the consequences of correcting the picture of *Homo economicus* to include motivations of caring along with self-interest, to recognize the significance of dependency in addition to independence, to recognize our social natures in addition to our "choosing" behaviors? I do not believe that the point of these economists recognizing our dependency and interdependency is to promote an "ethic of care," distinguishable from a focus on legal rights to safety net programs. Quite the contrary. If Congress were to consider proposals that would obliterate all tax support for social programs or all wage support legislation, replacing them with appeals to citizens to voluntarily share from their resources out of a sense of *caring*, I and the economists I have cited would argue strongly that such a direction would replace justice with charity, unwisely. Tax-funded programs, minimum-wage laws, and comparable-worth policies are coercive, requiring compliance, and such coercion is justified by the demands of justice. People who have more than sufficiency owe something of their extra to those who do not have enough to live in community with dignity. Need makes claims on justice. To protect the dignity of the poor, tax-supported programs or wage-support policies should be administered through bureaucracies that are in large part impersonal. The corrective to poorly administered welfare systems is not interpersonal intimacy with charity workers who care. It is well-administered public policy whose reach includes all strata fairly.

The point of our dependency and interdependency is that caring for the vulnerable is a crucial part of a healthy community. Men should participate in this caring, too, at a level that goes far beyond "helping" women do reproductive work. Policy should be consistent with an economic ethic that puts a higher value on reciprocity, between labor and capital, between land and capital, and between the reproductive and productive spheres of our work. Such reciprocity will not count in economic terms until economists, with moralists and social scientists, develop modes of measuring value that goes beyond what *Homo economicus* values.

One possible way to implement such reciprocity between the reproductive and productive spheres of our work is to legislate and mandate what we might call "full-cost wages." Full-cost wages are modeled on full-cost pricing in the arena of environmental economics: acknowledging that fully legal production and consumption practices have resulted in the dumping of waste into the air, water, and soil, full-cost pricing involves putting an economic value on harm done (to real-estate value, to health, to recreation, as examples), which manufacturers pay through effluent taxes, resulting in higher prices for their products as they go onto the market. The higher prices result in either less consumption, which results in turn in less production (and therefore less pollution), or better research and development to identify less-polluting methods of manufacture. The effluent tax is politically derived and administered by a government agency (the Environmental Protection Agency), thus requiring a role for government. It depends not on the goodwill of either manufacturers or consumers, but on incentives (to avoid the tax) to stimulate more ecologically sensitive behavior. Yet such an approach cannot depend on self-interest narrowly conceived. The political will to mandate such effluent taxes depends on a vision of shared health and wholeness for ourselves, our children, and the biosphere, a vision we recognize will result in money coming out of our pockets. We will pay the higher prices because it is the right thing to do. To make such a vision possible, we acknowledge that all businesses have to play by the same rules, whether their persons in charge are capable of valuing such a shared vision or not.

Full-cost wages, I propose, could depend on a similar logic. First, acknowledge that productive institutions (manufacturing, construction, service) depend for their ability to function on reproductive activity. These activities include food preparation, cleanliness, provision of shelter, socialization, mental health, and at least a modicum of happiness of the labor force; plus childbearing and child rearing (future workers) and care of elders (people we care about). Then, acknowledge the tendency in the wage-labor market for wages to be bid down to low levels, such that even full-time wage earners cannot support themselves and their families above conditions of poverty. Finally, acknowledge the dependency of all productivity (whether private or public) on the health of the social fabric. Thus we can justifiably mandate (through political means) a minimum wage at a level, adjusted routinely and with a regional factor, such that all persons working thirty hours per week could support themselves and two (three? one? let's agree on the principle, then argue the details) other persons above the poverty level.

The thirty-hour paid work week will likely result in higher prices, and it will exacerbate tension caused by capital flight off-shore. So the political will necessary to pressure for full-cost waging will need to be internationalist in its scope. These are real difficulties.

However, full-cost waging will make less substitute child care necessary and thus make more feasible the expectation that every able adult, whether male or female, will be involved in the care and nurturance of their children and other domestic labor *and* involved in the paid labor force. This picture of the way to value reproductive labor seems fairer to me than the model of taxing wage earners (those in the paid labor force) to fund public assistance for adults not in paid labor to care for their children.

Full-cost waging plays a key role in my view of authentic welfare reform, because I see it as the most promising way to acknowledge and value reciprocity between the reproductive and productive spheres of our work. This approach is not remuneration of domestic labor through tax-funded public assistance. It emphasizes fairly remunerated work for both women and men, along with domestic labor for both women and men. I hope that girls will grow up expecting to be in the paid labor force most of their lives, and that boys will grow up expecting to take direct responsibility for children and elders for most of theirs.[27] Full-cost wages should, however, be one piece of a network of mutually reinforcing programs that, all together, include the following:

- *Social safety net:* There will always be a need for social safety nets that provide for people who simply cannot work, even if sufficient well-paying jobs were available. The injured, the chronically ill, the handicapped, and mothers of infants who do not have paid maternity leave deserve a level of support that sustains their dignity, regardless of the economic status of their families of origin.

- *Comparable-worth policies:* Within the paid labor force, the jobs associated as women's jobs tend to parallel the reproductive role in the home: nursing, food preparation, teaching and socialization, support work. Even when the content of a job category is not associated with the mothering or feminine role, when women predominate in that job the pay goes down relative to the same job category in another firm when it is filled mostly by men. Comparable-worth programs evaluate job descriptions in terms of skills needed, responsibilities entailed, risks involved. They help to counteract the gender bias in the wage structure.
- *Full-cost wages:* Raising the minimum wage and redefining full-time work so that thirty hours would constitute full-time work. Whatever increased costs would result from lowering the work week should be passed along to consumers, so that prices internalize the true cost of workers' time, needed as it is in nurturing self and others as well as in production.
- *Universal health care:* Any serious effort to replace public assistance as the main means of support for poor women and men with children recognizes that, in order for work to raise a family above poverty, a higher minimum wage, along with access to health insurance and child care, must be packaged.
- *National commitment to preschool and after-school programs:* Preschool education for children aged three and above, provided by educated teachers and staff, should be a part of the public school system. Caregivers and teachers should be certified to do this important work, and facilities should be appropriate to guarantee the emotional and physical safety of children, depending on their age. Preschool child care should also move in time to more reliance upon licensed centers, less reliance on unlicensed home-business care. The licensing procedure provides accountability to parents and to the public that facilities and programs are appropriate for little children. Likewise, after-school programs staffed by certified staff should be on the school campuses or very nearby, to provide back-up care for children. These educational and care programs can be paid for with a combination of sliding scale parent fees, and local and state subsidies. With the thirty-hour work week, and both parents (whether married or not) participating in child care, center care could conceivably be limited to twenty hours per week, which is recommended for young children, and perhaps for all children.
- *Insured child-support enforcement:* In the event of divorce or lack of marriage, absent parents should be held financially accountable, regardless of income level. All payments (a percentage of wage income) would be collected like taxes through automatic wage withholding by the employer. If the income from the custodial plus the absent parent is not sufficient to support the child, the government would make up the difference.

- *Parental leaves:* People would earn (by a specified number of months on the job) the right to parental leaves with full or semi-full pay plus benefits for periods (say up to six months) for childbirth or care of a sick family member or elderly parent. Men should be encouraged to take these leaves so that women are not viewed as liabilities in the labor force.

All together, these components of a "welfare program" constitute a wage-labor strategy, one that involves labor-market reform, but that nevertheless presumes that men and women with children will lean heavily on wage labor. This way of guaranteeing the economic support of children should be seen as the norm, a norm that makes provisions for exceptions.

We must continue to encourage church and other publics to break down rigid gender-role stereotyping so that men as well as women will see the rightness and opportunities for joy in being engaged in domestic work along with "productive" work. We must also persuade church and other publics to limit human impact on the earth's biosphere because it is right to do so. Full-cost pricing and full-cost wages are ways of implementing right-making directions. These are the tools at our disposal to show we care not only about the health of our homes, but also about the health of this planet, our home writ large.

Notes

1. According to Nancy Fraser, more than 81 percent of households receiving AFDC are headed by women. More than 60 percent of families receiving food stamps or Medicaid are headed by women. Seventy percent of all households in publicly owned or subsidized housing are headed by women. See Fraser's discussion in *Unruly Practices: Power, Discourse, and Gender in Contemporary Social Theory* (Minneapolis: University of Minnesota Press, 1989), 147.
2. Ibid., 148.
3. Randy Albelda, "Introduction: The Welfare Reform Debate You Wish Would Happen," *Feminist Economics* 1, no. 2 (summer 1995): 81.
4. Paula England, "The Separative Self: Androcentric Bias in Neoclassical Assumptions," in *Beyond Economic Man: Feminist Theory and Economics,* ed. Marianne A. Ferber and Julie A. Nelson (Chicago: University of Chicago, 1993), 42.
5. Ibid., 43.
6. Amartya Sen, *On Ethics and Economics* (New York: Basil Blackwell, 1987), 32.
7. England, "The Separative Self," 44.
8. Herman E. Daly and John B. Cobb Jr., *For the Common Good: Redirecting the*

Economy toward Community, the Environment, and a Sustainable Future (Boston: Beacon, 1989), 86.

9. Julie Nelson, *Feminism, Objectivity, and Economics* (New York: Routledge, 1996), 20. A similar discussion appears in Diana Strassman, "Not a Free Market: The Rhetoric of Disciplinary Authority in Economics," in *Beyond Economic Man,* ed. Ferber and Nelson, 62–63.

10. Simon Duncan and Rosalind Edwards, "Lone Mothers and Paid Work—Rational Economic Man or Gendered Moral Rationalities," *Feminist Economics* 3, no. 2 (summer 1997): 34.

11. Helen Longino, "Economics for Whom?" in *Beyond Economic Man,* ed. Ferber and Nelson, 167.

12. Nelson, *Feminism, Objectivity, and Economics,* 34.

13. Ibid., 35.

14. Ibid., 36.

15. Simon Duncan and Rosalind Edwards, "Lone Mothers and Paid Work—Rational Economic Man or Gendered Moral Rationalities?" *Feminist Economics* 3, no. 2 (summer 1997): 49–50.

16. Ibid., 56.

17. Ibid., 34.

18. Rebecca Blank, "Teen Pregnancy: Government Programs Are Not the Cause," *Feminist Economics* 1, no. 2 (summer 1995): 47–58. National Center for Health Statistics data from 1996 show that 3.9 percent of white teens have a child, and 9.2 percent of black teens do ("U.S. Teens Are Having Fewer Babies," *San Francisco Chronicle,* May 1, 1998, A2).

19. Ibid., 48.

20. Ibid., 50–51.

21. Heidi I. Hartmann and Roberta M. Spalter-Roth, *The Real Employment Opportunities of Women Participating in AFDC: What the Market Can Provide* (Washington, D.C.: Institute for Women's Policy Research, Oct. 1993), 1–10.

22. Barbara Bergmann and Heidi Hartmann, "A Welfare Reform Based on Help for Working Parents," *Feminist Economics* 1, no. 2 (summer 1995): 85–89.

23. Another increase has been proposed by Senator Edward Kennedy (D-Mass.), 50 cents a year in each of the next three years, bringing it to $6.65. This proposal has not been adopted as of this writing.

24. Teresa Amott, "Reforming Welfare or Reforming the Labor Market: Lessons from the Massachusetts Employment Training Experience," in *Women and Welfare Reform* (Washington, D.C.: Institute for Women's Policy Research, 1994), 35–40. A discussion of Amott's proposal is found in Deborah M. Figart and June Lapidus, "A Gender Analysis of U.S. Labor Market Policies for the Working Poor," *Feminist Economics* 1, no. 3 (fall 1995): 60–81.

25. Betty Reid Mandell, "Why Can't We Care for Our Own Children?" *Feminist Economics* 1, no. 2 (summer 1995): 99–104.

26. Theresa Funiciello, *Tyranny of Kindness: Dismantling the Welfare System to End Poverty in America* (New York: Atlantic Monthly Press, 1993).

27. For fuller discussion, see Carol S. Robb, *Equal Value: An Ethical Approach to Economics and Sex* (Boston: Beacon, 1995), esp. chaps. 2 and 7.

PART TWO

RACE, CLASS, AND FAMILY VALUES

[5]

The Production of Character

A Feminist Response to the Communitarian Focus on Family

Gloria H. Albrecht

PEOPLE NORMALLY DO NOT BOTHER to speak at length on that which is going well. Today, community claims the attention of U.S. society because many people live with the growing fear that our life together is becoming meaner, harsher, and more violent. Popular laments typically include references to teenage illegitimacy, fatherless homes, welfare dependency, urban violence, drug use, divorce rates, a cultural obsession with sex, a rejection of anything that limits one's freedom of choice (especially the constraints of marital and family responsibilities), a lack of morally responsible public role models, the frantic busyness of everyday life, an unlimited demand for entitlements, and the obsession with "making it." We have become, we fear, a nihilistic gathering of frenzied individuals.

Popular public descriptions are clearly dominated by those who see these issues as symptoms of a deeper problem: the loss of shared values which sustain a civil and ordered society. In his 1995 State of the Union address, President Clinton said that our civil life is suffering: "Citizens are working together less and shouting at each other more.... The common bonds of community which have been the great strength of our country from its very beginning are badly frayed."[1]

This description is not new. Twenty years ago Daniel Bell named our problem as the problem of community and located its origin within our culture.[2] According to Bell's description, wonderful energies are unleashed by the free, autonomous person pursuing self-interest in the marketplace. However, when such unlimited self-interest is pursued within our civil society, the result is a culture distorted by the chaos of hedonistic selves pursuing every impulse in an endless quest for personal fulfillment. What is needed, according to Bell, is a return to "the public household": a culture in which people are taught the limits of human finitude. In learning their interdependence with others, citizens accept restraints on their personal desires and acknowledge their moral obligations to others. What is needed, he writes, is the return to a sense of *civitas,* "a willingness to make sacrifices for some public good," a willingness that has been lost with the decline of family, synagogue, church, and community.[3]

More recently, the conversation has been entered by a group of self-described liberals and conservatives who call themselves the "new communitarians."[4] With Bell, they identify the problem of American society as an imbalance between the growing demand for individual rights and a reluctance to accept individual responsibility. Amitai Etzioni writes that between 1960 and 1990, American society "allowed children to be devalued, while the golden [calf] of 'making it' was put on a high pedestal."[5] The answer to this moral stagnation, he writes, lies in individuals making different choices... to choose to want less, to choose to buy less, to choose to work less, to choose to earn less. This requires a renewed commitment to the family. "The best place to start," the communitarian platform reads, "is where each new generation acquires its moral anchoring: at home, in the family. We must insist once again that bringing children into the world entails a moral responsibility to provide not only material necessities, but also moral education and character formation."[6] It is the family which teaches those values that form a responsible moral character: to respect others; that hard work pays even in an unjust world; that when you do what is right you feel better; and, most importantly, "to control one's impulses and to mobilize oneself for acts other than the satisfaction of biological needs and immediate desires."[7] The result will be a society of dependable workers and citizens who do not expect handouts.

The family is also the key to good community for Michael Novak. Novak describes humans as "social animals, shaped by the traditions and nourished by symbols, languages, and ideas acquired socially."[8] "More exactly than that," he writes, "each of us is a familial animal."[9] It is within families that individuals learn to accept human frailty in others and face their own foibles. It is within the family that one learns the duties of one's sex and one's social roles. In the family one learns courage, obedience, the just exercise of authority, the desire to earn one's rewards through merit, and the ability to delay self-gratification.[10] Thus, the good family transmits economic advantages to its children and motivates the individual economic agent to "herculean economic activities" by family-regarding self-interest.[11] Through the good family, an individual participates in an economic system which, over time and on the whole, rewards with economic success those families that teach these values.[12]

The differences between Bell, Novak, and Etzioni span the differences between neoconservative and neoliberal discourses. Yet they share a description of our society fragmenting under the assault of hedonistic individuals who are unfettered by any sense of moral responsibility for others. Their common response is to turn to the family as the original source of this moral crisis. As Allan Carlson, president of the Rockford Institute, has written, the family was "the social unit that reconciled liberty with order, that kept individual's interests in balance with the interests of community and posterity. We have already paid a huge price for forgetting that lesson, a price that ranges from high levels of crime to environmental degradation. The proper response, at both the policy and personal levels, is *a turn toward home.*"[13]

At this point it is necessary to caution that the way a problem is described reveals the often unnamed assumptions that are silently at work in the analysis. These assumptions include views of human needs and capacities and of appropriate political and economic orders. It is this underlying worldview that produces the description of the problem and then focuses the range of imaginable solutions. The contemporary communitarian description of our social problems and their focus on the family as the source of these problems is specifically based on unspoken assumptions rooted in certain basic tenets of classical liberal theory and the economic system of capitalism which embodies it:

1. That society consists of the separate and relatively independent spheres of government (the political), marketplace (the economic), and culture.
2. That the ethical climate of the society is produced by an amalgamation of the moral character of its individual members as displayed in individual choices.
3. That moral character is shaped or misshaped in the private sphere of culture where family, religion, and civic associations are located.
4. That the origin of our current social problems lies in the failure of families to form a moral character that sustains community (Bell's "hedonistic bourgeois society," Novak's "new class family of elites," and Etzioni's yuppie parents).
5. That the values which we once had and have now lost are a work ethic of self-restraint, the ability to delay self-gratification, and the control of

biological and emotional impulses (exemplified in the impact of the welfare system and its production of unwed mothers).

Unmasking and challenging these assumptions will help us untangle the ideologies behind the recent changes in the welfare system—changes that have endangered poor women and children in the name of preserving the work ethic and protecting families.

The Problem: A Redescription

A feminist liberative ethic analyzes such social descriptions in order to expose their underlying assumptions and to identify the social experiences from which such ideas make sense. In other words, analyzing how a discourse "sees" a problem reveals the "sense-making" assumptions out of which a group of people explain their society, shape themselves, and relate to others. As a Christian feminist using a liberative ethic of analysis, I offer a differing description of the problems facing our society, particularly our families. My differing description is a result of very different assumptions about society and the forces that shape it—assumptions resulting from different social experiences.

In *Moral Fragments and Moral Community*, Larry Rasmussen remembers reading Bell's book as "an epiphany." However, Rasmussen saw in Bell's description of the problem something Bell himself did not see. Rasmussen writes: "When Bell described modern culture and its moral ethos, I knew he was holding up to the light an X-ray of white, middle-strata psyches and society."[14] This insight points out that the communitarian account of lost community describes the experience of one community: "preponderantly middle-class white U.S. Americans heavily invested in the institutions and patterns of modernity."[15] It is a description of that community's sense of loss in a society where every aspect of successful life is modeled after the competitive, individualistic, self-interested, and instrumental relationships of a capitalist economy. This community now experiences itself as "autonomous creatures who, on the basis of their own wants and preferences, fashion their own world in a series of relationships they themselves make and unmake."[16]

In addition, Rasmussen's point reveals that the communitarian lament over their lost sense of community serves to deflect from view the experiences of those who have never shared equally in the "common" bonds of community. It ignores the history of the struggle of women, minority men, and the poor and working classes for participation in the decisions that shape social values and social institutions. "We" have not suddenly lost a sense of community or common values. Some of us were never meant to be a part of it—not if community implies mutuality and reciprocity in the cocreation of common well-being; not if shared values means a sharing in the processes that name values.

In the current debate about values and community now shaping secular culture and Christian ethics, therefore, it is important to distinguish among the views being produced from differing social locations based on differences of (at least) race, gender, and class. The demands of oppressed groups in our society for basic human needs, for economic security, and for equal voice in social decisions that effect them are ethically distinct from the self-interested demands of those who have had basic needs met and who traditionally have enjoyed such access.[17] Any ethical analysis that erases this difference (as these communitarian responses do) serves to maintain an unjust status quo.

For millions of Americans, the problems of our society are more accurately described as the problems of economic insecurity: declines in real wages; reduction of benefits and pensions; underemployment, unstable employment, and unemployment; the increase in part-time and temporary work; discrimination against women and men of color in the work force; the growing poverty among women who are the sole providers for children; the increasing disparity in income and wealth among sectors of the population; inadequate and unequal access to appropriate education and health care; exposure to pollution and toxic waste placed in one's neighborhood by others; and the unrelenting reduction of public support for families that lack access to sufficient income through employment. From the perspective of those who are marginalized in our society or whose labor is exploited by our society, injustice is the source of community destruction. It batters our civil associations, including the families which nurture us as social beings. From this contrasting description of our social problems, a liberative feminist analysis finds the unspoken assumptions of communitarians unacceptable.

Strong feminist analysis already has challenged the liberal myth of the separation of economic and domestic life.[18] The experiences of women's work makes this particularly clear. Capitalism (within patriarchy) has depended upon women to do the unpaid domestic and reproductive work that reproduces workers while serving (with minority men) as an expendable source of wage labor. At the same time, patriarchy (within capitalism) has depended on women's gendered identity to sustain the civilizing virtues of emotional intimacy, cooperation, regard for others, self-sacrifice, and so forth, because these virtues have no place in the economic sphere of competitive self-interest. These multiple roles have required some women—primarily single women, poor women, and women of color—to cross the boundaries of public and private spheres.

Crossing the boundaries provides a different perspective of society, one that Joan Kelly has called, "a unified, 'doubled' view of the social order."[19] It is a perspective formed by the experience of the interconnection between the so-called public/domestic and the so-called private/economic spheres. It exposes the false communitarian assumption of separate spheres that functions to hide both the realities of most women's lives and the power of the economy to continually reshape gender roles and family structures according to the needs of production.[20]

It is my contention that our current crisis is a crisis created by shifts in the requirements of economic production to which "the family" is responding in order to survive. In economic crises, a variety of family forms will result according to the concrete resources and explanatory worldviews available to families.[21]

Some examples from women's experiences of work will be illustrative. Historian Jeanne Boydston has shown how diverse forces in seventeenth-century colonial America caused shifts in productive relationships which created a new ideology of "economics."[22] While the household remained the center of seventeenth-century economic production, women's productive work there was dropped from the dominant concepts of "work" and "economics." By the mid-eighteenth century, one Jared Eliot concluded that the profit incentive was what separated activity that was "work" from indolence.[23] The nature and value of a woman's actual work did not change, but her position within the intersection of a "masculine" money economy and a "feminine" household made her "domestic" and her activities "not-work."[24]

Not until the nineteenth century did industrialization create an actual physical division between productive work and reproductive work to match the distinction that had already been accomplished ideologically. While this division between home and work primarily restricted the place of white, middle- and upper-class women, it cemented the myth of separate spheres into the social imagination and redefined the characteristics that society would require from each gender: the soft, nurturing, domestic "true woman," and the rational, competitive, aggressive, and public "economic man." Yet, as Stephanie Coontz argues, some women could be domestic "true women" only because the price of manufactured household goods was kept low by extracting surplus value from the slave labor of children, women, and men in the cotton fields; the industrial labor of women and children in the northern garment factories; and the domestic service labor of poor women.[25] The morality of "good" families (defined as those in which mothers could stay at home and teach their children the work ethic) required the "moral inadequacies" of "bad" families (defined as those in which mothers and children worked to support the family). Due to unpaid work (slavery) or poorly paid work (field, domestic, and factory work), the cash needs of poor and working-class families in the nineteenth century could not be met by the market labors of one person. Thus, wives and children transgressed the line between home and work. Rag pickers, scavengers, street vendors, daily domestics, taking-in work, and putting-out work contributed to the family's income. Women's unpaid domestic work also transformed the goods that came into the home into the instruments and products needed for family consumption.[26]

However, the dominant ideology of "the good family" in industrial capitalism had created a symbol system for good and failed families in which a married woman employed outside the home signaled an inadequate husband. Social-work agencies, addressing primarily white poverty in the early 1900s, denounced working mothers as the cause of husbands' abandonment of their responsibility to provide for their families.[27] Confronted with this worldview, poor families often gave up the middle-class ideal of nuclear family privacy for the shared economic resources of an extended family or for the income that could be gained by boarding strangers. It was the ideology of "the good family" that encouraged poor wives to work for extra income at home while poor, uneducated, young girls and their single older sisters flooded the mills for wages to supplement fathers' incomes. Stephanie Coontz's research shows that working-class families survived in the United States at the turn of the century only because the value of the work done at home by married women and very young children and the additional wages brought home by older child labor was added to the grossly insufficient wage of the adult male provider.[28]

One irony of this history is that the virtues currently identified by communitarian proposals as the necessary basis for communities of moral character and for the economic success of good families are the very virtues exemplified by these poor and working-class families. What communitarians fail to see is that survival itself has required the virtues of hard work, self-discipline, delayed gratification, and the ability to control biological and emotional impulses. However, as Jonathan Kozol has so well described in his book *Amazing Grace: The Lives of Children and the Conscience of a Nation*, these virtues are concretely different in the discourses that shape East Fifty-ninth Street in Manhattan and Brook Avenue in the South Bronx. Seven-year-old Cliffe lives in the South Bronx and knows God. Kozol asks him how he pictures God:

"He has long hair and He can walk on the deep water." To make sure I understand how unusual this is, he says, "Nobody else can."

He seems to take the lessons of religion literally. Speaking of a time his mother sent him to the store "to get a pizza"—"three slices, one for my mom, one for my dad, and one for me"—he says he saw a homeless man who told him he was hungry. "But he was too cold to move his mouth! He couldn't talk."

"How did you know he was hungry if he couldn't talk?"

"He pointed to my pizza."

"What did you do?"

"I gave him some!"
"Were your parents mad at you?"
He looks surprised at this. "Why would they be mad?" he asks. "God told us, 'Share!'"[29]

Cliffe (located in a different community) understands well the meaning of self-discipline and delayed gratification, but his meaning makes no sense within the market logic of our economy. It is not self-denial based on rational self-interest. At best it is the luxury of charity, which Cliffe and his family can ill afford. However, it is exactly this expression of hard work, self-discipline, delayed gratification, and belief in achievement through merit which history reveals among those whose lives and labor are being exploited by insufficient wages and the disappearance of work from neighborhoods. It is their values that should cast judgment upon those whose social privileges and "virtues" are dependent upon the products of cheap labor. The moral breakdown revealed by attention to the struggles of the poor can then be located in the unwillingness of the affluent to sustain work for others and to pay for it with living wages.

The end of the twentieth century presents another crisis for many U.S. families, one produced by the economic transitions toward a global and postindustrial economy: the shifting of economic sectors from manufacturing to service, geographic shifts of industries (from Rust Belt to Sun Belt and off-shore), and the increasing polarization of labor into high- or low-wage jobs. Today, families are threatened by the phenomenon of soaring corporate profits accompanied by stagnant wages, declining benefits, and increasing numbers of underemployed workers.[30] Recent attention to what is often referred to as an emerging black underclass belies the continuous history of poverty as a natural result of the capitalist system and an inadequate governmental response.[31] Looking at family changes among the so-called urban underclass, Maxine Baca Zinn concludes: "Families adapt to social and economic constraints by weaving together elements derived from their culture and the limited structural resources available to them. The results may be conceptualized as family strategies.... Family strategies can absorb many of the costs of race, class, and gender inequalities [but] still undermine family well-being. There may be a limit to what can be achieved by each line of adaptation."[32]

While these structural changes continue to disproportionately harm communities of color in the United States, they now also threaten middle-class white America. Finally, "we" have a crisis. Today white middle-class American families are clearly faced with the contradictions within patriarchal capitalism. In a postindustrial, global capitalism, the economy has an increasing need for workers who must tolerate bad work: lower pay, fewer or no benefits, part-time, low-skill work.[33] Under these economic pressures, real wages for men have declined, and more and more women have gone into the wage labor force to support their families. Karen Nussbaum, director of the Women's Bureau, concludes that "the last 10 years have been hard years for most working women and their families: the average working woman saw her real wages stagnate, her benefits contract, and the number of hours she worked grow longer. She is more likely than ever before to be working more than one job and with diminished job security.... The overwhelming majority of working women— 78 percent—earn less than $25,000 a year."[34] Thus, in different ways, at very different costs, middle- and upper-class families, as well as economically marginalized families of all colors, continue to resist, endure, and adapt in order to survive new economic pressures.

Conclusion

More of us are experiencing society as meaner, harsher, and more violent.[35] While the patriarchal assumptions of communitarianism provide no other place to turn for explanation than to the family (particularly the family in which a woman single-handedly functions as parent and provider), remembering the past struggles of oppressed groups within the United States exposes the falsehood of blaming families.[36] A feminist analysis of poor and working-class families requires that we redirect ethical attention from the communitarian focus on the family's (that is, women's) responsibility for public moral decay, and turn that attention toward the political economy. As the concrete place and set of relationships by which a society produces and distributes goods and services, the economy also participates in the material production of various types of family, gender identities, values, and, consequently, character. It produces a legitimating ideology by symbolically establishing a worldview through which people come to consciousness of themselves and others as "familied," as "gendered," as "worker," as "value-able" or "value-less."[37] I have argued for the necessity of analyzing this ideology as a socially produced description that gives us an explanation by which to understand ourselves and others. It provides values by which we learn to judge "good" and "bad" families. It shapes our capacity to see and name the social problem.[38]

I have argued that patriarchal capitalism is a description that explains and justifies both a sexist and racist division of labor and the removal of moral responsibility for social well-being from the political economy to family structures. While depending upon the strength of families, it calls us to ignore the economic demands that devastate some families. While praising family values, it requires values that actually work to destroy families. It requires values intended to reproduce human labor for a subordinate relationship to the demands of capital. For example, Etzioni tells us that hard work pays even in an unjust world and that we are not to be motivated by our biological needs.[39] Novak urges us not to expect our need for community to be part of our work life; delaying self-gratification and bettering oneself economically should be.[40] With historical examples, I have shown how patriarchal capitalism makes use of race, gender, and class to maintain conditions against which some people and families always have had to struggle. With statistics I have argued that the current economic transformations are threatening middle-class America and its ideal family with the same disregard for families and neighborhoods that poor people and people of color always have experienced in the United States. I contend that the erosion of community and the sense of social obligation that newly troubles middle- and upper-class Americans is a logical result of both the contradictions within patriarchal capitalism and of its stated values. Today more of us are feeling that threat.

From the perspective of women, and especially of poor and working class women, the basic assumptions of the new communitarianism render it unable to interrogate the political economy, to hold it accountable for the power it has to give life to families and neighborhoods, and to identify its abuse of that power. The communitarian myth of separate social spheres is particularly at work in welfare dismantling. By isolating the family as the primary originator of moral character, communitarianism participates in blaming the welfare system while ignoring the economic structures that provide both normative descriptions and material social options. Communitarianism ignores the larger web of social injustices which gives privileges and resources to those families defined as "good" while unjustly burdening those "welfare" families labeled "bad." In its refusal to see the material basis for the realities that families face in their responses to shifting economic demands, the new communitarianism merely perpetuates the cause of its own lament.

Notes

1. William Clinton, "The President's Address: We Heard America Shouting," *New York Times,* January 25, 1995, A17.
2. Daniel Bell, *The Cultural Contradictions of Capitalism* (New York: Basic Books, 1976). Bell defines culture as those aspects of a society in which the meaning of life (in response to the experiences of death, tragedy, limits, love, obligations, etc.) is explored symbolically, especially through literature, drama, rituals, and religion (see p. 12). The family is a primary social institution through which these meanings are transmitted.
3. Ibid., 25, 244f.

4. Amitai Etzioni, *The Spirit of Community: Rights, Responsibilities, and the Communitarian Agenda* (New York: Crown, 1993).

5. Ibid., 63.

6. Ibid., 256.

7. Ibid., 91.

8. Michael Novak, *The Spirit of Democratic Capitalism* (Lanham, Md.: Madison Books, 1982; reprint, 1991), 61.

9. Ibid., 161.

10. Ibid., 166–70.

11. Ibid., 163.

12. Ibid., 85. See also George Gilder, *Wealth and Poverty* (New York: Bantam, 1981), esp. chap. 6.

13. Allan Carlson, "The Family and the Constitution," *The Family in America* 3 (1989): 8 (emphasis in the original).

14. Larry Rasmussen, *Moral Fragments and Moral Community* (Minneapolis: Fortress, 1993), 86–87.

15. Ibid., 21, n. 1.

16. Ibid., 37.

17. I use the term *oppressed* informed by the definition provided by Iris Marion Young in *Justice and the Politics of Difference* (Princeton, N.J.: Princeton University Press, 1990), chap. 2.

18. See, for example, Stephanie Coontz, *The Social Origins of Private Life* (New York: Verso, 1988); Jean Bethke Elshtain, *The Family in Political Thought* (Amherst: University of Massachusetts Press, 1982); Susan Okin, *Justice, Gender, and the Family* (New York: Basic Books, 1989); Carol Pateman, *The Problem of Political Obligation* (New York: Wiley, 1979).

19. Joan Kelly, "The Double Vision of Feminist Theory: A Postscript to the 'Women and Power' Conference," *Feminist Studies* 5, no. 1 (spring 1979): 216. Paradoxically, women's capacity to transgress these boundaries was rooted in industrial capitalism's patriarchal construction of the "feminine," specifically in the "feminine" virtue of sacrifice for family. In the United States, some women's work in field, factory, office, and home for wages or barter is justified as a "sacrifice for family" while other women's isolation at home doing unpaid domestic labor (a different form of economic vulnerability) is also justified as a "sacrifice for family." What links together these contradictory social locations is this ideology of the feminine—that is, the appropriateness of women's self-sacrifice for the well-being of the family.

20. See Linda Kerber, "Separate Sphere, Female Worlds, Woman's Place: The Rhetoric of Women's History," *Journal of American History* 75, no. 1 (June 1988): 9–39. For an account of how particular forms of labor exploitation led to creative and adaptive forms of family among African American, Chinese, and Chicano communities in the United States, see Bonnie Thornton

Dill, "Fictive Kin, Paper Sons, and Compadrazgo: Women of Color and the Struggle for Family Survival," in *Women of Color in U.S. Society*, ed. Bonnie Thornton Dill and Maxine Baca Zinn (Philadelphia: Temple University Press, 1994), 149–69.

21. For an analysis of the relationship between the economy and family patterns in the urban underclass, see Maxine Baca Zinn, "Structural Transformation and Minority Families," in *Women, Households, and the Economy*, ed. Lourdes Beneria and Catharine Stimpson (New Brunswick, N.J.: Rutgers University Press, 1987), 155–71.

22. Jeanne Boydston, *Home and Work: Housework, Wages, and the Ideology of Labor in the Early Republic* (New York: Oxford University Press, 1990).

23. Ibid., 28.

24. Julie Matthaei, *An Economic History of Women in America: Women's Work, the Sexual Division of Labor, and the Development of Capitalism* (New York: Schocken, 1982), 33–34.

25. Stephanie Coontz, *The Way We Never Were: American Families and the Nostalgia Trap* (New York: Basic Books, 1992), 11. In 1840, 40 percent of the industrial labor force comprised women and children. See Claudia Goldin, *Understanding the Gender Gap: An Economic History of American Women* (New York: Oxford University Press, 1990), 50.

26. Boydston, *Home and Work*, 88–90.

27. Matthaei, *Economic History of Women*, 130.

28. Coontz, *The Way We Never Were*, 111, 235. A 1923 study of poverty-level families showed a labor force participation rate of 96.3 percent for fathers, 96.6 percent for sons, 95 percent for daughters, and 25.9 percent for wives. See Matthaei, *Economic History of Women*, 127.

29. Jonathan Kozol, *Amazing Grace: The Lives of Children and the Conscience of a Nation* (New York: Crown, 1995), 8.

30. For example, see Floyd Norris, "Paradox of '92: Weak Economy, Strong Profits," *New York Times*, August 30, 1992, section 3, p. 1. Norris reports the new highs reached by corporate earnings in the midst of a recession by laying off workers and reducing payrolls. He writes, "America is not doing very well, but its corporations are doing just fine." Where technology once replaced human muscle, it now replaces human brains. Today, the service industry faces the kind of technological upheaval that has reduced agricultural and manufacturing jobs. The big boom in employment in the 1990s is in temporary work and part-time jobs. See Teresa Amott, *Caught in the Crisis: Women and the U.S. Economy Today* (New York: Monthly Review Press, 1993), 36–37, 61–64.

31. Several recent studies have concluded that between one-third and one-half of the increase in poverty among families with children in the 1980s was due not to changes in family structure but to the decline in antipoverty impact of government programs (Coontz, *The Way We Never Were*, 260).

32. Baca Zinn, "Structural Transformation," 168. Similarly, Jeremy Rifkin, citing Sidney Willhelm's warning in 1970 that the racial outcome of the technological revolution would be to move black Americans "from exploitation to uselessness," concludes that "the commodity value of Black labor has been rendered virtually useless by the new automated technologies." See James Weinstein, "Worked Over," *In These Times* 26 (June 1995): 29.

33. The Women's Bureau of the U.S. Department of Labor reports that the majority of jobs created between 1975 and 1990 and the majority (nearly 94 percent) of new jobs which will be created between 1990 and 2005 will be in the service-producing industries. Twenty-two percent of all new jobs will be in the retail trade division, where many of the jobs will be part-time, offer low pay, require little training or skill, demand little work experience, offer limited advancement, and be extremely sensitive to shifts in the economy (U.S. Department of Labor, Women's Bureau, *1993 Handbook on Women Workers: Trends and Issues* [Washington, D.C., 1993], 232–33).

34. Ibid., iii. In 1986, the Joint Economic Committee of the U.S. Congress estimated that if large numbers of women (primarily married white women) had not entered the wage labor force in the past two decades, real family income would have dropped 18 percent between 1980 and 1986. See the Taskforce on Issues of Vocation and Problems of Work in the U.S., *Challenges in the Workplace* (Louisville, Ky.: Publication Service, Presbyterian Church [U.S.A.], 1990), 19. The shift to service work and corporate efforts to reduce the cost of labor (including downsizing, the off-shoring of jobs, greater use of part-time and contract workers, and reductions in benefits) continue to depress family income. In 1988, it took two wage earners in two-thirds of white and three-fourths of black households to earn a middle-class income (between $25,000 and $50,000). See Marvin L. Oliver and Thomas M. Shapiro, *Black Wealth/White Wealth: A New Perspective on Racial Inequality* (New York: Routledge, 1995), 96. Coontz estimates that if both parents were not working, more than one-third of all two-parent families would be counted as officially poor. (See Coontz, *The Way We Never Were,* 260.) In 1992, more than one-half of those mothers with children under the age of three were in the wage labor force; more than three-fourths of those mothers with children between the ages of six and thirteen were in the labor force. It should be noted, however, that there is still a large difference between the participation rates of black women and white women with preschool children. In 1990, black mothers of preschoolers had a labor force participation rate of 73.1 percent, compared to 57.8 percent of white mothers. (See *1993 Handbook on Women Workers: Trends and Issues,* 5, 12.)

35. For example, the poverty rate for all children has increased from 14 percent in 1969 to 21.8 percent in 1991, with much higher rates for children of color. (See James Newton Poling, *Deliver Us from Evil* [Minneapolis: Fortress Press, 1996], 86.) The United States now ranks twenty-first in the world in infant mortality. (See Coontz, *The Way We Never Were,* 2.)

36. We need to remember that in 1920, one-fifth of all American children lived in orphanages because living parents could not afford to care for them; that in 1960, one-third of all American children lived in poverty despite low divorce rates. (See Coontz, *The Way We Never Were*, 4–5.)

37. See, for example, Samuel Bowles and Herbert Gintis, "The Economy Produces People: An Introduction to Post-Liberal Democracy," in *Religion and Economic Justice*, ed. Michael Zweig (Philadelphia: Temple University Press, 1991), 221–44.

38. See Mary McClintock Fulkerson, "Feminist Theology and the Subjecting of the Feminist Theologian," presentation to the American Academy of Religion, Nov. 1993.

39. Etzioni, *Spirit of Community*, 91.

40. Novak, *Spirit of Democratic Capitalism*, 137, 93–94.

[6]

Family Values and Working Alliances

The Question of Hatred and Public Policy

Janet R. Jakobsen

THE CONTEMPORARY DISCOURSE OF "family values" has become so omnipresent within U.S. political culture that it is invoked by representatives of both mainstream political parties. In the 1996 presidential election, there was apparently no disagreement about the necessity of family values for America, despite the question of whether it takes a village or just a 1950s-style nuclear family, conjoined with "values." This bipartisan agreement is perhaps not so surprising given the ever-more-minute product differentiation between the two parties, but it is noteworthy given the fact that this bipartisanship was enacted legislatively in the 1996 welfare "reform" bill. This legislation (perhaps the largest social change yet of the post-Reagan era), passed by a Republican Congress but signed by the Democratic president, was funded in part by the bipartisan talk of family values that it materialized.

Talk of family values has become so omnipresent because it condenses an entire series of social relations. When enacted, "family values" is the sexualization of race, gender, and poverty, that authorized welfare reform. The complexity of relations condensed within family values is belied by the apparent obviousness of the invocation. In contemporary U.S. politics, the meaning of "family values" is so obvious, so commonsensical, that one doesn't have to say what is meant by either "family" or "values" or the conjunction. And yet, this naturalization of the term is precisely what allows it to operate in such a powerful fashion, allowing its invocation to cover over a series of incoherencies that it condenses.

What, after all, does "family values" mean? I have to admit a certain (and willful) bafflement. The documents that have codified its meaning, particularly the Contract with the American Family and its sibling, the Contract with America, which was used so successfully in the 1994 Congressional elections, might promise the possibility of, if not diminishing, at least articulating this bafflement, but these documents just do not make sense. To cite just one example, one point in the Contract with the American Family urges an end to, or privatization of (whichever comes first?), the Public Broadcasting System. Given the political right's frequent condemnation of the "filth" produced in Hollywood and on the internet and its relation to children, it seems just a little odd that the one source of consistent, "clean" (and nonviolent) children's programming would be targeted as evil in a document focused on the family. Similarly, welfare reform as a specifically "family" value can be read as contradictory. Certainly, the primary program to be cut—Aid to Families with Dependent Children—was conceived to provide support specifically for families in difficult financial situations. Only a very specific set of assumptions can make *cutting* support for families seem like a coherent expression of valuing the family.

Simply pointing out these inconsistencies, however, has not necessarily proved to be an effective strategy in resisting the power of the invocation or its political effects. When, for example, opponents of the 1996 "Defense of Marriage Act" (DOMA) pointed out that many of its proponents, while appealing to the language of family values, had themselves been married multiple times, the obvious contradiction had no effective impact on the vote itself. Similarly, with regard to debate over welfare policy, it is not enough to point out the inconsistencies in the rhetoric of welfare reform: to point out that the budget deficit could be addressed by cuts in other areas; to show that the stereotypes on which this rhetoric depends are precisely stereotypes (and in particular that they are racist stereotypes); to demonstrate the importance of reliable, affordable child care and health care; or to point out that an economy dependent on ongoing un- and underemployment has its costs. Naming these facts will not, in and of itself, counter the prevailing rhetoric, because the enumeration of facts does not address the complex of relations that are being reworked through talk of family values, nor does it address the ways in which the apparently obvious meaning of "family values" both pulls together and covers over the contradictions within this complex of relations. Simply to point out a contradiction does not intervene in the management of contradiction that makes for common sense and that makes talk of family values such a powerful discourse in the contemporary United States.

Unfortunately, however, the claims of those social movements which have opposed the right-wing uses of family values can also take on this supposedly self-evident but nonsensical quality. Take, for example, the popular slogan found on bumper stickers and T-shirts "Hate Is Not a Family Value." It seems quite possible that "hate" *is* a family value, and if the Defense of Marriage Act and the welfare reform bill are any indication, it may be central to family values. Apparently, if gay people get married (a relatively conservative act that affirms social structure), America's families will fall apart. Given the nonsensical nature of this argument (it makes sense to "defend" heterosexual marriage against gay marriage only if one believes that, given the option, the majority of people would choose gay marriage), something more than logic must be motivating DOMA. Somehow the denigration of homosexuality in relation to heterosexuality is necessary to hold families together.

The question is, what is the specific relationship between the moral discourse of family values and the affective invocation of hatred? There is certainly a distinction between hate groups and movements and the widespread sites of family values, including those middle Americans who experience themselves as not hateful and, in fact, as tolerant of "others." The political spectrum in the United States is not, however, merely a line-up of individual and distinct positions. It is, rather, a moral economy of positions that have meaning only in relation to one another.[1] Moreover, it is important to ask the specific question of the relationship between ongoing domination and hate. Why is it that America has been unable to eradicate various forms of domination, given that the American public thinks of itself as liberal in the sense of being fully democratic and understands its public affect to be a tolerance correlative to that liberalism?

Welfare reform has a complex relation to hate in that it both depends on the affective motivations for dominations and on the denial that hate is in any way part of the policy process. Thus, policies that are substantially draconian can be represented as not only *not* motivated by hatred, but as somehow beneficial to participants in government programs: welfare reform will "free" them from the "cycle of dependency." I will argue that these two facts—the distinction between hate groups and family values and the passage of legislation that does the work of hate—indicate the working of a complex economy in which the moderate disavowal of hatred can work to extend rather than extinguish its effects.

"Family values," thus, is part of a Christian-right discourse that serves as a connector between groups, movements, and discourses which might explicitly be referred to as "hate groups" and a moderate, Christian-identified public which remains invested in relations of domination but wishes to disavow connection to the affective dimension of domination—that is, hatred. The simultaneous disavowal and enactment of hatred works together to such an extent that even members of explicitly white-supremacist groups like the Ku Klux Klan might disavow hatred.[2] While the national offices of an organization like the Christian Coalition certainly would deny such outright hatred, the connector provided by Christian homophobia allows the disavowal to enable the functioning of the hate. Once the disavowal is made, there need be no responsibility taken for the connections between outright hatred named Christian and moderate homophobia traveling under the same name (Christian). Thus, the strong emotion and even violence linked to hate can remain part of explicitly Christian discourses. For example, at a political rally in Atlanta in 1993, a Christian minister proclaimed that he wouldn't be satisfied "until all of them [homosexuals] are carried out in body bags."[3] Similarly, bumper stickers like "I'm Pro-Life and I Shoot" or "Army of God and Atlanta Bomb Squad" (a reference to the bombings in Atlanta at a clinic that provides abortions and at a lesbian bar in 1997), remain part of the right-wing Christian activist culture.[4] This question of relation is so important because it points out how complicated it is to intervene in the rhetoric of the right. If denying that you hate anyone is one of the tools that enable hatred, if the right is happy to disavow hatred and to claim moderation and even tolerance, then simply opposing hatred will not be effective.

If a straightforward counterdiscourse will not provide effective intervention in the litany of claims made in the name of family values, how should activism and advocacy be framed and undertaken? A crucial starting point is to ask, why sexual regulation? Why is the containment of sexuality within the confines of "family" the most visible articulation of "values" in the current moment? Why is a major social change like welfare reform undertaken through a rhetoric focused on young poor women and their sexuality? The prevailing discourse simply takes for granted that American politics should be conducted through talk of sexuality. Is there, after all, anything more "American" than an obsession with sexuality *and* its regulation? In particular, is it not the primary concern of American "religion" to regulate sexuality? How did values about sexuality, rather than, for example, social justice become the primary purview of religion in America? The political centrality of sexuality and the connections between sexual regulation and religion often seem assumed, despite the fact that it is not the case that sexual regulation has taken this particular form (family values) at all times and places. It is not the case that all religions have been invested in this type of family values. It is not even the case that Christianity has always been invested in the particular types of sexual regulation currently trumpeted.[5]

Once again, however, the counterdiscourse can depend on these same assumptions. For example, the explanation for family values, within a radical field like lesbian, gay, and bisexual studies, often depends on some version of the naturalization of religion as sexual regulation, along the lines of "Oh, of course, they hate us, they're religious." And, yet, this very logic of reduction is precisely the claim the right wants to make, "Of course, we hate them, we're religious, and to be religious is to have values and to have values is to be conservative." In accepting the "of course they hate us," story (a story which produces a naturalized set of connections from religion through Christianity to sexual regulation), progressive politics can come to articulate the very claims that it would contest. This naturalization is not useful politically. In fact, it plays into one of the central claims of the right: that to be religious or Christian is to be invested in the particular set of values named "family," and that if you don't agree with these particular values, you don't have any values and can't be truly religious. This move not only hides the complexities of something we might call "religion," and undercuts those sites from within religious history and practice where resistance might be undertaken, it sets up an oppositional dynamic between sexual deviants and Christians that works not only to the advantage of the right, but which also constructs a "tolerant," middle-of-the-road, middle-class that tolerates hatred along with the hated.

"Family values" addresses a fear that political liberalism has evacuated all values, so the move to religiously inflected family values is a means of reasserting values of any kind. The condensed understanding of values makes it seem like the choice is family values or no values. Thus, the Democrats have taken up this language because to fail to do so would leave them open to the charge of valuelessness. By connecting values to something so supposedly common as family (after all, doesn't everyone have a family?), it is possible to assert values without the middle class's sense of itself as tolerant being challenged. Thus, the conjunction of family and values allows for a position that asserts sexual regulation under the continuing guise of tolerance.

Politics and Common Sense

The question faced by activists is how the assertion of something so common-sensical, so seemingly benign and even positive as ascribing a value to "family," can work as an ideology that allows for policies like welfare reform which actually have such detrimental effects on some families. Common sense is constructed through a network of binaries that organize conceptual categories and possibilities, that organize what can make "sense" in a given moment. And in the contemporary situation, these binaries enable sexual regulation through the invocation of family values. This network of binaries, like that between moral and immoral or hetero- and homosexual, is the discursive fabric that makes family values into common sense, into words that can be invoked to great effect without having to state their specific meanings. Catherine Bell theorizes the workings of such networks, arguing that the complex interrelations of the binaries are what allow the network to provide a (common) sense of "a loosely knit and loosely coherent totality."[6] Within such a network, the binaries both line up (she uses the example of light/dark, good/evil, culture/nature, male/female)[7] and don't precisely line up, so that in the process of shifting among binaries a series of claims are articulated with one another, but they can be defended on the grounds of the single binary that makes the most sense in a given moment or argument.[8] The oppositions are treated as homologies: light is to dark as good to evil, culture to nature, and male to female; but there is also slippage among the terms so that they are not precisely homologous. This slippage, rather than undermining the network, can actually reinforce it, however, by providing a shifting site of reference in the face of counterevidence. Thus, if men empirically show themselves to be not necessarily good, the terms can slip to the culture/nature binary and whatever "evil" men do—wars, for example—is now placed in the context of the (necessary and) good production of culture. The slippage to the culture/nature binary shifts the meaning of the good/evil binary so as to return male to its homologous relation to good. "Culture" becomes a node that articulates in two directions—to good and to male—and as such, it also stabilizes the meaning of "good" in relation to "male." The possible incoherence sparked by empirical counterexample is, thus, averted. Rather, the network of binaries allows precisely for the management of incoherencies. When one binary is challenged, threatened, insufficient, problematic, or itself incoherent, it is possible to discursively slip to another, thus protecting the network as a whole.[9]

The network of binaries invoked by and condensed into family values works to regulate a number of social relations which are not named directly, because invoking one opposition can invoke the network as a whole. Thus, for example, moral/immoral can be mapped onto social locations, like man and woman in Bell's example or hetero- and homosexual in the Defense of Marriage Act. The image of family can, in the case of the Defense of Marriage Act, be invoked to police homosexuality. But in the case of welfare reform, family values works to regulate heterosexuality, and by tying the regulation of sexuality to black/white and middle-class/poor binaries, it can work to regulate the (hetero)sexuality of poor young women of color. Through this regulation, discourses of race, class, and gender relations are elaborated even as they are invoked in condensed form.

If the image of appropriate family relations is restricted to the supposedly traditional but historically specific (even unusual) postwar American nuclear family, then sexuality, and in particular sexual "respectability," is made the marker for middle-class propriety to which all Americans should aspire.[10] The American dream of class mobility is here tied to sexual respectability. All Americans should aspire to the middle class, and the best means of doing so, regardless of economic resources, is to emulate the middle-class family. Therefore, all Americans should act as if they are living in middle-class families. The moralistic underpinnings of this mobility narrative imply that a personal and moral failing can be ascribed to those who are not mobile. This narrative has been further racialized, such that the empirical fact of race hierarchies in the United States is narratively explained not by reference to the historic and ongoing operations of racial domination, but to the supposedly unfortunate, but necessary results of a refusal by or an inability of people of color to adopt and enact middle-class family values.[11] As Patricia Hill Collins states, "The advice to the poor seems to be that the sole requirement to lift oneself out of poverty is to think and behave like white, middle-class men and women."[12]

These family values are strongly gendered such that both "family" and "values" should read through gender hierarchy. "Family" means only a patriarchal family with "appropriate" gender hierarchy in which caring for children is women's work but work that can only be accomplished successfully if supervised by a man.[13] The onslaught of talk about the apparently unavoidably negative consequences of raising children without fathers (itself a gendered discourse where single mothers supposedly produce girls who become single mothers and boys who become criminals) makes women's work to care for their children when single a moral failing rather than an accomplishment. This assumption plays into a history of descriptions of mothering in which women are both designated as the guardians of culture and mistrusted in their ability to carry out this task without supervision, a mistrust that is indicative of a cultural anxiety about women's autonomy more generally.[14] Thus, "values," when conjoined with "family" is an assertion against women's claims to moral autonomy. The slashing of Aid to Families with Dependent Children works to materially enforce the denial of women's autonomy by limiting the economic and hence relational possibilities for women to negotiate in or leave heterosexual relationships.

As a condensation of this complex matrix, the invocation of family values articulates in two directions. Through sexual regulation, race, gender, and class relations are also regulated as moral discourse about sexuality reinforces social hierarchies and dominations. Welfare reform enacts the economic and political changes of budget-cutting and shifting the role of government through a moralistic discourse focused on out-of-control sexuality and inappropriate familial form. These shifts in government reinforce class hierarchies as the elites benefit from shifts in tax policy while middle-class entitlements are protected and the poor pay the costs of reducing government. In the other direction, sexuality itself is regulated. Yet these economic and government shifts are accomplished through a discourse dependent on a racialized set of images of welfare mothers, images invoked in order to control the sexuality of young, single women of color and the number of children they have by limiting already severely constrained economic choices. The Defense of Marriage Act similarly constricts the options for any form of sexual relation that is not defined by heterosexual marriage by restricting the form under which a whole series of social benefits, from health care to citizenship, are available. Ultimately, welfare reform works to reinforce a racialized and patriarchal heterosexuality, naturalized as the (white, middle-class) "family."

In the case of family values, the network of binaries is quite extensive. In addition to the ties among moral/immoral, white/black, middle class/poor, and hetero-/homosexual, which are tied to the structure of "family," a set of binaries is condensed into the conjunction with "values." These binaries connect a set of structural issues by tying together terms like: religious/secular, moral values/economic value, Christian/non-Christian, and American/un-American, with moral/immoral, hetero-/homosexual, black/white, and middle class/poor. This complex network invoked through the claim for values accomplishes a number of things for the right. If, for example, to be American is to be Christian in a certain way, then non-Christians, or even those who are Christian in another way, will always be minorities that can only be tolerated within the broader American public. Moreover, members of religious minorities are American only insofar as they agree with dominant American (that is, Christian) values. So the points of similarity or overlap in values, not the differences among traditions, become the publicly acceptable articulation of all religions. These claims also pose the Christian-identified radical right as the site of the intersection between religion and values, such that any alternative configurations of these relationships (values, for example, that are not necessarily Christian) are erased. Thus, "family values" allows a reference to values that are effectively marked as religious and Christian without the need to name them directly as such.

This move is at once universalizing and specifying, or, more accurately, it enacts the universalization of a specific set of values, such that all values that travel under other names can be conflated with Christian values and further condensed into family values. All those that cannot be so condensed are simply placed outside the realm of recognizable values. They simply are not values. So, for example, Katie Cannon argues that black womanist ethics are often not recognized as moral, are labeled immoral or amoral, precisely because they are in resistance to capitalism, rather than enacting the dominant U.S. Protestant ethic that supports capitalist endeavor.[15] In other words, even Protestant Christian values if not in line with the secular-market version of Christianity are unrecognizable as values. The Christian Coalition has, in fact, had difficulty in its attempts to form Catholic and Jewish alliances precisely because the values that the Christian Coalition names as "Christian" or as "religious" are a particular version of Protestantism.[16]

An opposition is then established between the religious as the site of values and another nonreligious site supposedly free of values which could be termed the "secular."[17] The split between the secular and the religious, as it developed in the modern period, was often articulated as being about establishing a site of "freedom" from religious dogma. This freedom from religion included economic freedom from ecclesiastical authority, instituting the market as a site of economic activity outside of the oversight of the church.[18] Thus, the secular is the site of capitalism, where the market operates freely, driven only by economic value, not moral values. While individuals are expected to bring their own (Protestant) work ethic to their actions in the market, the market itself responds only to economic, not moral, incentive. The fear induced by this structural asymmetry is that the market, because value-free, will not recognize and may not reward hard work. This disconnection between economic and moral value can open the space for a moral discourse critical of capitalism, but I will argue that moral values can also be invoked as the buffer to the market. Specifically, the desire for family values is, in part, the expression of a desire to buffer the effects on the middle classes of the expansion of the market. The fear that a value-free market has evacuated all possible moral value is countered by the location of a nonmarket site of values named "family." This allows for a discourse of values that in being distinct from capitalism nonetheless does not challenge but rather works with that economic system.

Why Welfare? Why Now?

The notion of family values thus lays the groundwork for various forms of social retrenchment. In this sense, the fact that talk of "family values" is ubiquitous indicates that the field of contemporary American politics is predisposed in favor of intensifying social regulation. Regulation on social (but not economic) issues is the likely outcome of political struggles. Regulation is not, however, the necessary outcome. As activists, we need to ask both how to intervene effectively and why regulation takes the particular forms it does in the current moment. We cannot assume that the particular battles engaged by the right are the necessary outcome of social conditions. Rather, they are constructed *as if* necessary in order to make it seem only natural that politicians are talking about cutting the social safety net, thereby setting the terms of debate in favor of regulation before the debate is even engaged. For example, one of the central questions about welfare reform is how welfare has become the site for budget-cutting. Why are social programs that address poverty paradoxically treated as "luxuries" when budget-cutting is proposed as necessary? And why is the response to the economic changes that supposedly motivate budget-cutting not one of social solidarity? Why was there a language of social solidarity that could be meaningful, if not fully effective in terms of justice, during the hard economic times that led to the establishment of social programs? And why is such language apparently so unavailable in U.S. public discourse today? How is it that the moral language of "social" and "justice" has been transfigured into one of "family" and "values"? And how does the move to make family values coextensive with morality allow the work of hatred to be conducted under the auspices of the moral?

The rhetorical effectiveness of family values provides part of the answer. Talk that conjoins family and values not only serves to condense social relations, it also constructs the relationship between economic value and moral values. In particular, it works to manage a particular set of contradictions created by recent economic shifts—shifts which David Harvey has theorized as the move from the modern to the postmodern.[19] Harvey argues that the economic shifts through deindustrialization from an economy organized around industrial production to one in which capital is much more mobile are so fundamental as to be indicative of an epochal shift: from industrial capitalism to postindustrial capitalism and from modernity to postmodernity. In particular, Harvey argues that in the United States, the shift toward the "condition of postmodernity" has been a shift away from the Fordist compromise(s) between U.S. corporations, government, labor, and the "public" which connected U.S. national interest to the welfare of U.S. corporations. Fordism for Harvey is the relatively stable economic arrangement which enabled industrial production.[20] Thus, under Fordism it made sense to say "As goes GM, so goes the nation." The contemporary movement toward transnationalism as the mark of (U.S.) corporate structure has also prompted a reworking of the relationship(s) among the economy, the state, and the American "nation." Now, GM is more of a transnational, than an "American" company. These economic shifts have created a number of dislocations in the nation, most dramatically the deindustrialization of much of the United States, particularly in the Northeast and Midwest (traditionally sites of extensive labor movement and union activity), but also including a decrease in job security and an increasing disparity between economic classes. Moreover, the presumed tie between U.S. corporations and the welfare of the American nation has been undercut by transnationalization.

In reference to the modern period, it is common to speak of the "nation-state" as a single term. Because the nation-state developed in some conjunction with capitalism, the function of the state is usually understood as mediating between the market and persons subjected to the market embodied as the "public" or "nation." In the post–World War II Fordist compromise, this was certainly the case: the role of the state was both to mediate the compromise between corporations and organized labor and to constitute a single nation which this compromise sustained. Thus, the welfare state, particularly through its federal programs, was supposed to create a nation in which everyone had some sense of investment in the success of corporate America. Even as the terms of the agreement stabilized corporate power, they also opened up a discursive space in which checks on corporate "interests" could be articulated when corporations did not serve the "national interest." Thus, corporations in this period were the primary site of reference in the invocation of the term "special interests." This rhetoric of corporate special interests was not to say that corporations (or capitalism) were themselves problematic, but rather that they needed to operate within the terms of the national interest—the terms set by the "public," which supposedly included everyone and which supported families. Social movements of the 1950s and 1960s succeeded in accomplishing what they did, in part, by showing that not all "Americans" were included in the well-being of the nation. The terms of the agreement provided the discursive space to challenge through new social movements the all-too-real ways in which many Americans continued to be shut out of the supposed benefits of Americanness and to challenge corporations as sources of, if not oppression or domination, at least problems of constraint and danger, which needed to be addressed.[21]

Now, however, in the move to the postmodern period,[22] two major shifts have taken place: transnationalization and the shift in the relationship between the financial markets and industrial production, such that financial markets dominate industrial production in a new way, as indicated, for example, by the 1980s' mania for leveraged buyouts and the breakup and sale of corporate assets. These two shifts—transnationalism and the extension of the supremacy of finance—indicate changes in the way that the state works for the market, specifically the ways in which the state works now in the service of the financial markets as relatively autonomous in relation to the market for goods which drives industrial production.

What the combination of these two shifts implies is that the job of the state in relation to American business has shifted and the nation must in some sense be constructed separately from the state's relation to transnational corporations. Both of these tasks may still take place at the site of the government, but the restructuring of government that we currently see under way is reflective of the differentiation of these two tasks. As Harvey points out, the state's traditional job of working for capitalism and serving as a site for the constitution of the nation is now a contradictory one:

> Arenas of conflict between the nation state and trans-national capital have, however, opened up, undermining the easy accommodation between big capital and big government so typical of the Fordist era. The state is now in a much more problematic position. It is called upon to regulate the activities of corporate capital in the national interest at the same time as it is forced, also in the national interest, to create a "good business climate" to act as an inducement to trans-national and global finance capital, and to deter (by means other than exchange controls) capital flight to greener and more profitable pastures.[23]

These shifts are accompanied by a shift in the labor market that intensifies both class and race divisions in the United States as the sense of threat in relation to the loss of capital and industrial production overseas is articulated for and by middle America as a threat of: "Don't complain or *we* may soon all be out of a job." The effectiveness of this threat has been an apparently paradoxical embrace of corporate America just as it becomes even less socially responsible. Thus, we no longer can speak of corporations as enacting special interests, but rather those who would challenge corporate policy or the boundaries of middle America become the transposed site of threat and are now named "special interests."

Enter Reagan's America, where this fear on the part of middle America conjoined with the corporate interest in union-busting to cut back on the "high" cost of labor under Fordism can be used to slash federal programs. If, because of the loss of jobs tied to industrial production and the destabilization of job security, middle America no longer has access to the proceeds of U.S. industry, it is certainly not going to stand by while poor Americans receive any kind of support from the federal government. Thus, for example, just as low-income housing became more necessary because of deindustrialization in the late 1970s and early 1980s, it was slashed drastically by Reagan's policy, and we see the rise in homelessness that now seems inevitable and irreversible but that is in fact the result of policy decisions.

These shifts are also connected to a whole set of retrenchments around the social issues of 1960s' and 1970s' movement, so that we see through the 1980s not just the white flight to the suburbs that marked the post–civil rights retrenchment in major cities, but a flight of both whites and capital to the South and West as a means of reworking the social relations changed by the sixties. It is not a mistake that we now have all kinds of automakers, both "American"

(Saturn) and "foreign" (Honda, Nissan, etc.), setting up manufacturing in the less unionized, more white "rural" areas of states like Kentucky and Tennessee.

The question is why have these retrenchments worked in this way at this time? Why does it no longer matter if large segments of the American population have any stake in the nation? First, the threat of corporate movement, of jobs or of the corporation itself, is effective. Were it not, we would not see bidding wars between states over corporate location where any positive effects for "the community" are given back in the tax, zoning, and regulatory structure of the agreements.

Second, and perhaps more importantly, talk of family values provides one means of managing the dislocations caused by the shift to transnationalization and mobile finance capital by shifting the site of the nation away from the state and toward the family. In order for the state (the U.S. government) to continue to work on behalf of (now) transnational capital, it must now embody a transnational form of Americanness: American only insofar as transnational corporations are also U.S. corporations.

This contradictory task is managed, in part, by reducing the size of government to allow for the greater mobility of capital, yet there is also a need to constitute the nation at another site so as to manage reaction against transnationalization articulated as the loss of Americanness. In this climate, the primary site of Americanness is being shifted from the state to the family, which can come to embody the nation precisely because, under the discourse of family values, it embodies American values.

The shift that we see is a shift in primacy. Family values can be spoken of so self-evidently as a site of nationalism because of the long history of association between "family" and "nation." Now, however, moral values (named family) rather than economic value become the primary site of nationalism, because economic value, even "American" economic value, is fundamentally transnational.

The heightened discourse of Americanness indicated in moves against flag-burning, indecent (un-American) art, or protection of the military from infiltration by gays is all a means of reasserting the nationhood of America. If the "one nation under God" sanctified for public schoolchildren in the Pledge of Allegiance now occurs within the family rather than the state, then the investment in social control of familial form increases. If the slogan "as goes GM, so goes the nation," has now been replaced by "as goes the family, so goes the nation," then a high level of intervention in familial form is justified to protect the "nation."

This shift explains how we have (paradoxically?) moved into a period of smaller government that is also more, rather than less, invested in social control. Thus, we see a shift in regulation similar to the shift in primacy between moral and economic value(s): less regulation of corporations and an extension of regulation of familial form.

Efforts to "reform" welfare insofar as they are also attempts to enforce nuclear family structure, then, are also efforts to re-form the American nation. Re-forming both federal and state budgets by cutting welfare seems to make sense in this climate because it shifts governmental budget priorities toward subsidizing economic value, as embodied in transnational corporations, while enforcing nationalism through the proclamation of American values, as embodied in the nuclear family. Thus, the tension between American economic value and moral values that is raised by a shift to postmodernity in which economic and national interests no longer mesh, is managed by making national interests the subject of (family) values, thus allowing the state to support the transnational interests of economic value. Controlling both federal and state budgets by reforming welfare means that the state will continue to regulate this re-formed nation, while simultaneously leaving open the state's ability to subsidize corporations.

Yet why is the answer to the problem of transnationalization one of retrenchment rather than social solidarity? Why does the destabilization of the American middle class lead to a decrease, rather than increase, in the resources available to families through the social safety net? Harvey's story tells us something of the economic conditions that have prompted shifts in social policy over the past quarter-century, the ways in which shifts in the relations that produce economic value have opened the door to a (re)new(ed) discourse of moral values in the service of nation-building. It can also indicate how these shifts in the relations of production of both economic value and moral values lead to policy changes like welfare reform. What Harvey's story can't tell us is why the work of distinguishing Americanness takes the form that it does. Why do American (family) values also have to be the values that structure American domination?

Is Hate a Family Value?

To ask this question is also to pose the fundamental question of the relationship between economic (value-free) exploitation and (value-laden) domination. Economic exploitation is supposed to be free of determination by cultural values. It is supposedly based only on the profit motive and the operation of the market. Social domination, on the other hand, is value laden. It enacts the values of a given society.

For example, the race, class, and gender dominations enabled through the policy of welfare reform enact the value that men should be heads of households within a nuclear family structure. While it may seem natural to assume that exploitation leads to domination, that exploitation is the basis of social domination, if moral values can operate as primary to economic values, then the relationship between the two is much more complicated. Domination can structure economic value, just as economic value can structure domination.

If the terms are conflated, then the complexity of the relationship between economic value and social values is made invisible. Recognizing the constitutive role that domination plays in relation to exploitation, as well as the ways in which domination is the product of exploitation, points to the constitutive role that values play in relation to the production of value, the ways in which cultural values establish both what is produced and the relations of production—the social arrangements within which production takes place.

As Gayatri Spivak points out in "Scattered Speculations on the Question of Value," to understand how exploitation works, we must understand not only how a body that labors is exploited but how that body is produced.[24] If labor is not so denaturalized, we lose sight of the process by which bodies are made into labor power—bodies, in Mary Poovey's terms, "simply disappear into labor power,"[25] thus, reenacting the very disappearing act by which human beings become their labor that Marx would incite us to critique. Spivak rethinks domination and exploitation by reading domination as a tool of exploitation, in which the need to exploit bodies leads to social domination, and by reading domination as in some sense preceding exploitation, indicating the ways in which the exploitation of labor power is an effect of cultural values. She argues that cultural values contribute to the construction of bodies that labor through "desire," both the desire for consumption and the desire of the body disciplined in Weberian or Protestant terms to labor, to (in Spivak's terms) "consume the (affect of) work itself."[26] These desires make for "affectively necessary labor," such that the production of bodies that are both dominated and exploited "can no longer be seen as the excess of surplus labor over *socially* necessary labor."[27] Exploitation is never itself value free, because it is *both* dependent upon *and* structured by the values carried by the normatively inscribed—the dominated—body.

Spivak's argument demonstrates not only the importance of maintaining a complicated understanding of the relationship between exploitation and domination, it also points to the work that affect does in relation to social issues. It is on this basis that we need to inquire into the role that the affect of hate plays in relation to family values. If exploitation alone determined domination, if domination were only about the requirements of the market, there would be no need for hatred, but if domination also precedes and constitutes exploitation, then the affect necessary to the work of domination must itself be produced.

Talk of family values enables the particular forms of exploitation required by transnational capital by mediating between a liberal "tolerance" which is the public sphere corollary to (value-free) capitalism and the affect accompanying (value-laden) American domination. Thus, there is a chain of affect which moves from hate through family values to tolerance. Just as the relationship between exploitation and domination is often ideologically obfuscated so as to mask the interdependence of the terms, so also the affective stance of liberal tolerance works by being able to claim a distinction from the type of affect tied to domination that is named by "hate." The political discourse of a republic of freedom and democracy articulates with a sense that the U.S. public is not structured by either domination or exploitation but by tolerance of and even solicitude toward "others."

Family values provides the circuitry that enables policies like welfare reform (which might be seen as hateful) to be represented not only as impartial, but as somehow benevolent to those whose lives are affected. Family values accomplishes this particular task by taking up a middle—and, in this case, privileged—third position between tolerance and hate, and in so doing it materializes the tolerance of hatred. Thus, hate is simultaneously distinguished from and connected to tolerance. Middle Americans (the group which understands itself to be "tolerant" in the sense that it represents the "we" who tolerates a "they") can claim that "we" don't hate anyone, and yet support policies that effect domination—domination motivated not simply by the functionalist requirements of exploitation, but by the necessary affect of domination.

In sum, hate is part of a circuit of value(s) that runs from exploitation to domination and back again. Values serve not only as a cultural control on the market, the stable discourse of regulation to be appealed to in times of change, they also serve the socially constructive function of making crucial distinctions[28]—distinctions that signify Americanness even in an increasingly global society and distinctions that enable both domination and exploitation. The values of Americanness, for example, serve to distinguish between those persons whose lives are inscribed only in economic value, who are simply the subjects of exploitation, and those persons who have values, and so are empowered to be agents in relation to the market and economic value.

Domination works for America not (only) because it is functional in providing reserve supplies of labor and a consistent level of unemployment—in other words, not simply as a direct tool of exploitation. Domination works for America because it promises a site separate from exploitation in which some will be visibly marked as the exploitable and others will not; the circuitry that both separates domination from exploitation and still connects the two is currently called family values.

So, if "hate is not a family value," the two are connected in such a way that we can say that family values does the work of hate. Thus, welfare reform is empowered precisely because those persons who participate in Aid to Families with Dependent Children can be marked as lacking values. They themselves, rather than the social structure, are in need of reform.

In the current political climate, the connections among groups on the far right that might be specifically labeled "hate" groups, Christian-identified right-wing political organizations, conservative mainstream political actors, and "middle America" must be taken seriously, although not as part of a conspiracy theory. While there are conscious links among these sites, they also form a working economy in which persons and groups who would actively disidentify with one another may nonetheless take up positions that work together.

In the set of relationships that distinguishes and connects hate and tolerance, the middle is materialized as that social space between hate groups and the hated, who of necessity in this binary discourse must also be an "extreme." The middle, then, is the site of tolerance that disidentifies with both extremes and in so doing maintains the power to hold the extremes in place as marginalized in relation to the middle. The discourse of tolerance, by not openly naming the power of the middle, makes it seem natural, but the position it establishes is also unstable precisely because it does not openly proclaim its power or the values that are enacted through tolerance.

The work of the Christian right in relation to hate groups, hated groups, and the tolerant middle is to contrast the discourse of (family) values to tolerance as the absence of values. Establishing a position for values in contrast to both tolerance and hate expands the middle position to include both values and tolerance, and although it excludes hate, it opens the door to the work of hate under the name of values. To "defend" marriage against homosexuals or to "reform" welfare is not to hate anyone. It is simply to have values.

The Christian right stands between, is a connector for, middle America and hate. A chain is, then, established that runs from hate through values to tolerance to the hated. The investment of middle America in making this connection is incited as the desire for values. Middle America needs the right because it materializes something that is recognizable as values, and it does so under the name "Christian," thus protecting middle America from the fear that in a secularized context there are no values left.

Middle America needs values because without them all that is left is the market, and there is no cultural protection (for middle America) from its exigencies. Thus, even if hate is not a family value, "family values" materializes the connection between hate and public policy. Americanness constructs itself through this connection with, but difference from, "hate" per se.

Working Alliances

This network of differentiated but connected positions is precisely the social matrix that enables the contradictory alliances of the contemporary political right in the United States. The set of networked conceptual binaries—religious/ secular, moral values/economic value, Christian/non-Christian, white/ black, hetero-/homosexual, moral/immoral—forms the effective worldview of a network of political alliances that are internally contradictory but nonetheless "work." In particular, the alliance on the political right between fiscal and social conservatives has enabled a series of claims which might otherwise have broken down through their incoherence. The potentially libertarian interpretation of fiscal conservatism might counter the regulatory impulses of social conservatism, but instead fiscal and social conservatives came together to make the alliance that formed the "Reagan Revolution."

In this alliance, fiscal conservatism carries a double meaning that allows it to operate as the node at which the network is articulated, the connection that allows the alliance to work. Fiscal conservatism articulates in two directions. When articulated with/as libertarianism, fiscal conservatism enables the claim that the government should not be funding social welfare programs, because the government is always a site of regulation or control. Fiscal conservatism, however, also can be (and, in fact, often is) articulated in very socially conservative terms. Fiscal conservatism, even in its libertarian form, can fund a certain punitive impulse toward those who might receive government aid in the form of "welfare" (as opposed to middle-class "entitlements"), because those who accept government assistance are not participating in the freedom of the market.

Programs that assist the middle class are acceptable, because the middle class is acting out market freedom, and government assistance helps them continue to do so. Cutting off benefits will help welfare recipients because it will make them "free" persons. The libertarian sense of market freedom is easily articulated with a socially conservative (Protestant) ethic that recipients of government aid are undisciplined and greedy, in the sense of desiring to consume too much without having sacrificed in advance for the privilege of so doing. Interestingly, through this double articulation, fiscal conservatism connects and stabilizes the relation between libertarianism and social regulation.

This connection between libertarianism and social regulation effectively manages the contradictions of U.S. public discourse by allowing for the type of slippage among terms that Bell refers to in describing networked binaries. When faced, for example, with the question of welfare reform, the fiscal conservative can defend his or her position by focusing on only the libertarian side of the articulation: "I don't believe in sexual regulation," or "I'm not a racist. I just don't believe in big government. So, I'm willing to vote for a welfare reform bill that enacts racism, sexism, and sexual regulation for my own reasons: to be free of government control. The fact that social conservatives also want this bill—that's just politics." The alliance works in the other direction as well, in that social conservatives can enact their agenda through the language of fiscal conservatism and budget-cutting which formed the basis for welfare reform.[29]

The distinction between fiscal and social conservatives remains important for social conservatives as well, because social conservatives cannot fully embrace the market ideology of freedom. Thus, keeping the two forms of conservatism distinct allows the socially conservative side of the alliance to attack Hollywood for the loss of values implied in simply being driven by market value to produce the sex and violence that "sells."

Switching among binaries manages the potential contradictions of connecting the two positions. If, for example, the contradiction of promarket policymakers not following through on their own ideology when working for regulation of the internet is pointed out, then a switch is made from the freedom/regulation binary to the values/valuelessness binary. The need for values is asserted, and opponents are accused of promoting valuelessness. If, on the other hand, the value of social justice is asserted over against an ideology focused solely on the market, then freedom becomes the most salient term for conservatives, and justice is lined up with the binary oppositions on the side of "unfreedom." By asserting either values or freedom in a given situation, it is possible to take up a coherent position in each case despite the contradiction between cases. Thus, even though there may be persons/movements that are fiscally but not socially conservative, it is also possible for the same person/movement (and the same politician) to hold both positions, despite contradiction, by switching among binaries. In addition, each assertion lines up counterpositions of valuelessness and unfreedom, making counterdiscourse virtually untenable. If claims for social justice are always lined up as the opposite of freedom, then it is particularly difficult to sustain such claims.

The explanation, then, for the fiscal and social conservative alliance is not that they are the same, but that they work together. In fact, the disjunction between them is precisely why they work. To be allied is not to come to a consensus, to agree, but to work in and through and to depend upon differences. If fiscal conservatives had to identify actively with the socially conservative aspect of the right's agenda, or vice versa, then the contradictions of their positions would be brought to the fore. The libertarian argument, thus, is not simply a cover for social conservatism. Individuals and movements really are fiscally and not socially conservative. Others are socially conservative and willing to vote for tight fiscal policy because they see it as part of a socially conservative agenda. There are tensions among the positions—as, for example, James

Dobson threatens to undermine the Republican party for not maintaining a position that is conservative enough on social issues.[30] The distinction between the two positions can, however, work to manage the contradiction, and thus far it has done so. The separation among conservative positions enables them to speak to different sites in the political landscape, while their connection enables conservative dominance.

The network of binaries, thus, enables a network of conservative political positions that forms the working alliance that is the contemporary right. Talk of family values can condense a set of regulatory issues and social relations because it invokes not a single issue but the entire network. Once such a network is established, it is particularly difficult to intervene, because pointing to the contradictions of any given position will not be effective. The response will be to switch ground to the libertarian/big government, freedom/unfreedom binary, which alone doesn't contain the contradiction.

It is important to note that this particular articulation is overdetermined but not determined (not necessary), and, thus, it could be disarticulated. This alliance was not always so. In fact, the former post–New Deal Democratic alliance articulated precisely the same contradiction between fiscal and social conservatism in the other direction—socially conservative (white, southern) Democrats were willing to participate in the party of social programs in part because these programs were value-related: we will enact the Great Society, where "great" is the node that can be articulated with/as social "values" and economic or political (not really justice but) amelioration. The articulations, the connections or links, that make such alliances also make for political effectiveness. It is not necessary that issues be articulated in a conservative network. They could be articulated in another fashion.

Can We Work (in) Alliances?

The fact that family values represent the condensation of a complex matrix of social relations gives power to their invocation, but it also makes them vulnerable to intervention. If family values must carry the weight of multiple, contradictory relations, it opens the opportunity (albeit difficult to realize) of intervention; yet a particular type of intervention is required—an intervention in the network, not in a specific position or in the contradiction per se. The interventions need themselves to be networked in ways that not only can challenge the binaries, but take apart, rearticulate, and reposition the various aspects of the (dominant) network.

If the meaning of a particular term is fixed not by its own logic or commonsensical meaning but by its relationships to other terms—to its opposite and to the other terms in the network—then meaning can be shifted by shifting these relationships. For example, tying social justice to positive values rather than appealing to or depending on tolerance opens the possibility of shifting political discourse away from the binaries that fuel the right. The power to enact such a shift comes from the materialization of connections among positions and movements.

All too often, however, progressive advocates address sexual regulation, not as the condensation of a series of social relations but as a single issue. The battle against DOMA, for example, was frequently conducted as being simply about the regulation of homosexuality over against the assertion of a right to gay marriage. In this single issue formulation, gays should have access to the same benefits, such as access to employee health insurance plans, that accrue to married couples.

Yet there are other ways to formulate the issue triggered by the unequal distribution of benefits. Obviously, for example, a health-care system that made health care and/or insurance available to the entire public would shift the debate dramatically. But even if the issue of benefits were framed in the relatively conservative terms of access through employment, gay rights movements could focus on benefits that were designed so that a working person could include another person, not necessarily his or her spousal-equivalent. Then, these movements would, for example, address working people who are responsible for elder care in circumstances where their elders do not have health insurance, as well as gay domestic partners.

This type of strategy could articulate with feminist critiques of marriage as an institution which constitutes family values as patriarchal values in support of the state. Such a move lays the groundwork for connecting campaigns against sexual regulation. Gay rights activists, for example, need to become involved in the set of issues around race, poverty, and sexuality that are implicated in welfare "reform," not out of an altruism or correctness but because the interventions necessary to disrupt heterosexism and homophobia can only be effective if they are part of an alternative network of claims that can provide counterweight to the condensed network that is family values.

Similarly, welfare rights activists must recognize the ways in which sexual regulation perpetuates welfare policy. If "family values" works by making distinctions between those people who have sexual "values" and hence who deserve the benefits of citizenship and those who do not have values, then attacks on homosexuality in the name of family values work not only against homosexuals. They also work to create a structure of binary opposition between those who have values and those who do not, a structure that obfuscates all of the complexities of life choices in relation to social structures, in favor of a moralistic schematization of the world.

"Family values" works because it can connect various forms of sexual regulation under the banner of values. Supporting a radical politics of sexuality which makes room for various forms of social bonding, including but not limited to various forms of families, is a crucial component of an effective move to intervene in the discourse that has made welfare reform acceptable to the U.S. public. Alliance politics, thus, becomes not some future goal to be accomplished in the utopian moment of relating across differences, but the very basis of alternative possibility.

Notes

1. For the concept of "moral economy" and the argument about the interrelation of positions, see chapter 1 of Janet R. Jakobsen, *Working Alliances and the Politics of Difference: Diversity and Feminist Ethics* (Bloomington: Indiana University Press, 1998).

2. See, for example, Kathleen Blee's interviews with women who participate in hate movements (Kathleen Blee, "Reading Racism: Women in the Modern Hate Movement," in *No Middle Ground: Women and Radical Protest,* ed. Kathleen M. Blee [New York: New York University Press, 1998], 180–98).

3. Personal communication, Juliana Kubala.

4. *RESIST Newsletter,* June 1997.

5. See, for example, Carolyn Walker Bynum's work on the import of food symbolism in medieval Christianity and Beverly Harrison's history of Christian perspectives on abortion (Carolyn Walker Bynum, *Holy Feast and Holy Fast: The Religious Significance of Food to Medieval Women* [Berkeley: University of California Press, 1987]; Beverly Harrison, *Our Right to Choose: Toward a New Ethic of Abortion* [Boston: Beacon, 1983]).

6. Catherine Bell, *Ritual Theory, Ritual Practice* (New York: Oxford University Press, 1992), 106.

7. Ibid., 104.

8. Bell's analysis draws on the work of Pierre Bourdieu. For example, in the first seven pages of *Distinction,* Bourdieu offers the following set of binaries: sacred/profane, beautiful/ugly, tasteful/vulgar, quality/quantity, form/substance, liberty/necessity, upper-/lower-class (Pierre Bourdieu, *Distinction: A Social Critique of the Judgement of Taste,* trans. Richard Nice [Cambridge: Harvard University Press, 1984]).

9. My reading of Bell's concept of networked binaries and common sense is first worked out in relation to possibilities for specifically queer resistance to domination in my article, "Queer Is? Queer Does?: Normativity and Resistance" (*GLQ: A Journal of Lesbian and Gay Studies* 4, no. 4 [1998]: 511–36).

10. For an extensive consideration of sexual "respectability" and middle-class morality in relation to the history of nationalism, see George Mosse, *Nationalism and Sexuality: Middle-Class Morality and Sexual Norms in Modern Europe* (Madison: University of Wisconsin Press, 1985).

11. Probably the most effective articulation of this narrative has been its circulation in the form of the "Moynihan Report," the basic tenets of which have been repeatedly recirculated despite repeated interventions on the part of activists, particularly African American women activists, that demonstrate the problems with the narrative (Office of Policy Planning and Research, United States Department of Labor [Daniel Patrick Moynihan], *The Negro Family: The Case for National Action* [Washington, D.C., 1965]). Such interventions can be found as early as 1970, when many of the contributors to the anthology *The Black Woman* criticized the "myth of the Black matriarchy" (Toni Cade, *The Black Woman: An Anthology* [New York: New American Library, 1970]). Patricia Hill Collins, however, is responding to a television version of the Moynihan narrative presented two decades later by Bill Moyers in "The Vanishing Family: Crisis in Black America" (Patricia Hill Collins, "A Comparison of Two Works on Black Family Life," *Signs* 14, no. 4 [summer 1989]: 875–84; Bill Moyers, "The Vanishing Family: Crisis in Black America," CBS News Special Report, 1986).

12. Collins, "Comparison of Two Works," 878.

13. For example, one of the films produced by conservative Christian James Dobson and his organization, Focus on the Family, entitled *Where's Dad?*, encourages men to participate in their families. In an article that includes a description of this film, its "profound effect" on U.S. Representative Frank Wolf is reported to have made him choose to stay home on Sundays, thus indicating that caring for the children the rest of the week is not his responsibility ("A Righteous Indignation," *U.S. News & World Report,* May 4, 1998, 20–29).

14. See, for example, Linda Gordon, ed., *Women, Welfare, and the State* (Madison: University of Wisconsin Press, 1990), for histories of how moral narratives about women and family were incorporated in the formation of the welfare state. For discussions of anxieties over women's moral autonomy in the context of debates over reproductive freedom, see Harrison, *Our Right to Choose;* Faye Ginsburg, *Contested Lives: The Abortion Debate in an American Community* (Berkeley: University of California Press, 1989); and Janet R. Jakobsen, "Struggles for Women's Bodily Integrity in the United States and the Limits of Liberal Legal Theory," *Journal of Feminist Studies in Religion* 11, no. 2 (fall 1995): 5–26.

15. Katie Cannon, *Black Womanist Ethics* (Atlanta: Scholars Press, 1988).

16. In fact, the Catholic Alliance, auxiliary to the Christian Coalition, took up positions with which the Catholic bishops actually disagree on a number of issues (*New York Times,* November 5, 1995, A16).

17. These connections between the specific nature of reformed-Protestant values and the value-free market are also worked out in the context of a reading of the relationship between the Contract with America and the Contract with the American Family in Janet R. Jakobsen, "Family Values: Social Movements and Sexual Regulation," in *Religion and Sex in American Public Life,* ed. Kathleen Sands (New York: Oxford University Press, forthcoming).

18. John Guillory, *Cultural Capital: The Problem of Literary Canon Formation* (Chicago: University of Chicago Press, 1993), 328.

19. David Harvey, *The Condition of Postmodernity: An Enquiry into the Origins of Cultural Change* (Cambridge, Mass.: Blackwell, 1990).

20. See chap. 8, on "Fordism," in Harvey, *Condition of Postmodernity.*

21. So, for example, the late 1960s and early 1970s saw the growth of occupational health-and-safety issues as promoted by labor unions and countercultural movements against the constraining aspects of working for "the man" (Harvey, *Condition of Postmodernity,* 125–40).

22. See Harvey, *Condition of Postmodernity,* chap. 3, "Postmodernism"; chap. 9, "From Fordism to Flexible Accumulation"; and chap. 10, "Theorizing the Transition."

23. Harvey, *Condition of Postmodernity,* 170.

24. Gayatri Spivak, "Scattered Speculations on the Question of Value," in *In Other Worlds: Essays in Cultural Politics* (New York: Methuen, 1987), 154–75. I consider Spivak's argument in more depth in Janet R. Jakobsen, "Can Homosexuality End Western Civilization As We Know It?" in *Queer Globalization/Local Homosexualities,* ed. Arnaldo Cruz-Malavé and Martin Manalansan (New York: New York University Press, forthcoming).

25. Mary Poovey, *Making a Social Body: British Cultural Formation, 1830–1864* (Chicago: University of Chicago Press, 1995), 31.

26. Spivak, "Scattered Speculations," 162.

27. Ibid., emphasis in original.

28. Bourdieu, *Distinction.*

29. The shifts in controversies over arts-funding in the 1990s demonstrate how the alliance works in both directions. Arguments to cut public funding for the arts initially were made in the socially conservative terms of decency and preventing funding for obscenity, and are now made in the fiscal terms of the budget deficit (Laurel George, "Culture and Commerce in the New National Endowment for the Arts," Center for the Humanities Lecture Series, Wesleyan University, 1996).

30. See "A Righteous Indignation."

[7]

Agenda for the Churches

Uprooting a National Policy of Morally Stigmatizing Poor Single Black Moms

Traci C. West

It can be heard in casual conversations among friends and neighbors. There are sometimes references to it in comments that pass between strangers who share an airplane ride or who sit together waiting for their clothes to dry in the laundromat. We certainly hear it in the claims of elected officials and political analysts in the media. In a variety of public contexts, single black moms who receive welfare benefits are commonly depicted as a vile moral contagion destroying this society.[1]

This labeling of poor black women and girls as morally inferior not only demeans and objectifies them. It also helps to justify government regulations that experiment with withholding from these moms access to food and money needed for the physical and material survival of their families. The brutal measures are considered treatment that "welfare mothers" deserve. How can we bring to a halt, or at least vehemently protest, both the stigmatizing "welfare mother" rhetoric reinforced by the media and the sadistic material assaults that are institutionalized in public policy? In particular, religious ideas and leaders traditionally have contributed to shaping the moral agenda of this country. How might churches play a role in challenging this intense national drive to morally castigate poor black single moms?

Creating the needed change involves recognizing and uprooting the prejudices that are woven into the ways that "the welfare problem" is publicly formulated. There are especially resilient forms of sexism and racism that make the dehumanizing treatment of poor black women and girls seem rational and normal. Fed by a variety of cultural cues, we learn to view poor black single moms as objects rather than people. We learn to discount each mom as some thing that is shameful and that fits a category other than our own good, hard-working, deserving selves. Thus, a poor single black mom who receives welfare benefits is too often dismissed as simply a shameful other who resides over there, amidst a host of shameful activities and elements. Instead of accepting and perpetuating these false and debasing depictions of "welfare mothers," we must awaken our capacity to renounce them. We need to identify the specific ways that racial stereotypes and gender biases infuse common beliefs about the innate moral degeneracy of these individuals. The work of exposing and rejecting the rampant, devaluing myths about women and girls who receive welfare benefits furthers the likelihood of dismantling the cruel policies that are based on these distorted images.

Depending upon their racial and economic makeup, churches bear differing responsibilities in this effort. In white church communities, the members benefit directly from the continued disparagement of those labeled "the shameful other," because it reinforces the myth of their superior white racial status. Members of another community might internalize the embarrassment of being racially linked to the shameful other, as middle-class blacks often do. Alternatively, some live each day with all of the consequences of actually being the ones relegated to the position of the shameful other, as poor black single moms must. Each of these represents a wholly distinct vantage point. Hence, it varies greatly by context which strategies are required for impacting the attitudes internally among church members and for providing broader community leadership on issues of race, gender, and welfare policy. Nonetheless, all churches ought to share the common goal of leading a retreat from the popular consensus on maligning and inflicting limitless suffering on some of the economically poorest and socially most marginalized members of our society.

Confront the Blackening of Welfare

An incident that a friend of mine recounted vividly reminded me of the common racial associations that "the welfare problem" conjures up for most Americans. He described an encounter that took place just after President Clinton signed the purported welfare reform law, the 1996 Personal Responsibility and

Work Opportunity Reconciliation Act. My friend stopped at a self-service gasoline station located in a medium-sized southeastern town. When he went to the counter to pay for the gasoline that he had pumped, the comments of the white attendant took my friend completely by surprise. While handing back the change, the white male gas station attendant looked up at my black friend, and, in a sympathetic voice, he queried: "What the colored gonna do now that the welfare is ended?" This white man naturally assumed that welfare subsidies are a factor in the lives of all "colored" people, probably also supposing this to be the case for my friend. The attendant had additionally acknowledged, with some pity, that this new legislation would destructively impact the lives of the "colored." As the straightforward question of this man illustrates, "the welfare problem" is generally perceived as an issue that chiefly affects "the colored" people, and welfare reform is understood as a punitive measure against them.

Images of "Welfare Mothers"

The automatic racial assignment of "the welfare problem" to the exclusive domain of the black community is culturally reinforced in myriad ways. One method involves utilizing black women as public symbols. For, as titles of federal welfare legislation such as the 1995 Personal Responsibility Act strikingly demonstrate, our political leaders have decided to locate the problems that welfare policy seeks to address within the moral behavior of certain individuals. In other words, welfare policy no longer seeks to eliminate social problems such as poverty but rather targets the personal inadequacy of one sector of the population.[2]

On certain public occasions, politicians use black women as principle icons for what needs reforming and who needs to exercise personal responsibility. When President Clinton signed the 1996 Personal Responsibility and Work Opportunity Reconciliation Act, he was flanked by two black women who were former welfare recipients, Penelope Howard and Janet Farrell. They literally functioned as exhibits personifying the societal problem that this legislation was meant to reduce. Clinton pointed out the women in his speech at the signing ceremony, notifying his audience that such women are, in fact, capable of personal responsibility and of actually working.

The governor of New Jersey orchestrated the same type of exhibition during her televised 1997 State of the State speech. As Governor Christine Whitman discussed her welfare reform achievements and proposals, she pointed to Monica Jones, a black female former welfare recipient, who then stood up to serve as a live display. For political leaders of this nation to persuade the public that economic problems related to poverty are merely matters of deficient moral fiber among welfare recipients, the visual identification of a black woman serves as one of the most potent tools available.

In addition to these instances of public objectification, media-generated images can help teach the same lesson. Media images can instill the idea that the term "welfare recipient" refers to an individual with a moral problem, and that "welfare recipient with a moral problem" (hear the redundancy) equals black woman.

For instance, a degrading caricature of a black woman was presented in the *Boston Globe* to depict the "welfare mother" problem. A drawing of several blackened figures grabbing for cash appeared on the editorial page of the *Globe* beside an article written by Ellen Goodman entitled "Welfare Mothers with an Attitude."[3] The most prominent silhouette in the center of the illustration was a female with an Afro hairstyle, a wide nose, and a baby on her hip, who was also reaching up to get some of the cash. In this instance, the public is literally drawn an object lesson on "the welfare problem" and taught to focus on black women. The news consumer viewing this page is led to believe that "the welfare problem" is mainly embodied in black, big-nosed females who are greedy for cash like this one, and who sexually reproduce similarly greedy offspring.

Goodman's accompanying written editorial was probably supposed to be sympathetic to "AFDC mothers." However, much of the article provides examples of the kind of objectifying messages about poor women who receive welfare benefits that are typically found in the media. Furthermore, trying to unravel the details of these messages is an essential step in arousing our sensitivity to the public disparagement of these moms. In all likelihood, Goodman intended to dispel stereotypes with comments such as "Welfare mothers do not have more children than other mothers."

Yet the terminology "welfare mothers" and "AFDC mothers," which she uses here and throughout the piece, reinforces the idea of an interdependent relationship between mothering and welfare benefits. It fosters the perception that for individuals who wear this title, "AFDC mother," welfare is central to *why* and *what* they mother. It is as if when the women give birth, they see, instead of a baby, only the guarantee of welfare checks. The terminology builds a distinction between these mothers who are focused on "welfare" and normal, good mothers whose attention is on the children whom they have brought into the world. Thus, the name "welfare mothers" suggests that poor women and girls are implicitly guilty of the charge of procreating in order to receive welfare benefits.

The power of this suggestion is bolstered by the accompanying illustration of the silhouettes grabbing for cash and by Goodman's later discussion of the values these mothers lack. Yes, mistaken notions about the disproportionate number of children that "welfare mothers" produce are being corrected by Goodman. But, by calling them "welfare mothers," the status of these women as deviant, bad mothers is also maintained. So when examined closely, what seemed at first to simply be a debunking of myths about welfare mothers turns out also to implant reassurance in the consciousness of the reader that these deviant mothers are not producing more children than (normal?) mothers.

In addition, after we are convinced through the repetition of this language that there exists such a phenomenon as "welfare mothers," does that fact mean that there are also "welfare children"? The question is visually answered in the affirmative by the black silhouette of the baby who stretches out a tiny hand trying to grab some cash like its woolly-headed mother. Again, the written editorial reassures the public that children of (normal?) mothers will not be outnumbered by welfare children like the one that is pictured.

Later in the article, Goodman asserts the need to teach "middle-class values" to welfare mothers. She proclaims the importance of telling "AFDC mothers" that "No, we won't pay more for more children born onto the welfare rolls." This contention emphasizes the assumption that "AFDC mothers" are morally flawed in a manner that "middle-class" people are not. Again, without offering any proof, this argument about the need to tell them "no, we won't pay," presupposes that these mothers are instinctively concerned with gaining welfare benefits when they have children.

How do we know that they are using pregnancy for cash? Why isn't some proof of this accusation necessary? In the logic used here, since the women are poor, they are also condemned as inherently immoral (without "middle-class values"), which leads one to deduce that by their very natures, they are greedily focused on birthing children to gain welfare money. It is a circular argument that traps poor mothers inside of a degrading stereotype. They can never be seen as innocent mothers struggling to care for their children, since they are believed to be guilty of immorality the moment that they are born poor and black.

The tone of such analysis patronizingly treats these moms like children, who can perhaps be taught to do better. We—the good people, presumably the middle-class people, who are repeatedly juxtaposed to the welfare mothers—can try to teach them better values by saying "no" to them. Stripping "AFDC mothers" of the same human proclivities that "we" have in relation to mothering and morality in the ways noted above, solidifies their inferior status. Therefore, it is taken for granted that the rights and privileges of our superiority to welfare mothers include exerting control over them. We have the right and even the responsibility to tell them how to behave. Who is this *we*? It is those who have "middle-class values" to teach, those who in no way resemble that black silhouette with the Afro hairstyle and wide nose.

When any of us actively or silently agree to these assumptions about the innate human inferiority of poor black moms who receive welfare benefits, *whose* morality is clearly perverted? How do we who profess Christian faith deliberately inoculate ourselves with a gospel-based definition of innate human worth when we are surrounded by so many persuasive sources that alter that valuation for "welfare mothers"? How do we maintain an unwavering allegiance to the gospel notion of human worth, which never varies according to one's racial grouping, economic status, or any other category we construct in the societies of our human world?

Defining "Welfare"

Racialized messages about moral inferiority are not only conveyed by the concrete images of welfare mothers presented by politicians and the mass media for public consumption. The very term "welfare" has come to be generally understood as a description of a social problem that is primarily located in the black community. Welfare is usually included in a list of antisocial behaviors that certain people choose. These lists are so routinely invoked that, to the casual observer, this newly acquired definition of "welfare" no longer appears odd. For example, in a September 1996 speech, Gayle Wilson, the First Lady of the state of California, gave a speech on teenage pregnancy in which she listed "the attendant pathologies that accompany teen pregnancy," such as "homelessness, welfare, abused and neglected children."[4] In Wilson's analysis, welfare is viewed as a social malady that is comparable to the abuse of children!

These kinds of issues are regularly grouped together as a type of shorthand reference to urban black and Hispanic communities. And, when applied to these communities, there seems to be almost no limits on the pejorative use of the "welfare" label. In New York City, in April 1989, a white woman jogger was viciously beaten and gang-raped in Central Park by a group of black and Hispanic teenage boys. In the aftermath, one local newspaper printed an article castigating the entire community where these youths grew up, using this now almost standard practice of reeling off a list of community pathologies including welfare. *New York Post* columnist Pete Hamill asserted: "these kids...were coming downtown from a world of crack, welfare, guns, knives, indifference and ignorance. They were coming from a land of no fathers."[5] In Hamill's formulation of the social ills that he believes characterize poor black and Hispanic communities, he likens single moms and welfare to drugs and weapons. He does so to show how understandable it is that such "a world" produces such heinous behavior as gang-rape. There is no necessity for this reporter to offer justification for his utterly absurd claim that welfare is a contributing factor leading to certain young men carrying out a gang-rape. The combination of welfare and poor black and Hispanic single moms is simply presumed to nurture sociopathic behavior.

Welfare was also used as a handy target for blame when violence erupted in black and Hispanic communities in Los Angeles in 1992. In California, after jurors acquitted four white police officers of wrongdoing in beating black motorist Rodney King, tremendous civil disorder ensued, which included some loss of life, many physical injuries, and significant property damage. The top leadership of this nation seemed both unaffected by the videotaped brutality of the police beating (fifty-six blows to King were recorded in eighty-one seconds) and immune to the shock of the full acquittal of the officers. President Bush's press secretary, Marlin Fitzwater, and Vice President Dan Quayle assigned blame for the outraged response in Los Angeles which boiled over into tragic disorder in the spring of 1992 to the failure of welfare programs.[6]

As evidenced by these examples, when media and political leadership characterize welfare as a potent harmful force, it is almost always linked to race. In a major speech on Affirmative Action in July 1995, President Clinton decried the fact that too many children "are clearly exposed to poverty and welfare, violence and drugs."[7] President Clinton presents poverty, welfare, violence, and drugs as interlocking, equivalent forms of antisocial behavior. Apparently, we are to conclude that one goes out and applies for welfare just like someone decides to go out and sell drugs or commit violent acts. According to this usage of the term, welfare has evolved away from being a program established and conducted by the government, and, like others, aimed at helping to address the economic needs facing a particular sector of the citizenry. President Clinton probably would never bemoan the fact that children are "exposed to" unemployment compensation or Social Security. Welfare is considered a type of criminal behavior in which poor people choose to engage or which infects them with its deleterious power.

Moreover, why is this point about welfare included in a presidential speech about Affirmative Action? The subject of Affirmative Action has become a euphemistic way of talking about racial minorities. Of course in actuality, Affirmative Action programs redress discrimination against white women as well as people of color. However, the reality that white women have disproportionately been the beneficiaries of Affirmative Action programs seems to be readily ignored. So, too, the fact that whites have represented the majority of recipients of federal welfare benefits, is easily forgotten.[8] Therefore, it seems fitting that President Clinton would place a point about welfare within a speech on Affirmative Action: both topics have now become a means of identifying and discussing the problems of racial minority groups. In everyday parlance, discussions about race are synonymous with discussions about blacks. And public discussions about blacks often consist of discussions about "What's wrong with them? Why don't they try to better themselves?" (for conservatives) or "What can be done about all *their* problems?" (for liberals). These formulations rule out whites as the problem. That is, they rule out an understanding that views whites as the ones who possess the problems that we need to focus upon in order to eliminate racial inequities.

Therefore, as the issue of racial discrimination is most often raised in relation to Affirmative Action, the problem to be solved is more closely identified with racial minority groups than with the whites who perpetuate the discriminatory acts. It becomes even more evident in the context of a speech on Affirmative Action that a discussion of welfare is not only a thinly disguised reference to the subject of racial issues but also a reference to racial/ethnic minority groups. The behavior of whites as a racial grouping is seldom if ever the obvious focus of conversations about "the welfare problem." The invoking of welfare can cover over white actions as perpetrators of police brutality (referred to above) or hide a sizable white presence among recipients of the same programs. No, the term "welfare" is used to isolate black and Hispanic racial groups and particularly to label poor single moms of those groups as tainted with pathology.

To depict welfare as bad behavior tremendously distorts reality. No matter how many times this notion is repeated by newspaper columnists or by the president of the United States, in actuality, "welfare" simply does not refer to any type of antisocial behavior. Welfare benefits are government subsidies, like Medicare or corporate tax deductions. Just as elderly people, regardless of their income, apply for Medicare benefits to pay for their health care needs, people who do not have enough money to feed themselves and their children must go through an elaborate process to qualify for welfare benefits. To insist that poor people are behaving pathologically or criminally when they apply for and receive welfare benefits is to promote a mean-spirited falsehood.

Exposing some of the racial prejudices built into the terminology and framing of welfare policy is only a first, partial step toward undermining some of the vicious and dishonest claims that are made about welfare. The receptivity of American audiences to believe and be politically guided by those prejudices also has to be confronted.

Challenge the Barrier of White Prejudices

The depth of white prejudices, in particular, needs to be acknowledged and "unpacked" for there to be any chance of effectively shifting the moral agenda of welfare policy from attacks on poor moms toward the elimination of the poverty conditions with which these moms must contend. Deeply held, pervasive stereotypes about blacks and Hispanics represent a key obstacle to this shift. Many studies reveal the extent to which whites believe that a desire to be dependent on welfare benefits is an innate character flaw which blacks and Hispanics possess.

A 1991 general social survey conducted by the National Opinion Center at the University of Chicago reflects the salience of white stereotypes about the relationship between welfare and racial minorities. When white respondents in the study were asked to evaluate whites in comparison to blacks on whether each group preferred living on welfare assistance or being self-supporting, over half of the white respondents ranked blacks and Hispanics toward the end of the spectrum indicating a preference for welfare. Of whites surveyed, 78 percent thought blacks were more likely to prefer living on welfare over being self-supporting, and 74 percent thought Hispanics were more likely to prefer living on welfare. In a 1992 Anti-Defamation League national survey of white attitudes toward blacks, 76 percent of those surveyed agreed with one or more antiblack stereotypes.[9] The eight categories that respondents were given included such descriptions as "more prone to violence," "prefer to accept welfare," "having less native intelligence," "less ambitious." Fifty-five percent of whites agreed with two or more of the categories, and 30 percent agreed with four or more.

Such prejudices grant whites permission to be indifferent to the dire survival struggles of poor black single moms who rely on welfare funding. The stereotypes justify the dismissal of the women's full humanity and their right to dignity and respect. When one starts with the presupposition that "these people" desire welfare because they are lazy and dumb, the discussion of welfare policy has been poisoned with pernicious lies before it has even begun.

Negative racial attitudes can powerfully impede white people's ability to think clearly about political and economic policy, including consideration of their own self-interests. Yale political science professor Martin Gilens conducted a study of "race coding" and white opposition to welfare.[10] He found that the racial attitudes of whites are the single most important influence on their welfare views. He discovered a specific correlation between negative views of black welfare mothers and substantial opposition to welfare funding. According to this study, whites' impassioned negative beliefs about black welfare mothers generated greater opposition to welfare spending than comparable views of white welfare mothers. Negative views of blacks in general forcefully shape whites' beliefs about "welfare mothers." One of his most important findings was that white perceptions of blacks as lazy have a larger effect on their welfare policy preferences than does economic self-interest, beliefs about individualism, or views about the poor in general.[11] The judgment of whites about how to construct national policy is fundamentally distorted by their racist views.

Moreover, it is crucial to understand the function of these stereotypes and prejudices by whites in relation to their own white identity. In their study of white racism, sociologists Joe Feagin and Hernàn Vera emphasize the fact that whites do not merely create negative myths about blacks, they also simultaneously invent positive myths about themselves. Remember, prejudice is a prejudgment on insufficient grounds which can either be in favor or opposed to someone or something. As whites make negative assessments of "others," they cling to positive images of themselves. Feagin and Vera explain that white individuals usually see themselves as "not racist," as "good people," even while they think and act in antiblack ways.

Sincere fictions are both about the other (those fictions are usually called "prejudice") and about one's group and oneself.[12] Hence, a reference to single black moms as "those lazy welfare mothers" is not just a slur against the women, it is also an implicit assertion about whiteness. The statement may demonstrate a personal-identity need by a white individual to feel good about her/his own whiteness. Unfortunately, the goodness of whiteness is understood as possible only in converse relationship to the badness of blackness. A statement by a white educator offered in the Feagin and Vera study illustrates the creation of white "fictions." When asked her opinion of programs that compensate black Americans for discrimination, the white respondent changed the subject to the "welfare system," saying:

> There is this welfare system that enables young mothers...who can't support their children anyway. I see that system intact. And a lot of ways [it] encourages poor people to have children, and they don't have to work. And I see public housing, and Headstart...and free daycare, and free services, and free medical.... I guess this is my prejudice; it's toward education: I don't think you need to have money so much, just have some values towards certain types of things, like education or intellect, or something like that. Instead of, you know, just loafing, and watching TV, and getting welfare.... And you know, getting fat, and being angry, and taking your anger out on robbing people, and killing people.[13]

While this woman depicts black mothers as sitting around doing nothing but watching TV and obtaining almost every basic family need for free, she also asserts a self-description. She represents herself as "having values" directed toward education and an intellect. This teacher was asked a question about discrimination against black Americans, and, in response, she launched into a speech about their moral weaknesses and simultaneously pointed out her own moral virtues. She apparently has a need to affirm the value of her white racial identity, which, for her, comprises the same category as moral identity. In other words, in this woman's frame of reference, one's race determines one's morals. She affirms her own moral/racial identity by underscoring its superiority to black, lazy, fat, robbing, killing identity.

Even white women who are recipients of welfare benefits may find some comfort in asserting their inherent superiority to (black) "welfare mothers." The topic of racial dynamics among women welfare recipients once surfaced during a class session that I was teaching. During this session, a white woman student admitted that she had received welfare benefits at an earlier point in her life. She then testified to conversations with other white female welfare recipients in which they characterized most black women who also collect welfare benefits as lazy. Though she was now not at all proud of these sentiments, the student explained that this group of white women felt "Yes, we are on welfare, but at least we are not like the black women." These white poor single mothers found affirmation of their moral value in their whiteness.

Similarly, in a report on poor single mothers, a white female welfare recipient is quoted as conceding that she "probably" benefited from prejudice against (black) "welfare mothers," but sees justifiable reasons in that occurrence. For "Lori," it was "humiliating" and "horrible" just to find herself at the welfare office surrounded by "these people." She says, "I'm a snob and I'm sitting among the homeless filling out these forms."[14] In one comment, she marvels at how "these people" are able to fill out all of the forms, since "I think it takes a high IQ" to figure them out. "Lori" described one incident in which a rule was waived for her that would have barred her from child care benefits. She explained that the social service official was willing to ignore the regulation, most likely because "I was a well-dressed white woman that didn't talk slang and wasn't missing my teeth, and I looked like I was serious—and I said I really need help."[15] Even as she violates regulations so that she may fraudulently receive welfare funds, this woman offers a derogatory caricature of those "other" welfare recipients, whose race, dress, and manner do not merit the same treatment.

The rampant prejudice accounted for in these studies and examples is especially significant for the work of predominantly white faith communities involved in constructing a church-sponsored agenda on welfare policy. Since negative images of blacks are often the single most important driving force shaping white opinions of this government policy, intensive antiracism work has to be an *ongoing*, nonnegotiable aspect of the community's work. Deep issues involving the way that white racial identity needs are encrusted with prejudice have to be confronted forthrightly in white communities across the spectrum of economic groupings. The welfare issue is not only insidiously formulated as a black social problem in our country. It is also specifically culturally loaded with intense biases against blacks, which must be confessed and dismantled before any relevant policy issues can be authentically addressed.

Interrogate the Call to Moral(?) Action by Political Leaders

One of the more confusing aspects of trying to decide what kind of welfare policy is right and good is the constant use of the term "morality." Especially for those who place a high priority on their commitment to practicing a religious faith, just the mention by public officials of the need to promote moral behavior in America commands immediate attention and agreement. Moreover, few political issues have been couched in more references to morality than public discussions of welfare policy. This concept has become a handy political tool for many popular welfare reform advocates. They employ varied and sophisticated strategies to manipulate public audiences. More precisely, elaborate myths about the immorality of poor black mothers are devised by political leaders to create a sense of urgency about the need for action against these women and girls.

Even federal legislation can sound almost like an altar call for people of good conscience to recognize this supposed spreading blight and seek to control it. For example, the 1995 Personal Responsibility Act utilizes statistics to blame poor black single moms for violent crime.[16] These statistics are cited in the section of the act called "Reducing Illegitimacy." This introductory section explains that "it is the sense of the Congress" that the sexual reproduction of single poor women and girls and the related list of "negative consequences" the act offers represent "a crisis in our nation" which this welfare policy seeks to remedy. The legislation specifically asserts that "the greater the incidence of single parent families in a neighborhood, the higher the incidence of violent crime and burglary."[17] In an even more explicit reference targeting black single moms, the act states: "the likelihood that a young black man will engage in criminal activities doubles if he is raised without a father and triples if he lives in a neighborhood with a high concentration of single parent families."[18] Thus, the Congress of the United States promotes the absurd claim that the mere presence of black single moms in high concentrations within a neighborhood causes crime to skyrocket. There is no reasoning given for how these mothers induce high crime rates other than their mere identities and presence as single black mothers. Why is it tolerable for federal policy to be based on such a dehumanizing, prejudiced belief? Why is it so comfortable for our national leaders to single out this one population of American citizens to objectify and insult? In short, where can one find a rationale for federal policy, written into Congressional legislation, that refers to the impact on communities and on the nation of a high concentration of white males in a given vicinity?

Furthermore, creating statistics that link violent crime to single moms is obviously an arbitrary decision. Crime statistics could also be linked with the degree to which people in a neighborhood suffer from hunger, with the quality of schools, or with the quality of housing conditions, for example. Formulating a correlation between single moms and crime serves the particular agenda of stigmatizing and targeting poor black single moms as blameworthy for social ills. The strategy is to further a political agenda through frightening statistics that urgently announce a moral crisis descending upon the whole nation via these poor single moms.

In other types of justifications for welfare reform, poor black single moms are widely caricatured as a group of horribly deficient parents. In this strategy, the cause of "welfare reform" is advanced by convincing the public that poor black single moms are all sadistically abusive parents who produce sociopathic children and that welfare benefits for these families function primarily to perpetuate this cycle. For instance, Newt Gingrich based his call for welfare reform, in part, on the notion that mothers who receive welfare benefits are such awful parents that their children would be better off in orphanages.[19] Gingrich used horrendous examples to represent to the public the welfare problem that he sought to remedy legislatively. Defending his orphanage idea, he explained:

> The little four-year-old who was thrown off the balcony in Chicago would have been a heck of a lot better off in Boys' Town; that 11-year-old who was killed after he killed a 14-year-old might have had a chance.... The children you see in DC killed every weekend might be better off in a group home or a foster home.... We say to a 13-year-old drug addict who's pregnant, you know, "Put your baby in the Dumpster, that's OK."... Now wouldn't it have been better for that girl, instead of dumping her baby in a Dumpster, to have had a place she could go to and say, "I'm not prepared to raise a child."[20]

The Speaker of the House of Representatives offers appalling images of mothers and children as typical lifestyles of those who receive welfare benefits. Like the instances I noted earlier, this serves as another method of defining "welfare" as intrinsically linked to violent behavior. The public is led to understand that not only do these adolescent monsters try to kill their own children, but the mothering of any and all poor inner-city women and girls who depend on welfare benefits to help their families naturally spawns the killing of youngsters by others in their neighborhoods. Based on these examples, Gingrich argues, "wouldn't it have been better" if his "reform" proposals had been implemented. The political agenda is openly presented as a moral choice: which do you want—homicidal mothers producing homicidal children or welfare reform?

Presidents Ronald Reagan and Bill Clinton offer yet another version of this strategy from the highest level of political leadership in our nation. Instead of listing multiple reprehensible examples as Gingrich did, presidents Reagan and Clinton preferred the tactic of offering one archetypal, distorting image of a poor urban (black?)[21] woman, which they liked to repeat over and over again in their speeches.

President Reagan chose to cite a story about a welfare "chiseler," guilty of illegal and unethical behavior who was prosecuted for her crimes. Reagan invoked "a woman in Chicago" who "has 80 names, 30 addresses, 12 social security cards.... She's got Medicaid, getting food stamps, and is collecting welfare under each of her names. Her tax-free cash income alone is over $150,000."[22] Would as many Americans be persuaded by an argument for legislatively eliminating the presidency on the basis of Richard Nixon's lies and criminality as were swayed by Reagan's "welfare queen" argument? I don't think so.

President Clinton's version of this tactic differs in that he depicts a (black?) "welfare mother" with an attitude of repentance. He shares with his audiences a story of a former welfare recipient who witnesses to reforming herself and "now has a job." President Clinton likes to relate a personal conversation with a former welfare recipient who tells him that she wants the president to set up job-placement programs for people like her. According to this Clinton narrative, the woman says, "If you don't make us do it, we'll just lay up and watch the soaps."[23] She also tells him that what makes her proudest of having a job is that "when my boy goes to school and they ask him what does your mama do for a living, he can have an answer." First, Clinton cleverly achieves his political aims through citing a welfare recipient's *own* admission that she will only abandon her preferred lazy lifestyle if forced to do so by the government. She asserts the need for the government to reform her seemingly natural slovenly tendencies. Second, the woman indicates how her own child previously suffered because of his mother's shamefulness (prior to the government intervention forcing her to do something for a living). In short, she names herself as shameful and innately lazy, albeit through the mouth of the president of the United States, who was attempting "to end welfare as we know it" when he recounted "her" story. In both the Reagan and Clinton strategies, one woman is considered to stand for an entire group.[24] The presupposition is that if we understand this one case, we understand all of "them." The recipients of welfare benefits are easily lumped together under one umbrella of inherently deficient character.

The citizen listening to these arguments is compelled to become a partner in the struggle against the immorality. She or he may be most persuaded by the statistical verification of a spreading crime wave due to the presence of these mothers in neighborhoods, or the threat of homicidal maniacs embodied and incited by the mothers, or a confession and personal plea by one of them to be protected from her own indolent proclivities. Any aspect of this picture of immense depravity spurs one toward immediate action against the population identified as the problem. Unfortunately, these depictions of poor black single moms are at best grossly overstated generalizations of the most negative behavior, which very few have the capacity to carry out. Most importantly, the terms of morality have been appropriated by political leaders who sway the nation by offering large quantities of misleading information and by attaching some of the most vicious stereotypes that can be concocted.

We need to reclaim the idea of morality, demanding that truthfulness become a requisite element built into public presentations of moral issues. However, such a reclaiming process means overcoming the temptation to retreat into cynicism about political leaders, the media, and the possibilities for changed priorities in our local communities. Such cynicism is chiefly upheld by a misguided view that lies that are publicly advanced about certain poor women do not have a direct, negative impact upon one's own selfhood and cannot be overturned by deliberate, joint efforts of those interested in doing so. Such cynicism is truly a threat to our collective moral health.

Question, Embrace Inclusive Community, Protest . . .

Our ability to recognize politically popular falsehoods masquerading as moral claims can be developed by posing thoughtful questions of ourselves. The goal of the questioning is to activate one's conscience for critically evaluating the view of reality that is presented by political leaders in order to provoke and nurture less-distorted, alternative views. This process of moral formation should occur in a collaborative manner that allows both individual and corporate conscience to emerge. For example, we need to learn to challenge the disparaging terms used in discussions of welfare. We might probe the assumptions that underlie the terms we consume through questions like those that follow.

WHAT LABELS, IMAGES, AND STEREOTYPES?   What labels, images, stereotypes, terms, jargon, or adjectives describing personal traits or characteristics are applied to those directly involved with welfare policy? List all of the labels that you can think of that are attached to the following person(s) because of their direct connection to welfare policy: (1) welfare recipients, (2) legislators, (3) the president, and (4) members of the press. It might be helpful to close your eyes and picture the persons that belong to each category within the particular setting that most directly connects them to welfare policy, and then freely associate the identifying labels that come to mind.

From what sources did you learn these labels? Which categories were harder to find labels for? Why? What language should be used to describe the traits of each? When should a reference to the morality of the person be invoked? Why? For example, should the morality of a legislator who wants to cut food benefits to poor mothers and children be part of the terminology used to identify him or her publicly? Why or why not?

For each category, how are the labels and images that you have listed related to race? For example, discuss why and how the racial/ethnic background of a president who makes welfare reform a major priority, matters? Even if it is not openly discussed in the newspaper, what difference does the president's race/ethnicity make to the public, to the way he or she shapes the issue, to the president's political effectiveness in achieving "reform"?

For each category, what aspects of your religious faith and practice might be a helpful resource for evaluating the labels that you use and hear others use for persons directly involved in welfare policy? Give specific examples.

WHO IS LABELED, IMAGED, STEREOTYPED? Which racial/ethnic communities and economic groupings are labeled in relation to welfare? List them. Then, make a second list of the racial/ethnic communities and economic groupings that are not labeled in relation to welfare. For both lists, how and why are the family structures and moral values of members of these groups labeled? Which labels are appropriate? Why?

Exactly where do your criteria for making the judgments and assumptions about the morality of persons and families who do not receive welfare benefits come from? Make a detailed list of the sources that help you to form your opinions about this group of people.

What aspects of your religious faith and practice might be helpful in deciding how you should make these judgments?

The Larger Myth-Making Agenda

Discerning which labels we use and which ones we take for granted comprises only a small fraction of the myth-making process that leads to punitive welfare policies against single poor black moms. Nevertheless, the practice of interrogating the morally loaded terms and images constructed about both those considered "welfare" people and those considered to be nonwelfare, "normal" people, should be fostered. Especially when this practice is developed in a group setting such as an open community forum, an adult Sunday-school class, or a youth group, there is a strong potential for cultivating the needed resistance to the brutal policies.

Alongside of this effort of insistently posing questions, we must also work to transform divisive definitions of community. We need to put on "eyeglasses of faith" that evoke in us a commitment to building a just and inclusive community ethos. This must be a commitment that, as Christian ethicist Larry Rasmussen describes, "sets in motion those dynamics that draw us into webs of association that bind us together, sensitize us to needs beyond our own, and call forth active response to and with others."[25] In order to participate in this kind of embracing, engaging mode of relating to one another, we must openly confront the alienating, rigid barriers of racism and vast socioeconomic disparities that exist between us. Ultimately, in stepping fully into this kind of commitment, we come to recognize any assault on poor single black moms as constituting an assault on *our* community.

To achieve this, there is a need to continually resist popular notions like "*We* have to teach *them* values so *they* don't continue to receive so many of *our* tax dollars." We are bombarded with ideas like this one which discourage acknowledgment of the breadth of claims made on communal resources by the nonpoor. Feminist legal theorist Martha Fineman explains that "the public nature of perceived inadequacies of single mothers justifies their regulation, supervision and control. Private families, by contrast, are protected."[26] Middle-class families have access to government entitlement programs such as FHA or VA loans at below-market mortgage rates. Since these families live up to "normal" social expectations, they are considered to have earned the right of privacy from state supervision and control which "deviant" families are subject to.[27] All families with children who file federal income tax returns receive government financial assistance. A tax credit deduction is given by the government to these families simply because they have children they claim as dependents.[28] A poor woman applying for welfare benefits should be as entitled to tax moneys as those mothers of any economic background who file for tax-deduction benefits.

Out of this appreciation for how a variety of moms financially benefits from our shared base of community resources, we come to realize that "welfare mothers" exist to the same extent that "tax-deduction mothers" do. Making this acknowledgment might be a starting point for dialogue among mothers across socioeconomic barriers and might create possibilities for building coalitions. Mothers might unite actively against the way that entitlement to community resources has been rescinded for certain moms in the enactment of welfare reform legislation. This kind of dialogue could plant the seeds for solidarity and advocacy of radical change to increase economically just and respectful treatment of poor moms as well as nonpoor ones.

In predominantly black communities, racial and economic forces combine to create special pressures to view the interests of poor single black moms who collect welfare benefits as distant from or opposed to those of members of the community who do not rely upon those resources. Paying attention to divisive community dynamics prompted by economic disparities, Christian ethicist Cheryl Sanders calls for a remoralization process in African American communities that is centrally sponsored by black churches. Among other key issues that will demand response in this remoralization, Sanders identifies the following dilemma: "if the tendency of those with wealth is to distance themselves from poor neighborhoods, churches, and people, how does one teach, preach, and promote reconciliation in between the affluent and the poor within the African American community?"[29]

For blacks, the particularly potent nature of white racism against those who receive welfare can intensify antagonism toward the poor by those in middle- and upper-class income brackets. Pursuit of the illusive goal of white acceptance, which one needs in order to be considered successful in this country, provides incentive for blacks to disassociate themselves from those "tainted" poor single moms.

Black community antagonism against the poor rooted in class biases can also join with peculiarly gendered dynamics, in which black single moms are blamed for the troubles that poor black males face. In particular, the emphasis on black males as an "endangered species" in the media and by several black community leaders has led to theories blaming the deficiencies of single black moms in the raising of their sons for this crisis.[30] For African Americans, internal depictions of "our" community must not echo popular views of these moms as the problem population. Unfortunately, whether through programs that paternalistically try to "fix" the welfare recipient or by sponsoring economic development plans with the stated aim "to rid our community of welfare dependency," black churches can also perpetuate the falsehood that black moms have committed some shameful wrong in using government benefits to help support their families.

An authentically inclusive community ethos is one in which poor single black moms hold leadership and shape policy discussions about day care, education, welfare benefits and other aspects of communal life. Because of the formidable amount of hard work demanded of them as they struggle to take care of their families, most of these women have developed keen skills in navigating bureaucratic social agencies and have demonstrated courageous perseverance against scornful public opinion and vicious attacks by political leaders. Poor black single mothers have something to teach us all.[31] Community practices that honor, celebrate, and build on the costly lessons of that experience are imperative.

Finally, we must raise our voices in protest. In 1995, Nicholas Politan, a federal judge in New Jersey, cleared the way for New Jersey's law denying benefits for children born after a mom initially applies for benefits (a precursor for like provisions in the 1996 federal law). He explained how his ruling was consistent with what "the nation is crying out for."[32] We must make our unqualified dissent with the punishment and stigmatizing of black single moms heard by speaking up in our informal conversations with friends or strangers, as well as in the formal religious or civic public gatherings we attend. We must raise our voices in protest using any internet sources, print, radio, or television media to which we have access. Inflicting further suffering on moms and children in our communities who have the least resources is not what everyone in this "nation is crying out for." Is it?

Notes

1. I would like to express my appreciation to Jody Caldwell, Kyung-in Kim, and Pauline Wardell-Sankoh for their research assistance and to Jerry Watts, who served as an invaluable dialogue partner on this project.

2. In analyzing the "war on welfare" that has emerged since the 1970s, Nancy Ellen Rose notes the deliberate decision by Clinton-administration advisers to choose to focus on eliminating welfare dependency rather than poverty as the administration's main objective. This decision was made by David Ellwood and the White House Working Group early in the process of devising the Clinton approach to welfare policy (*Workfare or Fair Work? Women, Welfare and Government Work Programs* [New Brunswick, N.J.: Rutgers University Press, 1995], 172).

3. Ellen Goodman, "Welfare Mothers with an Attitude," illus. Barrie Maguire, *Boston Globe,* April 16, 1992, 19.

4. Gayle Wilson, "Looking at the Nineties through the Eyes of the Fifties," speech given at Radisson Hotel, Sacramento, Calif., May 29, 1996, sponsored by the Comstock Club, Sacramento, Calif.

5. Pete Hamill, "A Savage Disease Called New York," *New York Post,* April 23, 1989, 4.

6. Michael Wines, "White House Links Riots to Welfare," *New York Times,* May 5, 1992, A1, A26; Seth Sutel, "Quayle: Welfare to Blame," *Boston Globe,* May 14, 1992, 13.

7. "Remarks of President Bill Clinton Regarding Affirmative Action," White House briefing, Washington, D.C., July 19, 1995, [database online] *Dialog File 660: Federal News Service,* Washington, D.C.

8. U.S. House of Representatives, *Background Material and Data on Programs within the Jurisdiction of the Committee on Ways and Means* (Washington, D.C.: U.S. Government Printing Office, 1994).

9. Anti-Defamation League, *Highlights from an Anti-Defamation League Survey on Racial Attitudes in America* (New York: Anti-Defamation League, 1993).

10. Martin Gilens, "'Race Coding' and White Opposition to Welfare," *American Political Science Review* 90, no. 3 (Sept. 1996): 593–604.

11. Ibid., 593. See also Martin Gilens, "Racial Attitudes and Opposition to Welfare," *Journal of Politics* 57 (Nov. 1995): 994–1014.

12. Joe R. Feagin and Hernàn Vera, *White Racism: The Basics* (New York: Routledge, 1995), 135.

13. Ibid., 151.

14. Valerie Polakow, *Lives on the Edge: Single Mothers and Their Children in the Other America* (Chicago: University of Chicago Press, 1993), 82.

15. Ibid., 83.

16. *Personal Responsibility Act of 1995,* 104th Congress, 1st Session, H.R. 4.

17. Title I, Sec. 100, Para. 3(P).

18. Title I, Sec. 100, Para. 3(O).

19. This suggestion does not represent a new public policy idea. In devising welfare policy in the 1960s, the morality of welfare recipients was a focal issue. A 1967 Senate Finance Committee report noted that "some children now receiving AFDC would be better off in foster care homes or institutions than they are in their own homes. This situation arises because of poor home environment for child upbringing in homes with low standards, including multiple instances of births out of wedlock" (*Senate Report No. 744, 90th Cong., 1st sess., [1967],* quoted in Lucy A. Williams, "Race, Rat Bites and Unfit Mothers: How Media Discourse Informs Welfare Legislation Debate," *Fordham Urban Law Journal* 22, no. 4 [summer 1995]: 1159–96, 1180).

20. *Meet the Press,* NBC, December 4, 1994.

21. I have already noted above the way in which language about welfare is racially coded so that a Gingrich, Reagan, or Clinton example of a welfare recipient's immorality is popularly understood as a reference to African Americans. The politicians and the public mutually reinforce this prejudiced perception.

22. "'Welfare Queen' Becomes Issue in Reagan Campaign," *New York Times,* February 15, 1976, 51.

23. Remarks by President Bill Clinton at the National Legislative Association of Counties Legislative Conference, Washington, D.C., March 7, 1995 [database online], *Dialog File 660: Federal News Service,* Washington, D.C.

24. The use of the Ventura case in Massachusetts by the governor represents another example of how one story about one family comes to stand for all persons receiving welfare benefits, and most importantly comes to directly influence policy. Governor William Weld (R-Mass.) sent copies of a newspaper story to legislators during debate about welfare reform. The story was about a Hispanic mother of five who was accused of abusing her four-year-old son by putting his hands in boiling water and then leaving him for days without medical treatment (Don Aucoin and Scot Lehigh, "Weld Using Story on Welfare Reform to Aid His Case on Need for Welfare Reform," *Boston Globe,* February 25, 1994, 14). With the use of this story by Weld and other legislators, a two-year time limit was placed on the receipt of welfare benefits for persons over the age of eighteen, by a vote of twenty-five to one in the Mass-

achusetts Senate. For a detailed study of this example and how media informs welfare policy, see Williams, "Race, Rat Bites and Unfit Mothers."

25. Larry Rasmussen, *Moral Fragments and Moral Community: A Proposal for Church in Society* (Minneapolis: Fortress, 1993), 105.

26. Martha Albertson Fineman, *The Neutered Mother, The Sexual Family and Other Twentieth Century Tragedies* (New York: Routledge, 1995), 190–91. For a historical discussion of how issues of motherhood and race have been translated in welfare policy, see Jill Quadagno, *The Color of Welfare: How Racism Undermined the War on Poverty* (New York: Oxford University Press, 1994), esp. chap. 5, "The Politics of Motherhood."

27. Fineman, *Neutered Mother,* 191.

28. This analogy was offered by Lucy A. Williams in her opinion editorial "Welfare: Save a Dollar, Lose a Child," *Boston Globe,* May 12, 1994, 15.

29. Cheryl J. Sanders, *Empowerment Ethics For a Liberated People: A Path to African American Social Transformation* (Minneapolis: Fortress, 1995), 108.

30. Afrocentric psychiatrist Frances Cress Welsing exemplifies this trend in *The Isis Papers: The Keys to the Colors* (Chicago: Third World Press, 1991). As she describes in a vehemently homophobic argument about the feminizing of black males, "[A]s Black females are left to rear Black male children alone, the alienation, hate and disgust felt towards adult males are visited upon their sons subtly" (88). Welsing works with black mothers of black male children so that they will learn to raise strong men and stop "making babies of their sons and husbands" (92). For a refutation of multiple racist/sexist arguments that are used to scapegoat black women, see bell hooks, *Killing Rage: Ending Racism* (New York: Henry Holt, 1995), esp. 77–85.

31. This idea is developed more extensively in Barbara Omolade, *The Rising Song of African American Women* (New York: Routledge, 1994), esp. 67–78.

32. Robert Rudolph, "Aid Limits Upheld for Moms in New Jersey Welfare Program," *Star-Ledger* (Newark), May 5, 1995, 1.

PART THREE

ANALYSIS OF RESPONSES OF CHURCHES AND ACTIVISTS

[8]

Welfare as a Family Value

Conflicting Notions of Family in Protestant Welfare Responses

Elizabeth M. Bounds

FROM THE EARLIEST POORHOUSE ARRANGEMENTS, welfare provisions in this country have been about everything *except* enabling poor people to have access to adequate work, food, clothing, and shelter. As Joel Handler, a welfare policy scholar and advocate, explains, "Welfare policy...is not addressed to the poor—it is addressed to us. It is an affirmation of majoritarian values through the creation of deviants."[1] The recent welfare debates have amply proved Handler's point: few of the dominant voices paid any attention to one of the most fundamental requirements of poor women and men, access to a decent job at a living wage. Instead, the promised "end to welfare as we have known it" was conducted as an intense moral crusade.

Yet, although these debates have played out some old themes, there have been new emphases and intensities. The most potent image has been of black teenage nonmarried mothers who have moved from being Reagan's "welfare queens" to being dehumanized in Congressional debates as "crocodiles" or "wolves" who bring up children "unfit for the company of cats."[2] The notion of unfit mothers had always been present in welfare policy, since one of the most important "majoritarian values" it has reinforced from its inception has been the white bourgeois family. However, the symbolic force of these images takes on a new intensity. The behavior of these paradigmatic women has been credited as the source of the dissolution of the family, the work ethic, and the moral heritage of the Founding Fathers. And the solutions demand a cleansing punitive morality, necessary, it is claimed, for our national survival.

Such intensity, I would like to suggest, is a response to shifts in social and economic structures in ways that have undermined the consensus underlying the welfare state. Globalization has made it impossible for the national welfare state to provide the employment and the protections that were part of the consensus over its formation and legitimation.[3] The loss of consensus over the welfare state opens up a possibility for positive change, since the welfare state institutionalized many forms of gender and racial domination. However, as the recent welfare debates have demonstrated, it also has enabled the loss of an assumed minimal provision and protection of the poorest members of our society. In this chapter, I will suggest some of the ways these tensions have focused on a key institution: the family.

I have chosen this particular focus because during the welfare debates I was struck by the relative silence and invisibility of the old-line liberal Protestantism which is my context. In contrast to the hypervisibility of conservative Protestants, liberal Protestants seemed to be sidelined and shy. While this contrast is partially due to the declining public role and overall numbers of the liberal Protestant denominations,[4] I would also argue that conservative Protestants were able to best articulate the meld of race, gender, and economic anxieties that come together in the evocative appeal to the "family."

From their inception, welfare policies were constructed to support particular notions of work linked to the model of the white bourgeois family, while stigmatizing different family forms. However, changes in the relationship of the public and private spheres, in the economy, in racial formations, in women's roles, have all created insurmountable difficulties for continuing to maintain the white bourgeois family as the model of the "proper" family against which all families could be morally evaluated. The conservative emphasis on the family reasserts the security of the bourgeois family form, which they claim can be reconstituted simply through "personal moral responsibility." This turn to morality allows the illusion of control and the possibility of blaming "others," while masking the economic forces at work.

To explain this hypothesis, I first will describe the ways in which the main welfare program, Aid to Families with Dependent Children (AFDC), was established on the basis of certain assumptions about women, families, and citizenship. Then I will discuss how changing social and economic circumstances have dissolved such legitimation, leading to the current attacks on welfare as undermining, rather than strengthening, bourgeois family forms.

Such analyses will enable me to consider the particular problems facing Protestant Christian churches as they engage in the welfare debates. Following the political right, the conservative Protestant campaign for welfare reform has come to attack welfare policy as government interference that has endangered the bourgeois family. By contrast, the less audible liberal Protestant public voices have deemphasized the family questions and focused on social and governmental responsibility to the poor. While I find this an important corrective to conservative views, my analysis will suggest that the liberal churches need to engage questions of the family and its role as part of their concern to support positive welfare reform.

Christian churches in this country invested and continue to invest heavily in the bourgeois family form, which was vital to the Protestant ethic. Nineteenth-century Christian teaching often stressed the important interrelation of family/religion/nation: as one Protestant wrote in 1858, a disordered home "brutalizes human nature, dishonors God, subverts the principles of constitutional society...and overthrows both church and state."[5] The "family pew" continues to symbolize for Protestants "the dream of a loving, happy, churchgoing family as the hope of a Christian nation,"[6] an ideal implicit in the life of most liberal Protestant congregations and explicit in most conservative Protestant churches.

The welfare state emerged from a period in the late nineteenth and early twentieth centuries in which responsibility for provision for the poor was transferred from religious social reformers operating on the basis of charity, purity, and moral reform to the state, where some of these shaping motives remained but were transformed into state bureaucratic apparatuses. These transfers to the state, although marking the diminishing public status of religion, also encoded some of the basic Protestant values of family and charity as part of the state welfare framework. Part of the renegotiation of the welfare consensus is thus linked to recognition of the eroding cultural authority of the Protestant ethic, which necessarily requires Christian communities to renegotiate aspects of their identity.

From Virtuous Widows to Welfare Queens

To understand the ways in which models of the family undergird the current welfare arguments, it is important to look back at two key developments in nineteenth- and twentieth-century American history. The first is the emergence of citizenship on the basis of a society divided between public and private spheres. The public sphere, the arena of citizenship, was a place of "free" men, unencumbered of the dependency that would endanger the autonomous use of reason in decision making. The private sphere, the world of the family, was, by contrast, a "world of particularity, natural subjection, ties of blood, emotion, love and sexual passion"—the world of women and of motherhood.[7] Women whose economic or sexual activities did not conform to this world were morally stigmatized as "bad" women and/or "unfit" mothers. And men whose economic and sexual activities did not conform to the corresponding public world of autonomous, independent men were feminized—and thus stigmatized—as dependent and inferior. Thus, the two spheres not only determined social gender roles but structured two forms of citizenship. Although both were understood as essential to national strength and survival, one form included formal access to the civil and political rights of citizenship while the other was a female citizenship-as-dependence.

The family wage system, the second key development and an underlying assumption of all welfare provision, emerged from these divisions. The independence deemed necessary for citizenship required a reconceptualization of wage labor from a mark of dependency (on the employer) to independence. Through working-class struggle, economic independence became defined as the ability to receive the family wage, which would maintain not only the male worker but a household of dependent women and children.[8] Middle-class Protestant women reformers joined the working class in seeking protective legislation for women and a family wage for men, which appeared to bring economic structures in line with domestic ideology. Men would be able to be the sole family breadwinners, freeing women to be the angels of the home, or, in other words, providing essential unpaid reproductive and moral tasks such as childrearing and household maintenance while dependent upon male income. This combination represented the "American way," the embodiment of the Protestant ethic, and it demonstrates the way in which this ethic was gendered. Since, however, wages for many men were never "family"-sized and since many women had no men to support them, this domestic model was never available for a large part of U.S. society, allowing it to serve as a punitive badge of race and class status, demonstrating the way the Protestant ethic was *race*d and *class*ed.

The symbolic family wage and its accompanying domestic ideology were crucial in the initial formation of the U.S. welfare system. The welfare consensus assumed a model of work which entailed a family wage and a bourgeois family form. As feminist historian Linda Gordon has put it, "assumptions that . . . women would marry, remain domestic, and be supported by their husbands imbued virtually all...welfare programs."[9] From the earliest poorhouse provisions, the fear has been that too-generous welfare provision would undermine the work ethic necessary for male citizenship and participation in U.S. society (which included responsibility for dependent women and children). Even when changing attitudes suggested that dependent mothers and children should be helped by the state, it was understood that such help must strengthen, not undermine, "proper" families supported by their male breadwinners. In the 1920s and 1930s, the mostly Protestant middle-class white women behind the Aid to Dependent Children (the predecessor of today's AFDC) understood themselves as helping "deviant" immigrant families achieve, or at least not threaten, the family model and family wage. They argued that this type of welfare provision by the state would not provide incentives for immoral single motherhood and that these dependent women ought to be able to stay at home to fulfill their domestic role.

This vision of dependent mothers shaped by white, middle-class ideology lies behind our two-tier welfare system, in which one track has enabled those categorized as independent male breadwinner-husbands to claim entitlements based on rights, while the other track has permitted those categorized as dependent female mother-wives to experience state intervention to help their needs only if the breadwinner is unavailable. The ideology of this system, promoted by the New Deal government, continues to enable many Americans to view Social Security payments as "entitlements," which are "deserved," while welfare is a charitable handout, even though both systems draw from a common tax fund.[10]

From its inception, the privatized family model assumed by the welfare system created contradictions for its intended recipients. The professional arguments against mothers' employment, although aimed "to win support for mother's aid," resulted in the "stigmatization of mothers who worked," who seemed "less deserving of support," which reinforced prejudice against poor and nonwhite women whose circumstances forced them to do waged work.[11] As Gordon sums it up, "Already victimized by the failure of the family wage system, the charity of public assistance system added to [single mothers'] disadvantages—such as low wages and responsibility for children—by emphasizing domesticity as their only maternal virtue."[12] Single mothers were doubly stigmatized since they were both dependent (that is, poor) and *improperly* dependent, since their dependency could not be relieved "naturally" through the family system but required action by society or the state. This deviant dependency became linked with ideas of laziness, greed, and female sexual immorality, carried out by "morals testing" to determine if the single mother was able to provide a "suitable home."[13]

Tension around the notion of the virtuous welfare mother became even more evident as more women from families outside the white bourgeois world entered into the welfare system. For the first decades of ADC, African American women basically had no access to these programs, since part of the political compromise that enabled the Social Security Act was a virtual exclusion of the southern black work force.[14] States were permitted to use "suitable home" or "man-in-the-house" rules, which were generally enforced against African American women.[15] With the postwar migrations from the rural South to the urban North and the civil rights legislation of the 1960s, greater numbers of African American women were admitted to the welfare rolls. In 1931, 96 percent of ADC families were white and 3 percent African American; by 1975, 40 percent of AFDC recipients were white, 44 percent African American, and 12 percent Hispanic.[16] Differing African American and Hispanic American family structures, with greater reliance on extended family for child raising and an extended work history for women, were at odds with the family model assumed in AFDC policy. The model of the dependent mother was also challenged by welfare activism in the 1960s, chiefly through the National Welfare Rights Organization, which made the new suggestion that welfare provision, rather than charity, might be an entitlement or a right, claimed on the basis of the family nurture provided by women. Simultaneously with entrance of these new populations and new claims, came a series of five changes that have affected U.S. families profoundly.

First, women (especially married women) were an increasing presence in the work force, which was now publicly acknowledged. In 1950, three-fifths of U.S. households had a male breadwinner and female homemaker; by 1990 more than three-fifths of all married women with dependent children were no longer homemakers but fellow breadwinners.[17]

Second, the number of single-parent households began to rise, due to both divorce and reduced rates of marriage. Rising rates of divorce resulted in a 37 percent increase in the number of woman-headed white families between 1960 and 1970, and a 40-percent increase between 1970 and 1980. Declining opportunities for black male employment meant an increase of 37 percent and 35 percent, respectively, in black female single-headed households during those same two decades.[18]

Third, "male" high-wage blue-collar jobs began to be replaced by "female" low-wage service-sector jobs (a shift most devastating to African American workers). The availability of high-wage blue-collar jobs and semi–white-collar jobs, generally held by white men, began to decline and to be replaced by low-skilled service jobs, more likely to be held by white women and minority persons.[19]

Fourth, due to shifts in birth rates and immigration patterns, the percentage of the white population began to decline while that of blacks, Asians, and Hispanics began to rise. In this decade, the non-Hispanic white population decreased by 3.0 percent while the black population rose by 0.3 percent, the Asian by 0.8 percent, and the Hispanic population by 2.0 percent.[20] While these numbers may seem small within the given number of years, this is a steady trend and has already been exaggerated by persons who fear these changes.

Fifth, shifts in economic production and distribution have meant that the share of income going to the top one-fifth of the U.S. population rose by 13 percent between 1979 and 1996, while the share going to the bottom one-fifth fell by 22 percent. The result contributes to what economist Richard Freeman has termed the "apartheid economy," where there are increasing geographic divisions between the haves and have-nots.[21]

These changes, wrapped up in the complex phenomenon of globalization, leave us, in Anthony Giddens's phrase, living lives in contexts of "manufactured uncertainty," affected at all levels by a variety of global forces. David Harvey speaks of the increased flexibility of capitalism, which can rapidly put new technologies into use and which can move capital increasingly rapidly around the globe. These changes have privileged certain groups whose technological expertise is required and enabled the displacement of other groups whose work is expendable. They have also required the increasing use of female labor throughout the globe.[22] The presence of women in the work force and the connected shifts in family forms have made the notion of a stable heterosexual two-parent unit supported by the man and nurtured by the woman at home increasingly difficult to maintain and justify. The traditional forms of family are being restructured in the face of reshaped relations and social contexts. No longer are marriage and family assumed, but, for vast numbers of our population, are decisions or choices. As a recent study of religion and family has put it, cultural and economic structures have been "pushing families toward a democratization of intimacy, work, value formation, and parenting."[23] Thus, it is harder to preserve the assumption of a certain form of family, the white two-parent heterosexual isolated unit, as "natural." Direct ideological work is required to mobilize emotional allegiance to a form contradictory to economic and social structures. Appeals to family values help people negotiate a postindustrial economy that demands a flexible work force by maintaining belief in the protection of the family as a haven in what has become an even more heartless world.[24] This belief must be supported through moralizing divisions that divide the good insiders from the bad outsiders. As has historically been the case, the "deviancy" of the poor is the fault line of this divide, a deviancy loaded with race and gender connections.

These demographic, economic, and social changes have shifted the terrain for the welfare conversation. Kathy Rudy suggests that from the 1950s, "anxiety over the loss of separate spheres and the integration of sexes and races was articulated in the celebration of whiteness and traditional domestic feminism...staving off the claims of those who had been excluded."[25] Starting in the late 1960s, new arguments against welfare have emerged which preserve traditional concepts of poverty as a moral failing but now cast state welfare provision as the destroyer of the bourgeois family. As welfare analyst Lucy Williams puts it, there has been "a powerful coincidence of two events: the growth of the Right's attack on welfare, and the arrival of African Americans and other people of color on the welfare roles,"[26] a coincidence, I have argued, embedded in the sharp economic and social changes in capitalism over the last decades.

Welfare policy has become located in the midst of a series of contradictions. The demand for low-cost labor creates pressures to push persons, including mothers of young children, into the kinds of unskilled menial jobs that are the bulk of those provided by workfare. Middle-class fears about the stability of their own work and economic situation in this world of "manufactured uncertainty" reduce notions of charity and reinforce the always available sense that welfare is a handout to the shiftless and lazy funded by the hard working and respectable. Yet, over against these forces pressing for increased welfare-to-(any)work programs, which necessarily separate women from their children, are claims for family values that promote the traditional presence of women at home. While the ideological world of early ADC policy stigmatized women for going to work and not being "good mothers," the current ideological climate around welfare reform doubly stigmatizes them for not being good mothers (the common attack on poor women) *and* for being lazy—that is, not good workers (an attack traditionally made on poor men). The legitimation or compromise underlying both the power of the Protestant ethic and the legitimacy of the welfare system is being pulled apart.

Family Values or Poor People?

These current contradictions have been visible in Protestant participation in the welfare debates. The historical, theological, institutional connections between Christianity and the care of the poor bring churches into the welfare debates. Yet their perspectives on provision for the poor are also marked by their investment in traditional family forms, their role as nongovernmental providers, and (in the case of the Christian right and the mainline Protestant churches) a dominantly Euro-American culture. The two examples discussed here, statements by the Family Research Council (FRC) and the Evangelical

Lutheran Church in America (ELCA), negotiate the contradictions and interests in quite different ways. The FRC, a voice on the religious right, supports conservative economic and family forms but must mediate between promoting what the economy demands and the FRC's family ideology. The ELCA, one of the historically mainline liberal Protestant denominations, raises some questions about the economy but tends not to talk about family at all. It raises, rather, a different set of problems as it cannot speak to the lived tensions of the experiences of many of its middle-class and working-class members or, possibly, challenge some of their assumptions concerning the nature of the family.

Let me turn first to the family-values campaigns of the Family Research Council, which was formed in the early 1980s to represent the conservative Christian perspective on Capitol Hill. While it is a division of the evangelical Focus on the Family (run by James Dobson), its lobbying and research work is done in the language of national politics, without explicit theological or religious references.[27] Thus, it provides a particularly good perspective on the social and moral views underlying conservative Christian approaches to welfare, which was a central focus of the FRC's work during the welfare reform debates.

For the FRC, welfare is a subset of its primary concern, the current "crisis" of the family. Reading through their literature,[28] the family crisis appears to be, at bottom, a crisis of morality. What is at stake is the central value of U.S. society—freedom. This is not a freedom of pluralized values and self-fulfillment, but a freedom based on personal responsibility and self-restraint. It is, in fact, the freedom of the Protestant ethic, where self-denial leads to both prosperity and virtuous behavior and counters the innate human tendency towards pleasure ("the individual preference for pleasure over pain, privilege over duty").[29] In order to uphold the Protestant ethic, the FRC supports a free-market (rather than a globalized) version of the capitalist economy, in which the freedom of the market promotes prosperity and morality, guaranteed by a bourgeois family structure.

The welfare crisis, in the eyes of the FRC, arises from two related social problems. One is the loss of what FRC calls the "natural married-couple family" through divorce, single parenthood, and "disappearing fathers."[30] The FRC is somewhat cautious about explicitly stating the gendered nature of this natural family, putting a heavier emphasis on common parental responsibilities. Yet it is clear that the "natural" behavior of young men is toward "irresponsible sexual behavior" unless "socialized into responsible adult behavior" and "self-restraint," while the "natural" behavior of young women seems headed toward marriage unless prevented by the "unnatural" intervention of the government welfare check.[31]

This sexual ethic is evidently (if only implicitly) class- and race-biased. Jennifer E. Marshall, the welfare policy expert for FRC, writes of the dangerous weakening of a universal reliance on "bourgeois virtues," including the virtue of the family form. While she insists these virtues are "available to all, regardless of race and class," she invokes Mary Ellen Richmond, a social worker who argued that "The way to integrate the deviant into society... is to educate and indeed direct them toward the shared values of the mainstream culture."[32] It is significant that in the 1920s Richmond opposed the original plans for "mother's aid" because she feared that such aid would promote family forms deviating from the Anglo-Saxon bourgeois norm.

The family is understood as the place for moral education, an education that can only be provided by the "natural" pair of married heterosexual parents operating as a self-sufficient unit. As Ralph Reed, the former head of the Christian Coalition, puts it, "The intact family is the most effective department of health, education, and welfare ever conceived." There is no mention, of course, of who has traditionally done most of the healing, educating, and caring. In the FRC's words, "The role of the traditional two-parent family is essential in sustaining the institutions of a free society precisely because it is the vehicle by which values are transmitted from generation to generation."[33] Since we now live in a "culture that values sexual liberty over the marital bond,"[34] these values cannot be transmitted, which jeopardizes American (Christian) civilization.

The second social problem that the FRC recognizes as leading to the welfare crisis is the damaging relationship of government and family, particularly through the welfare system. The council argues that the government undermines the institution of the family through bureaucracy and regulation. It opposes government intervention on a range of moral issues; for example, advocacy of parental rights over compulsory government-provided education, particularly provision of sex education. In the FRC's model, government stands over against institutions of family and community, politics over against morality. It is silent, however, on certain forms of government provision, such as Social Security, which evidently pose no moral problems.

The FRC's understanding of the two problems affecting formation of poor families shapes its two-fronted attack on welfare, one prong focusing on family structure, the other on the overall communal context. The most prominent argument is that government welfare provision promotes what the FRC calls "a culture of illegitimacy" within family life. Illegitimacy used to be controlled by "natural economic consequences," however the provision of government benefits regardless of marital status of recipients "subsidizes illegitimacy." The current welfare system encourages family disintegration and discourages personal responsibility by guaranteeing a right to cash benefits regardless of behavior and "perpetuate[s] a welfare system that makes it harder for men and women to pursue virtuous living."[35]

The attack on illegitimacy highlights the gendered nature of the FRC's moral analysis. The moral disorder caused by welfare lies in the way it removes the limits on naturally unrestrained male sexuality and misdirects the natural or appropriate dependency of women. Without constraint, men's sexuality can never be responsible: "If society does not stress the importance of marriage, what father will not have his pleasure now and avoid the pain and pressure that lie between him and rewards he only dimly grasps?"[36] Indeed, "If not socialized into responsible adult behavior and, as it turns out, into responsible sexual behavior, young men are dangerous."[37] This last comment not only genders but races morality, since it is linked to a quote from James Q. Wilson about the ways the "underclass" (generally a reference to urban African American teenage men) reproduces itself. For men, there must be the "deferred gratification" of the Protestant ethic, which socializes them not only into family responsibilities but also into work.

"Women on welfare," on the other hand, "should have equal opportunity to follow the playbook that for centuries has been surest guarantor of human happiness," "the traditional anti-poverty program called 'marriage.'"[38] What is wrong with young women on welfare is not so much that they are sexual or even that they are mothers, but that they are *improper* mothers—that is, their motherhood is not carried out within a bourgeois family structure, including, in particular, economic dependence upon men. The model of motherhood is the same white bourgeois model underlying the original formation of ADC, which condemns women for work or sexuality carried out apart from male economic control. The policy focus of FRC is not, however, to limit welfare payments to "good" women who are not to blame for their manless condition, but to reduce or eliminate benefits through family caps, reducing pregnancies, and promoting reliance on men. Women are not exempt from work since the FRC has supported workfare provisions for "older mothers," along with men.

The FRC's second argument against welfare is an expansion of the problem of the culture of illegitimacy. Welfare provisions not only distort the primary institution of the family but affect individual autonomy and the communal nature of the social order. The welfare system makes it impossible to raise free people, because it interferes in the "natural" family form and the "natural economic consequences" of moral behavior by "suppress[ing] a sense of personal responsibility" and creating a "culture of dependency" that deprives individuals of freedom and the personal moral responsibility necessary for economic responsibility.[39] Government provision is "tribute" money which creates alienated relationships through bureaucracies that have "eroded community cooperation and displaced the 'one-on-one practice of compassion.'"[40] Further, liberal government policy is "political salvationism," which has preempted "traditional morals" in communities.[41] Private charity enables relationships "as fellow human beings" and forms part of the community which fosters good families and "right habits of the heart."[42] The FRC says transformation of welfare will restore individual freedom and vitality of community, restoring functions of community and church.

For the FRC, there is a linked set of equivalencies which form their moral framework. Throughout its work, it emphasizes the central role of "family, virtue, and freedom," which can be seen as "natural" = "moral" = "freedom." A biologically based bourgeois family, a conservative morality of responsibility, and an economy of free-market capitalism all come to seem "natural" in contrast to the "unnatural" formation of the liberal welfare state. This natural/unnatural division is also written as a moral/political division so that any historical and social reconstruction becomes impossible. Appeals are made to nature and common sense, neither of which needs to be questioned: "The family we seek to rebuild must be the one that nature and commonsense tell us is best for children: a father and mother, joined in marriage, striving to the best of their ability, with the reinforcement of tradition and public policy, to remain together for life."[43]

The welfare problem is not a problem of poverty but a problem of morality. The history of the welfare state as an effort to patch up some of the side effects of capitalism is occluded, as is any understanding of the current forms of mobile global capital which undermine the strong national community the FRC celebrates.

The FRC's proposals allow it to be both cheap and moral: cheap because it supports the deep cuts in welfare and the overall use of workfare; moral because it argues for combining these cuts with targeted restrictions, such as family caps, that would punish nonmarital sexual behavior and "renew the ethic of individual responsibility and personal compassion that will restore moral authority to the Founders' notion of liberty."[44] The council's proposals also allow for the support of capitalism by limiting the cost of the unemployed, while still endorsing the bourgeois family form.

In "Working Principles for Welfare Reform," affirmed in March 1994 by the Board of the Division for Church in Society of the Evangelical Lutheran Church in America,[45] there is a quite different placement of poverty, family, work, and government. Instead of making welfare a moral problem, the ELCA states at the beginning of the document that "Poverty is the underlying problem welfare programs seek to alleviate," which stands in contrast to the FRC's insistence that the real problem is morality. This different starting point enables the ELCA to point to at least some of the structural constraints involved in the welfare issue.

While both the ELCA and the FRC stress the reality of human interdependence, they have very different understandings of the implications of this reality for the role of government. The FRC believes that government must stand apart from the practice of human compassion within the sphere of civil society, leaving this to private charity. The ELCA insists that "government has the responsibility to help meet the needs and uphold the rights of those who are at the margins of the economic system." They also suggest that the common good is created both through government policies and private or civil activities.

The ELCA avoids any suggestion of moral inadequacy in its discussion of the poor, remarking that "none of us are truly 'self-sufficient,' 'deserving,' or autonomous" and stating that "Welfare policies that make distinctions between persons who are 'deserving' and those who are 'undeserving' need to be questioned." The ELCA's emphasis on the positive sense of dependency and its repudiation of self-sufficiency as an overriding moral good moves away from the traditional emphases of the Protestant ethic. In sharp contrast to the FRC, the ELCA states that there is a right to basic provision: "All human beings are entitled to the basic necessities of a dignified, humane existence and/or to the means of securing such." While agreeing with the need for policies that encourage responsibility ("Welfare policies should nurture the power to act responsibly"), the ELCA envisions policies based on incentives rather than restrictions ("Coercive or punitive measures should not be used to compel human action"). The importance of work is stressed, but in the context of a critique of workfare in light of the reality of a low-wage job market and the necessity for job training. While the FRC implies that any kind of work is morally beneficial, the ELCA sees the need to consider the ways in which demeaning work can affect people's lives.

Support of families is part of the ELCA proposal, since they "are the basic communities in which personhood is fostered." However, this is one point among several, rather than the focus of concern. Instead of emphasizing the moral necessity of marriage, the ELCA states that "Policies that require or encourage parents to remain unmarried or to separate in order to qualify for welfare programs must be changed." In this light, it insists that single parents of young children should not be required to work "if they decide that the good of their children, and thus the social good, is best served in their circumstances through the work of nurturing their family, rather than through efforts to become economically self-sufficient." Like the FRC, the ELCA is criticizing the ways in which welfare policy can hurt families, but unlike the FRC it does not connect such criticism to any explicit defense of the bourgeois family form. Further, it calls for "Quality, affordable child care," a demand that is invisible in the FRC program.

The ELCA positions the church and Christianity quite differently from the FRC. It envisions a society where government has responsibility to the poor, where work must enable dignity and self-support. While also concerned with social morality, it does not locate the source of this morality solely in the "personal responsibility" of individuals. Nor does it make the bourgeois family responsible for the moral well-being of the nation. Instead, it sees personal and social responsibility in dialogue and finds that the government can play a positive moral role, rather than just operating as a moral check.

Although it has moved away from the Protestant ethical emphasis on individual work and a "good" family, the ELCA still does not confront some of the issues at stake. In spite of its awareness of the broader context of the welfare issue, the ELCA backs away from naming economic exploitation, the loss of good work, the stigmatization of those on welfare, and the reality of different family forms.

Conclusion

The family is (or, in the words of the Christian right, "family values" are) a fault line in a struggle over adjustment to pressures of globalizing economy, where companies are mobile and jobs ephemeral. The tension becomes particularly clear in the intersection of welfare issues and family values where the pressures of the economy on the poorest are repackaged as moral faults in their family life. The fears of the middle class and working class about their own economic security and their own family transformations are projected on those who have no political power—women on welfare. Welfare is not about "personal responsibility" but about changes in the status of the welfare state. The dismantling of welfare, especially through attacks on "deviant" families, is a way of mopping up the effects of capitalism by blaming them on the poor.

As I suggested at the beginning of this chapter, a focus on the family raises particular issues for Protestant Christian churches, which have historically been invested in the bourgeois family form as part of the legitimation of their own moral authority. The erosion of this authority requires renegotiation of their position. For conservative Protestants, this means strongly reasserting their moral authority, refashioning the Protestant ethic over against any governmental authority, and turning back to traditional family forms. Yet this form in its historical origins was partnered with the family wage, which no longer exists. Thus the FRC champions the moral form of family, insisting that women be dependent on men in an economy that no longer supports this; the practical effect is denying support to single poor women. It and other conservative Protestant groups manage this contradiction by insisting on the "natural" or "commonsense" connection of bourgeois family, morality, and economic "self-reliance." One price of this management has been the FRC's attack on any form of government support. Another price has been the intense attack on the moral character of poor people.

While the ELCA supports the continued role of government in protecting the poor, it does not directly engage with any of these undercurrents, keeping silent about just what family or what poor people are being discussed. Because of power of the "natural" or "commonsense" connection, it is necessary to intervene more directly in the debate. There is a need to revisit the presuppositions of the Protestant ethic, which was a particular combination of work, family, morality, Christianity, and nationhood that still is an implicit assumption in much liberal Protestant thought. There is a particular need to rethink the dynamic of dependence and independence present in this ethic. Nancy Fraser and Linda Gordon remark on the ways in which dependency has become increasingly stigmatized in our postindustrial society. "Everyone," they say, "is expected to 'work' and be 'self-supporting.'"[46] Equality of opportunity can be claimed in ways that rewrite the ongoing structural inequalities as personal failures. The family becomes the only place where we can be "dependent," yet that "good" dependency is tied into the bourgeois family form, which can be used punitively against women—especially poor women of color.

For liberal Protestants to contribute to welfare debate, we need to name the moral, economic, and social forces at work as part of a reconstruction of the Protestant ethic. We need to affirm flexible family forms and condemn the stigmatization of poor people of color. We have permitted conservative Christianity to monopolize public moral discussion with its notion of family and its notion of economy, and thus we are debating notions of morality devoid of acknowledgment of the effects of the economy, politics, race, class, and gender. We need to name a morality that takes these forces into account, that names the shifting relations of government/civil society/economy. There is no doubt that poor families need support: any engagement with the lives of poor women brings one into contact with women who struggle valiantly to ensure the minimal conditions of well-being for their families. But an exclusive emphasis on punitive morality will not build an economic and social context where these women can realize their hopes. And a punitive definition of dependence falsifies our common interdependence (on families, friends, social structures, governments).

Churches must take a lead in naming kinds of truly "family friendly" welfare policies that involve the work of government, business, and civil society in the interdependent business of our lives. We need to be part of a conversation that insists there can be no *personal* responsibility without renewed *social* responsibility.

Notes

1. Joel Handler, *The Poverty of Welfare Reform* (New Haven, Conn.: Yale University Press, 1995), 8–9.

2. Mary McGrory, "Wolves, Studs, and Nazis," *Washington Post,* April 2, 1995, C4.

3. Anthony Giddens, *Beyond Left and Right: The Future of Radical Politics* (Stanford, Calif.: Stanford University Press, 1994), 135–40.

4. For an account of the shifting fortunes of oldline Protestantism, see Wade Clark Roof and William McKinney, *American Mainline Religion: Its Changing Shape and Future* (New Brunswick, N.J.: Rutgers University Press, 1987). For discussion of the shifting relations of liberal and conservative Protestantism, see James Davison Hunter, *Culture Wars: The Struggle to Define America* (New York: Basic Books, 1991), and Robert Wuthnow, *The Struggle of America's Soul: Evangelicalism, Liberalism, and Secularism* (Grand Rapids, Mich.: Eerdmans, 1989).

5. Quoted in Colleen McDannell, *The Christian Home in Victorian America* (Bloomington: Indiana University Press, 1986), 113.

6. Janet Fishburn, *Confronting the Idolatry of the Family: A New Vision for the Household of God* (Nashville: Abingdon, 1991), 20.

7. Carole Pateman, *The Disorder of Women: Democracy, Feminism, and Political Theory* (Stanford, Calif.: Stanford University Press, 1989), 43.

8. Nancy Fraser and Linda Gordon, "'Dependency' Demystified: Inscriptions of Power in a Keyword of the Welfare State," *Social Politics* 1, no. 1 (spring 1994): 11.

9. Linda Gordon, *Pitied but Not Entitled: Single Mothers and the History of Welfare* (Cambridge: Harvard University Press, 1994), 3.

10. Ibid., 31.

11. Ibid.

12. Ibid., 291.

13. See ibid., 282. It is important, however, to recognize that poor women have never simply accepted the role of deserving or undeserving poor. In their actual negotiations with the welfare framework, they did and continue to demonstrate creative agency in using the system to enable them to escape domestic abuse, to help them support their children, to try to move ahead with their lives. See, for example, Mimi Abramovitz, *Regulating the Lives of Women: Social Welfare Policy from Colonial Times to the Present* (Boston: South End, 1988).

14. Abramovitz, *Regulating,* 226–27, 318–27.

15. Lucy Williams, *Decades of Distortion: The Right's 30-Year Assault on Welfare* (Somerville, Mass.: Political Research Associates, 1997), 3.

16. Joel F. Handler and Yeheskel Hasenfeld, *The Moral Construction of Poverty: Welfare Reform in America* (Newbury Park, Calif.: Sage, 1991), 70, 113.

17. Judith Stacey, *In the Name of the Family* (Boston: Beacon, 1996), 6. See also, Handler and Hasenfeld, *Moral Construction,* 136.

18. Handler and Hasenfeld, *Moral Construction,* 114.

19. The real wages of low-income workers have fallen 20–25 percent over the last twenty-five years, and the starting salaries of college graduates have also declined (Richard Freeman, "Unequal Incomes," *Harvard Magazine,* January–February 1998, 64).

20. The U.S. Bureau of the Census, Population Division, release PPL-91, "United States Population Estimates, by Age, Sex, Race, and Hispanic Origin, 1990 to 1997."

21. Freeman, "Unequal Incomes," 62, 64.

22. David Harvey, *The Condition of Postmodernity* (Cambridge, Mass.: Blackwell, 1989), 189–97.

23. Don S. Browning, Bonnie J. Miller-McLemore, Pamela D. Couture, K. Brynolf Lyon, and Robert M. Franklin, *From Culture Wars to Common Ground: Religion and the American Family Debate* (Louisville, Ky.: Westminster John Knox, 1997), 65.

24. I have been helped in forming these ideas through the draft dissertation work of Ann Burlein and earlier drafts of the essay by Janet Jakobsen appearing in this volume.

25. Kathy Rudy, *Sex and the Church: Gender, Homosexuality, and the Transformation of Christian Ethics* (Boston: Beacon, 1997), 28.

26. Williams, *Decades of Distortion,* 1.

27. See Matthew Moen, *The Transformation of the Christian Right* (Tuscaloosa: University of Alabama Press, 1992), 132.

28. All of the FRC literature cited below (notes 29–44) is found on their Web site, available at http://www.frc.org. The material is divided into different series, which are cited as appropriate.

29. Charles A. Donovan, "First Comes the Baby Carriage," *Perspectives.*

30. "Why Does the FRC Exist and What Do They Stand For?"

31. Jennifer E. Marshall, "Observations about America's Welfare Crisis," *At the Podium.*

32. Jennifer E. Marshall, "Sanctioning Illegitimacy: Our National Character Is at Stake," *Insight.*

33. Jennifer E. Marshall, "Illegitimacy: Compassion's Offspring," *Perspectives.*

34. Donovan, "Baby Carriage."

35. Marshall, "Observations."

36. Donovan, "Baby Carriage."

37. Marshall, "Observations."

38. Jennifer E. Marshall, "The Legacy of the New Jersey Family Cap," *At the Podium,* and "Capping Welfare Payments: Subsidizing Illegitimacy Isn't Pro-Life." The second article attempts to answer the charge that family caps would promote abortions by arguing that only marriage and compassionate charity will ultimately prevent abortions.

39. Marshall, "Legacy" and "Observations."

40. Marshall, "Capping."

41. Ibid.

42. Marshall, "Observations," "Legacy."

43. Donovan, "Baby Carriage."

44. Marshall, "Legacy."

45. Evangelical Lutheran Church in America, "Working Principles for Welfare Reform" (Chicago: Division for Church in Society of the ELCA, 1994); available from http://elcasco.elca.org/des/welfare.html. All subsequent citations in this section are from this document.

46. Fraser and Gordon, "'Dependency,'" 15.

[9]

Poor Women, Work, and the U.S. Catholic Bishops

Discerning Myth from Reality in Welfare Reform

Mary E. Hobgood

THE 1995 U.S. CATHOLIC BISHOPS' STATEMENT entitled "Moral Principles and Policy Priorities on Welfare Reform" makes an important contribution to the welfare policy discussion and the development of welfare ethics. This discussion continues to be of crucial importance as the Personal Responsibility and Work Opportunity Reconciliation Act of August 1996 becomes implemented at the state level throughout the nation.

In an effort to continue the work of developing welfare ethics, I argue in this chapter that a critical analysis of political economy challenges the central assumption driving U.S. welfare reform and has the potential to enhance Catholic welfare ethics. By examining the radical restructuring of work, rising corporate subsidies, and the ideological function of welfare, I support the bishops' policy goals while I expand the moral principles at stake and redefine the scope of the problem. I also identify the political challenges the bishops' proposals will actually pose.

Bishops' Letter on Welfare Policy

The bishops claim that "poverty has national dimensions and consequences" and that private and religious efforts to address poverty, while important, are inadequate.[1] Therefore, the bishops advocate strengthening the federal social safety net for poor children and their families. The bishops believe that the proper goal for welfare reform is to promote productive work that enables families to leave poverty behind. To achieve this goal, they support such new investments as a children's tax credit, a strengthened earned-income tax credit, education, training, and other concrete forms of assistance. The heart of the bishops' welfare policy consists of decent jobs with health and child-care benefits that permit families to live and work in dignity.[2]

Since welfare restructuring is significantly impacting the poor, especially women and children, it is a moral issue that the bishops do well to address. Indeed, the Urban Institute, an eminent research group studying poverty, predicts that the 1996 federal welfare bill will push 2.6 million people into poverty, including 1.1 million children. Moreover, the bishops' proposals, which affirm full employment, above-poverty wages, and a strengthened social safety net, are laudable and necessary social justice goals that can provide grounds for moral criticism of the new legislation.

Unfortunately, the bishops' proposals for dignified jobs and benefits are not informed by an analysis that probes the structural causes of poverty. Such analysis is essential not only if we are to identify wider economic policies pertinent to authentic welfare reform but also if we are to identify successful strategies needed to achieve such reform. Thus, while their 1995 statement—like the earlier pastoral letter "Economic Justice for All"—provides a moral beacon for Christians concerned about economic injustice, the bishops are not successful in orienting Christian moral thinking amid the treacherous currents of global markets and ideological maneuvering.

In the pages that follow, I will offer such an analysis, drawing attention to what I take to be its four principal benefits. First, I will use such analysis to show that the heart of the problem is deeper than welfare costs and the desirability of making people self-sufficient by putting them to work (although both the federal legislation and the bishops' letter cast the issues in these terms). Rather, the government is dismantling welfare as a response to the restructuring of social relations by advanced global capitalism. In particular, welfare dismantling responds to the more fundamental problem of work and the destruction of better-paying jobs in a global economy that is hostile to workers.[3]

Second, an analysis that probes the structural causes of poverty will enlarge the number of moral principles that are pertinent to welfare ethics. To those already identified by the bishops, such as the right to meet one's basic survival needs and the duty of government to protect the poor, structural analysis adds the principle of restitution, or returning to the poor what has been stolen from them.

Third, a structural reading of welfare not only unmasks the dynamics of increasing economic misery and the moral principles that these dynamics violate but also corrects stereotypes or myths about poor women. This is especially relevant to poor women of color, who have suffered twice over: once by always being made to shoulder a disproportionate share of the worst work in this economy, and then, a second time, by being held morally blameworthy for their economic misery—misery that is actually the result of unjust economic policy. Rather than simply lament the temptation to view the poor as "easy scapegoats of our society's social and economic difficulties,"[4] Catholic welfare ethics needs to unmask these myths so as to offer Christians a welfare story that reflects a more complex and accurate view of social relations.

Finally, an analysis of the specific mechanisms, organizational patterns, and mythology that support poverty and keep people in bondage helps Christian ethics to develop better-informed strategies concerning what we ought to do to achieve the bishops' policy goals, especially given the current legislation. By offering an explanation of how welfare functions within late twentieth-century global capitalism, we can begin to identify the extent of the ethical and political challenges that morally principled, woman-friendly welfare reform will actually pose.

Labor, Work, and Welfare: A Social Analysis

Dominant political discourse claims that the root of social problems—from crime to high taxes—is welfare, and the solution is forcing people to work by shredding the social safety net, which has been in place for the past six decades. To enact this goal, the first part of the August 1996 welfare legislation (a set of federal guidelines to the states) mandates cutting $55 billion over the next six years in programs that primarily will affect poor legal immigrants, low-income children with disabilities, working poor families, and the elderly poor. But, as former assistant secretary for Health and Human Services Peter Edelman says, as a way of putting people to work, these cuts, which mainly affect working families, are "wildly inconsistent with the stated purposes of the overall bill... [and] are just mean, with no good policy justification."[5]

The second part of the new welfare bill converts the Aid to Families with Dependent Children (AFDC) program into Temporary Assistance to Needy Families (TANF). Federal money (a total of $16.4 billion to fiscal year 2003) will be given to the states in fixed block grants that will be decreased if people are not moved off the rolls. This new law mandates a five-year lifetime limit on welfare benefits, and, because states can define "the needy" in any way they wish, they can decline to give any cash assistance at all. States must impose a work requirement of twenty hours of community service per week after two years and thirty hours by the year 2000. Severe penalties are put on out-of-wedlock births, and participation in higher education is no longer considered legitimate work. Finally, there is no requirement that states document the effects of the programs they will enact according to their individual interpretations of these federal guidelines.

In this chapter, I wish to challenge the central assumption of both the new welfare legislation and the bishops' proposals that the problem is welfare and the solution is putting people to work. Rather, I wish to argue that the real problem is *work,* and the social relations that are being restructured by advanced global capitalism. Only from a more critical perspective can we see why current capitalist interests are "reforming" or dismantling welfare as a "solution" to the larger problem of work and economic crisis.

Welfare comes into public discourse as a "social problem" in order to reinforce prevailing ideology that affirms dominant values and social arrangements when advanced global capitalism is eroding them. As a prelude to exploring the history and ideology of welfare, I will examine the radical restructuring of the labor market that has been underway for the past twenty years, as well as simultaneous increases in government support of corporations. Together these provide the background for further arguing that the shaming of poor unmarried mothers (especially young, poor mothers of color) is essential to maintain cultural norms in an economy that is eroding work and the material basis for the work ethic, male-dominant marriage, and the racially segregated work force.

The Restructured Labor Market

Driven by the engine of profit seeking, capitalism is a revolutionary force in world history that continually reshapes the world into new configurations. Capitalism is also a historical institution that promotes commonly held expectations or rules of behavior (social roles) which human agents decide to fulfill or obey.[6] Capitalism is an institutional "mask," if you will, that human agents wear so that a few can own and control production and investment and can produce for profit rather than for what the larger society might decide is useful and sustainable. The agents who fulfill capitalist social roles include producers and consumers, investors and money managers, and those who direct global finance and trade, like the members of the World Bank, the International

Monetary Fund, and the World Trade Organization. Capitalism also requires a state apparatus that will absorb the resistance to the negative fallout from capitalist operations and maintain a social environment favorable to business.

In the drive for increasing profits, those who control the institutions of transnational capital restructure the workplace and the composition of the global working class. The creation of new decentralized technologies and the ability of investors to move capital around the globe instantaneously have transformed the appearance of capitalism since the early 1970s. The human agents in charge of mobile and highly technologized capital have created policies to enact deindustrialization, relocate industrial plants, segment labor markets, establish alternative systems of labor control, and automate production—all of which have seriously weakened the position of workers.[7]

During the last two decades, the fallout for workers from the new situation of global capital has been hidden by political rhetoric in the United States. The dominant discourse, shaped by former Labor secretary Robert Reich, among others, has promoted the "skills-mismatch rationale" for the lack of better-paying jobs with good benefits.[8] We are told, in accord with traditional neoclassical economic theory, that if workers were more highly skilled or had the right kind of new skills, the market would provide better jobs in order to take advantage of them. In reality, while the labor market is requiring a smaller sector of very highly trained workers, global capital is generating increasing amounts of low-wage work. As workers within and between nations are forced to compete against others to do this low-wage work, the United States is rapidly resembling other Two-Thirds World nations in becoming a cheap labor haven for corporations.

For example, a recent study by the U.S. Labor Department found that retraining for better-paid high-tech jobs under the Trade Adjustment Assistance Act failed to raise wages. In fact, more than three-fourths of the retrained workers earned less after three years than in their pre-layoff jobs.[9] This may be a consequence of the fact that more than three-fourths of all new jobs created between 1979 and 1989 were in low-paying retail trade and service industries.[10] One-half of total projected job growth through 2005 is expected to be in occupations that do not require more than a high-school education.[11]

Because mass production is often not as profitable as smaller units of diversified production with quick turnover potential, corporate leaders find that long-term commitments to workers are counterproductive. The Bureau of Labor Statistics reports that dislocated workers in the mid-1990s numbered over 3 million per year.[12] While 30 percent of all college graduates march straight into unemployment or underemployment, the United States General Accounting Office reports that the number of illegally employed children under the age of fourteen has nearly tripled since 1983.[13]

As educated workers are laid off and children's unskilled labor is illegally exploited, the public is misled regarding the number of adults without work. While the official unemployment rate in 1994 was just over 6 percent, the actual jobless rate, according to MIT economist Lester Thurow, was 15 percent.[14] Lance Morrow of *Time* magazine says that corporations want high unemployment to keep wages down and a work force that is "fluid, flexible and disposable."[15]

This restructured labor market—now resembling a pyramid rather than a ladder—is built around a core of better-paid, high-benefit, and often overworked employees who manage a much larger web of full-time, part-time, and contingent low-wage workers. Thus we have increasing overwork, underwork, and unemployment existing simultaneously. Overtime is rising such that the average United States full-time worker puts in an extra month of work compared to workers twenty years ago, while the fraction of the labor force working part-time but desiring full-time work has increased more than sevenfold.[16]

How these trends are reflected in the double shift for women is receiving increased attention from researchers. Harvard economist Juliet Schor cites a Boston study which showed that employed mothers averaged over 80 hours of housework, child care, and employment per week. Her own studies show that gaining a husband adds 4.2 hours of domestic work per week to a woman's schedule.[17] Sociologist Arlie Hochschild studies mothers employed outside the home who are fixated on the topic of sleep like hungry people are fixated on food.[18]

In this restructured labor market, the poverty rate is increasing not only for the lowest strata but also for many families that in previous generations could count on some level of economic security. While productivity is up 15 percent since 1990 and corporations are experiencing record profits, 80 percent of United States workers have endured a 20 percent drop in wages since 1973.[19] Dollars that should be going into wages and salaries for the people who produce the products and services are going instead to the richest 10 percent, who own 90 percent of outstanding corporate stock and have seen their dividends increase since 1980 by over 250 percent.[20] According to a Children's Defense Fund study, since 1973 the earnings of U.S. men aged twenty to twenty-four have fallen over 30 percent, and their marriage rate has declined by 50 percent. This study documents that poverty rates more than doubled in one generation for three groups: young white families with children, families headed by married couples, and families headed by high-school graduates.[21]

The deep erosion in earnings since 1973 also affects the approximately 30 million people who do the full-time, year-round jobs that no one else wants, such as those in fast food, janitorial service, and the lowest rungs of hospital labor. Working full-time for their poverty, they cannot afford decent housing, adequate nutrition, health care, and child care. Deeply intertwined with the welfare poor, they often live with them and rely on their food stamps and subsidized housing to survive.[22] Like the working poor, studies show that the overwhelming majority of AFDC receivers have desired not increased benefits, but jobs that pay more.[23]

For those who "choose" welfare, the average benefit in 1993 ($4,476 annually) was less than 40 percent of the poverty threshold for a family of three in the United States.[24] Both AFDC and food-stamp funding ($32.2 billion in 1991) reach fewer than two-thirds of all poor children in the United States.[25] Medicaid ($52.5 billion in 1991) has been a bit more protected since it uses the poor to fund hospitals and doctors.[26] Nevertheless, even before the new legislation, more than 25 percent of those who officially qualified as poor received no government assistance of any kind.[27]

Given such meager benefits, it is not surprising that although only 20 percent have reported non-AFDC income, between 40 and 50 percent of welfare recipients have been working outside the home.[28] One study found that 40 percent of recipients combine welfare with half-time employment, the same amount of employment on average as nonpoor mothers of small children. This is especially the case for women receiving welfare who are not disabled or caring for a disabled relative, and who are living in an area where the local unemployment rate is low.[29]

These statistics shed light on many issues pertinent to the bishops' discussion of welfare. An exploration of the radical restructuring of the labor market explains why poverty has deepened significantly in the United States over the last twenty years. It also helps to resolve the moral ambiguity of poverty.

In their effort to "lift up the moral dimensions and human consequences" of welfare,[30] the bishops try, in liberal fashion, to balance the need for greater personal responsibility on the part of the poor with the need for greater social supports from state and federal government. However, as my analysis of the political economy makes clear, poverty is not primarily a matter of lacking the personal values of work and independence. Women on welfare want decent work like everyone else. Whenever possible, they are active agents who, in the face of a discriminatory low-wage labor market, combine employment and welfare for the survival of their families. Mandatory work policies, a central feature of the government's welfare "reform," insult the poor who are already working very hard under heavier economic and cultural burdens than other workers endure.

The bishops rightly lament the temptation to view the poor as "easy scapegoats of our society's social and economic difficulties."[31] Yet without a systemic analysis of the function scapegoating serves, the bishops are reduced to individual moral exhortation. This does not help the ever-larger numbers of economically at-risk people who lack a social analysis to decipher what is really going on in the economy and who are ready to blame those groups targeted by politicians and the corporate-controlled media as the reason for their own economic vulnerability. At a time when increasing numbers are enduring overwork or low-wage work and when at least 40 percent of workers fear loosing their jobs, people often need to engage in the arduous task of justifying a system that is detrimental to their own well-being.[32] Influenced by the dominant analysis that is designed to punish those in subordinate positions, people experience understandable rage toward those who are presented as not pulling their own weight.[33]

This analysis also points to some of the difficulties that will be involved in implementing the bishops' proposal for full employment, which flies in the face of downsizing trends. Investors make more money with fewer workers, especially fewer workers who make above-poverty wages. It would seem, therefore, that assumptions that the poor lack motivation to work, or that the poverty problem can be solved by simply putting people to work, need serious reassessment. Also in need of reassessment (as I will show in the following section) is the assumption that the present government will provide the supports needed by the poor.

The Problem of Corporate Subsidy

In addition to the radical restructuring of the labor market, another factor pertinent to the current shaming of the welfare poor is the significant increase in public "aid to dependent corporations." The phenomenon of rising corporate welfare during the last half of this century has its roots both in capital mobility and in the increasing competition among capitalist firms facing the problems of overproduction and sustaining effective demand in a world with increasing inequalities of income.

Roaming the planet for the best business deals, those with capital to invest can hold nations and their workers hostage to their demands. Investors who can destroy massive amounts of above-poverty-wage work in the search for profits are increasing the gap between those at the bottom and in the eroding middle strata, and those at the top of the global economy. However, their drive to cut costs by decreasing wages seems to imperil the system itself. Who will buy the products that make the profits if potential customers keep losing economic ground?

Consequently, corporate investors are replacing mass production with highly diversified, smaller units of production that have the potential for rapid turnover. They hope that the rising income of those few at the top levels of the economy will make up for the loss in income of increasing numbers of disposable workers. This means that competition is ever more keenly felt as global businesses vie for the lion's share of potentially saturated global markets. Hence, the relentless push for "free-trade" agreements and the assumption by United States policymakers (who get elected through corporate-financed campaigns) that taxpayers should subsidize the profits and socialize the costs of doing business.[34]

Statistics on corporate welfare reveal the deepening dependency of big business on the public dole. The tax shifts during the Reagan and Bush administrations transferred the costs of state activities from big firms to low- and middle-strata households. Corporate contributions to total income-tax collections have steadily decreased since the 1950s. Once comprising 39 percent of total tax revenues, corporations in the 1980s paid only 17 percent of total taxes collected, and their projected share by the year 2000 is 11.1 percent.[35] During the 1980s, corporations would have contributed $130 billion more every year (enough to wipe out the annual federal deficit) if their taxes had not decreased from the previous decade.[36] In 1991, nearly 60 percent of U.S.-controlled corporations, and 74 percent of foreign firms doing business in the Unites States, paid no federal taxes.[37]

In the early 1990s, all money spent each year on AFDC and food stamps (under $40 billion), combined with that spent each year on Medicaid (just over $50 billion), amounted to less than the yearly subsidies enjoyed by corporations. As of this writing, progressive legislators have put the Corporate Responsibility Act before the 105th Congress; this act addresses the over $100 billion in annual corporate welfare, specifically targeting $800 billion over the next seven-year period.[38]

An even larger aspect of corporate welfare is the increased appropriation by the business elite of more-hidden forms of the economic surplus belonging to workers. Especially since 1970, when the post–World War II business boom ended, corporations have had to rely on external financing for their operations. As a result, major sources of the investment capital of British, U.S., and Canadian firms, for example, have come from their control over the pension plans, savings accounts, insurance policies, and the interest on credit-card debt of ordinary workers.[39] It is clear that the entire economy is hostage to the profits of a few.

As low- and middle-income wage earners pay for rising profits to corporate investors through their higher taxes, decreasing wages, and lack of control over their own pensions and other economic surplus, the corporate-controlled media focus on the welfare poor as the cause of their impoverishment. An alternative social analysis reveals, however, that the ethical concern is not a parasitic poor stratum but those with power in the political economy who profit at the expense of the majority. A structural analysis of the political economy demonstrates that the overwork, enforced leisure, and increasing economic vulnerability of the majority is primarily financing not welfare for the poor but the increasing shares in income and wealth enjoyed by the relatively few at the top of the economy.

The Ideological "Solution" of Welfare

Given that AFDC constituted less than 1 percent of the U.S. federal budget and less than 3 percent of state outlays, and given that the average benefit has been 40 percent of the poverty threshold, welfare policy is not primarily about meeting the needs of the poor.[40] Welfare, and rhetoric about welfare "reform" now at the state level, try to legitimize a political economy that is both destroying higher-wage work and rewarding the business activities of the rich with extensive subsidies.

Historically, welfare has provided inadequately for poor women and their children, since its purpose has been to promote the male-breadwinner family (a social arrangement that now prevails in fewer than 15 percent of U.S. families).[41] Welfare was designed to partially compensate for the supposedly temporary loss of the male family wage among those who were accustomed to upper-working-class or middle-strata incomes.[42] Consequently, welfare rhetoric is primarily about the public production of symbols that affirm dominant values and social arrangements—especially the entire social system of class, race, and gender subordination. Revitalizing welfare rhetoric is especially necessary when the economy is eroding the material base for sustaining these values and arrangements, including women's economic dependence on men, and men's dependence on employers and the unpaid labor of women.[43]

From its inception in the 1930s, welfare has served a twofold function: to control and stigmatize deviant behavior as it legitimized the male-dominant family, the work ethic, and the proliferation of people of color at the bottom of the economy. The specific ways in which welfare functions ideologically, however, change as the needs of capitalism change, as a historical review will demonstrate.

The system of "mothers' pensions," the precursor to AFDC, supported male dominance, racism, and class elitism by awarding pensions only to those mothers who were widowed from husbands who had worked. In this way, widows who were predominately white and from the middle strata were rewarded but also kept out of better-paying jobs in a shrinking Depression labor market.

At the same time, this system refused pensions to poor mothers who were divorced or had never married—a group disproportionately comprising women of color. Gwendolyn Mink observes that the origins of the American welfare state lie in a racist response to the perceived lack of moral fitness of those women who did not conform to white, middle-strata maternal values.[44] These women were needed to do the work that no one else wanted in the low-wage agricultural, mining, and domestic-labor markets, which were also removed from coverage under Social Security or unemployment compensation.[45] The labor of poor women of color was readily exploited while they simultaneously were blamed for violating the patriarchal domestic code.[46]

The proportion of women of color receiving AFDC rose dramatically in the 1950s and 1960s, primarily for two reasons: One was the massive displacement of sharecroppers forced off the land due to the mechanization of southern agriculture. They entered northern cities just as jobs and low-cost housing were disappearing due to automation, capital flight and "urban renewal." The second reason women of color—especially African American women—gained access to AFDC was due to their political mobilization in the civil rights and national welfare rights movements, which made it harder to discriminate against them and their children.[47] Since that time, even though more AFDC mothers have been white than African American, racism dictates that the public face of welfare is an African American woman.[48]

Now that labor market needs have changed drastically, what is socially sanctioned must also change to serve the needs of corporate investors. We cannot understand the national obsession of the last two decades with so-called welfare reform and workfare unless we see the confluence of these three realities: the enormous proliferation of low-wage work; a relatively expanded AFDC system dating from the 1960s; and the changed labor patterns of middle-strata women, whose work is no longer exclusively childrearing.

The decades following the 1960s saw the expansion of AFDC into communities of color with the simultaneous massive entry of white, middle-strata women into the labor force. Since it now took two or more middle-strata incomes to do what one used to accomplish, caring for children was no longer the only culturally sanctioned work relegated to these women.[49] As a consequence, lower-strata women (who historically were denied earlier forms of welfare because they *were* in the work force) cannot expect the state to fund them for work in the home. In other words, poor women used to be shamed and penalized because they didn't stay home like middle-strata women. Now their social safety net is being removed when they stay home with their children and do not have middle-income jobs like middle-strata women! Here we see the classist and racist subtext of so-called family values. Social conservatives insist on children's needs for a mother's care, but not if the mother is a poor woman of color.[50]

The current focus on the welfare poor, however, serves different purposes from what appears on the surface. A primary function served by welfare "reform" is not to move people out of poverty through work but to make welfare so meager and so despised as to increase the incentive of those at the bottom of the economy to endure work that denies conditions of human dignity.

Despite the political rhetoric, about 70 percent of recipients traditionally have moved off welfare in two years, although increasing numbers (currently about 22 percent) have been cycling on and off welfare because of unstable employment, poverty-level wages, lack of benefits like health care or social supports like child care.[51] In addition, many women cannot enter the work force, either because they have children under the age of six or because they themselves have disabilities or are caring for a disabled child or relative. There is a second reason why these women will not work their way out of poverty: if they do find work in a highly depressed labor market, the work they are most likely to get will pay poverty wages, and most states will find it too costly to subsidize this work by paying for child care.

To the extent that programs do force people to work outside the home for their poverty, the programs exacerbate the crisis for workers in myriad ways. For example, critics of the newly passed Wisconsin Works (W-2) program (which forces mothers of children as young as twelve weeks to work in any available job) argue that it is detrimental not only to the mothers and children immediately involved but to all workers and their children. Such programs subvert the minimum wage and jeopardize the jobs of minimum-wage workers, make the public subsidize low-wage employers, increase the pressure for substandard day care, and create incentives for workers to collude with employers to keep wages low, since earning more may mean losing what benefits are left.[52] If the conditions of work continue to erode and if low-wage, low-skill work expands even further, it is more than likely that programs like W-2 will increase as welfare is all but eliminated in order to force the most vulnerable into these jobs.

The current effort to dismantle welfare is a solution that the corporate elite and the politicians who work for them require in order to maintain social order when so many people who are currently working are living in misery. Shaming poor unmarried mothers, particularly those of color, and targeting them as public enemies eroding civic order and undeserving of a social safety net accomplishes at least three things for corporate interests.

First, it increases the incentive to work at poverty wages in an economy that is generating a disproportionate amount of low-wage, part-time, and contingent work.

Second, by targeting the unmarried poor in an economy that is rapidly reducing the pool of marriageable men (that is, men who earn above-poverty wages), policymakers affirm marriage and the patriarchal family. Dominant discourse on welfare supports not only any job under any circumstances but any marriage under any circumstances. If the unmarried can be targeted for their personal sexual immorality, then the basic dynamics of an economic system that is destroying the material basis for family life remain invisible and unchallenged, and marriage remains the main route out of welfare.[53] The social vulnerability of women and children escalates when what little alternative women have had to exploitative and abusive employers and husbands is dismantled.

Third, by targeting despised racial groups, dominant discourse promotes racial hostility to counteract the potential solidarity of people across racial/ethnic lines who find themselves sharing a common class position at the expanding bottom of the economy.

In short, the deep hostility toward the female-headed household in poverty uses racism and sexism to focus attention away from the problem of class elitism in the political economy, a problem that is manifested in the deteriorating labor-market structure and the increasing flow of wealth to people at the top of the economy. Poor unmarried mothers of color serve as the symbolic repositories of all that is a threat to individualistic, competitive, workaholic, sexually repressed (and obsessed) capitalist culture. They are the shock absorbers whose despised status helps to maintain discipline in the deteriorating capitalist workplace. The shaming of poor unmarried mothers of color is necessary to affirm dominant class, race, and gender arrangements in a political economy that cannot provide better jobs, higher wages, and universal health care, even to increasing numbers of white men, without jeopardizing the profits accruing to those at the top of the U.S. class structure.

Social Analysis and Ethical Principles

This kind of critical social analysis is needed to augment the laudable welfare policy goals of the U.S. Catholic bishops. The concrete study of the structural dynamics of contemporary economic arrangements does more than uncover important factual information that ethicists and policymakers must take into account; it also alters the theoretical matrix within which the debate about justice and welfare is carried on. Social analysis enhances the search for welfare justice by helping us sort out what belongs to whom. But more importantly, it enables us to see that restitution of stolen resources is an ethical principle that is highly relevant to this debate.

The bishops operate from three assumptions pertinent to welfare policy: (1) people deserve to have their survival needs met; (2) people deserve to have access to dignified work in order to participate in economic life, and (3) government has a duty to protect the poor. As Carol Robb has pointed out, these principles are rooted in the notion that "private property cannot be amassed or used in ways that are contrary to distributive justice and the dignity of all persons."[54]

The assumption that surplus should not be enjoyed when others' basic needs are unmet has a long history in Christian ethical tradition. One finds it in the work of Thomas Aquinas, who taught that "in cases of need all things are common property."[55] One finds it in Catholic social teaching in the principles of the accountability of private property to the common good and of capital to just, productive relations. One finds it, as well, in much recent work in Christian economic ethics, such as *Toward a Christian Economic Ethic,* by Prentice Pemberton and Daniel Rush Finn,[56] and Carol Robb's *Equal Value: An Ethical Approach to Economics and Sex.*[57] Christian ethicist Beverly Harrison sharpens this principle when she says that "no one has a right to luxury or even less essential 'enhancement needs' if those needs are satisfied at the price of others' basic dignity or physical survival."[58]

A structural analysis of political economy, however, expands the principle of just distribution to show that the poor are deserving not only because they are poor in the midst of affluence but because they themselves have created the wealth in the society. That is, as long as profit and "return on investment" are the basic operating principles of the economy, the overwork, underemployment, and unemployment of the majority will serve the profits of shareholders and the corporate elite. Those who have in excess of what they need have no right to it, not only because those who have more should share with those who have less but because what they are sharing rightfully belongs to those whose exploitation and marginalization have served to create it in the first place.

However, without a social analysis that uncovers the structural relationships between wealthy persons, social institutions, and the various sectors of the economically vulnerable and the poor, a moral evaluation of how property or capital is amassed at the expense of others cannot be articulated. We remain ignorant about how the generation of wealth for a minority requires the overwork of some, the enforced leisure of others, and the economic vulnerability of the many. People in need have a justice claim on others because the affluence of the few is being built on their collective backs and stolen from them.

Even though managerial capitalist culture promotes contempt for weakness and a need to punish and control others (phenomena beyond the scope of this chapter), I do not think that conspiracy against workers and poor people is the issue here. Making the highest possible profits for investors is the issue, as well as sustaining a self-justifying analysis of capitalism that makes people fear that any alternative would be worse than what we already have. Indeed, studies show that neither the highest-income population nor the most highly educated are knowledgeable about the structural causes of poverty.[59] More-explicit structural analysis by Christian social ethicists not only would address this ignorance but also would disclose more clearly what justice demands of us.

As scripture scholar Walter Brueggemann reminds us, biblical justice entails a right reading of social reality, of who has the power and who has the goods, so that we can sort out what belongs to whom and return it to them. This is especially pertinent to those who have controlled what belongs to others for so long that they mistakenly believe it belongs to them. If doing justice is the primary expectation of the biblical God, we need critical analysis to help us do it. The work of ethics uses social analysis to sort out what belongs to whom; the work of justice is "giving things back," enacting the restoration.[60]

Discerning the Myths in Welfare Rhetoric

As I suggested above, rhetorical complaints about the irresponsible poor often have a very precise (if unrecognized) ideological function in deflecting blame for economic misery; the resources of social analysis can help Catholic welfare ethics expose the myths that function as deceptive moral justifications of violations of justice. Three such myths focus on mothers as a group and on teen mothers and African American unmarried mothers in particular.

The first myth is that the only work is paid work. Critical economic analysis shows how wealth for the few is maintained in part by rapidly deteriorating public work, but also by the completely invisible domestic work of caring for children, the sick, and the elderly. This work encompasses perhaps one-fourth to one-third of all economic activity.[61] The myth is that this "women's work"—not even measured by mainstream economic theory—is not *real* work and so is denied social status and remuneration. Vandana Shiva says we must unmask the myth that mothers, who raise the next generation of workers and taxpayers, are economic parasites and do not deserve a share of social wealth.[62] Philosopher Nancy Fraser agrees when she observes that "the real free-riders in the current system are not poor solo mothers who shirk employment. Instead they are men of all classes who shirk carework and domestic labor, as well as corporations who free-ride on the labor of working people, both underpaid and unpaid."[63] The responsibility to make women's work visible and to honor their claim to a fair share of economic resources cannot be divorced from the responsibility to support all families and to restructure "women's work" so that it is no longer relegated to women alone and to poor women of color more than any others.

The myth of the African American welfare queen—another myth central to the dominant discussion on welfare—illustrates how those who are economically exploited are then paradoxically and perversely blamed for situations and behaviors that only express their oppression and exploitation by the powerful. This myth, relentlessly promulgated by politicians and the media, is particularly unjust since black women have shouldered a disproportionate share of social labor in this country. First they were enslaved workers and forced breeders of slaves for over two centuries. Then the only work open to them was on the lowest rungs of agricultural, factory, and mining labor, which no other workers would do. More recently, they have been domestics who have had to spend more time raising white people's children than their own. As a group, black women continue to bear a disproportionate share of low wages and poverty today.[64] In her history of black women, work, and the family, Jacqueline Jones documents black women's struggle over the centuries for the freedom to care for their own families without interference from slaveholders, welfare bureaucrats, or workfare-minded politicians.[65] What should be learned from this resistance?

Also in need of unmasking is the myth of the irresponsible teen who is having multiple babies in order to increase her welfare payments. Contrary to the dominant view, the percentage of total births to teen mothers (all races) was *less* in 1990 than in 1980, and this decline has been steady since the 1970s.[66] In addition, research has found consistently that over two-thirds of teen mothers have children by men who are over twenty-one years of age, and the younger the mother, the wider the age gap. While dominant ideology waged by powerful white men is blaming teen mothers for being economic parasites and for destroying family values, thousands of teenagers are suffering sexual abuse in the home.[67]

This analysis makes clear that poverty is essentially a form of structural violence sustained by economic, political, and cultural institutions that violate a wide range of Christian ethical principles and thrive on stereotypes that mask the true nature of social relations. Those involved in an ethical evaluation of welfare need to educate people as to how the political economy mediates the violence of poverty and unjust social relations, upheld (and concealed) in this process by destructive social myths.

Social Analysis and Liberating Praxis

In addition to expanding the moral principles at stake in welfare ethics and critiquing the cultural myths that support poverty, a critical economic analysis reveals the scale of transformation, both immediate and long-term, required for authentic reform and social transformation. The struggle for welfare justice will require enormous effort, even though we know what is needed and even though we already have the resources to afford all people in the United States an above-poverty standard of living. Critical analysis not only reveals the extent of the challenges we face, it also gives people an alternative story about our collective situation, a story that is essential if we are to sustain the moral passion necessary for the costly social changes recommended by the Catholic bishops.

False Consciousness, False Problems, False Solutions

The problem of addressing welfare and poverty in the short-term is neither lack of knowledge about what to do nor lack of resources to do it. For example, in 1991, the U.S. Census Bureau determined that about $70 billion ($37 billion in addition to the $32.2 billion of AFDC and food stamps) would have raised the income of all poor families with children to the poverty line that year.[68] A similar estimate of $86 billion was proposed for a 1996 program by the Institute for Women's Policy Research. This program would provide all low-wage workers and parents who do not work outside the home with the health insurance, child care, housing assistance, and other supports necessary to attain an above-poverty standard of living. These necessities could be financed by shifting funds from programs that support those at the top of the economy, like programs for the Pentagon, the CIA, and agricultural subsidies to wealthy farmers.[69]

The problem is, rather, ideological and political. It is ideological because the lie that "nothing works" or the mantra that "money is no solution to being poor" supports an economic system that requires poverty, unemployment, and low-wage work to keep profits up.

The problem is also political, as evidenced by the particular shape of current programs that, like the bishops' proposals, advocate putting the poor to work. These workfare programs—such as the federally enacted Work Incentive Program (WIN), and state programs such as the Employment and Training Program (ET) in Massachusetts and the Greater Avenues for Independence Program (GAIN) in California—have had occasionally modest but usually dismal results. Such programs only begin to work if they operate within a relatively tight local labor market, if expensive support services like child care are actually funded, and if participants have at least some college education and can be placed in administrative and professional jobs.[70] Scholars who have studied pre-1996 experimental workfare observe that while these welfare reform programs have demanded that AFDC mothers work outside the home, they (like the economy itself) are structured so that most will fail to escape poverty through employment. The successes that a few will experience will appear to validate hard work, and the many failures will appear to confirm dominant ideology about the depth of the degeneracy of the poor who, despite the supposed opportunities offered by these programs, still fail to leave poverty.[71]

It seems, therefore, that workfare persists in the new welfare legislation not because it reduces welfare rolls significantly but because the able-bodied unemployed are a threat to current assumptions. They threaten not only the work ethic but the perception that the capitalist market economy can provide work for all its citizens so that they can escape poverty. Given the uncritical support of work programs, which are expensive even when they (usually) fail, it would seem that they serve primarily a symbolic purpose to uphold cultural norms, the economic status quo, and continued belief in a deeply flawed system.[72]

Moreover, it is quite likely that the future of welfare will be dependent not on the adequacy of workfare but on the state of the economy. More draconian measures like the previously mentioned Wisconsin Works program (W-2) which reduce benefits to almost nothing and "force low-skilled mothers of small children into full-time sub-minimum wage jobs with warehouse care for their kids" will be the face of the future.[73] As Sister Noel Doyle, SND, a religious working at Project Hope in Dorchester, Massachusetts, has said: "What we are seeing is nothing less than institutionalized domestic violence" at the national level.[74] Such violence will escalate if hostility to workers persists and investors increase their dependency on the public subsidies, low-wage work, and enforced leisure afforded by the masses. How these programs affect the hopes, dreams, aspirations, and basic survival of poor parents and their children is a matter that does not have to be documented according to the new legislation. It is largely ignored because the current consensus has us believe that the poor have forfeited their right to the free exchange of their own labor by accepting welfare.[75]

If the bishops do not wish their program to be, at best, merely symbolic or, at worst, supportive of forms of wage slavery and increasing public irresponsibility for children, they need to be cognizant of these realities as they respond to welfare reform and the struggles that are increasingly in store as states interpret the new federal guidelines. It is unlikely that a just welfare reform will result from policy prescriptions that are not grounded in a systemic understanding of poverty and the need for disciplined, sustained political strategies to exert mass pressure on policymakers.

Building a New Order

Policies that address the violence of poverty and build genuine welfare reform will require the creation of a new postindustrial welfare state that gives poor women and their children an alternative to abusive spouses, employers, and state officials.[76] It will necessitate significant public control over corporations, macroeconomic policies aimed at creating high-quality permanent jobs, shorter work weeks, universal child and health care, a social security system for all children and adults who work in the home, lower military spending, and more-progressive tax policies. Many of these are identified in the bishops' proposals. They are not only the minimum required to establish basic justice in the land, they are essential for the long-term well-being of the society as a whole and the economy itself.

However, getting these measures passed and implemented will require more fundamental change than the bishops and traditional liberal political groups admit. It will require especially the enactment of democratic forms of decision making about economic priorities. This is essential in an economy where rising stock prices, productivity rates, and corporate profits are in fundamental opposition to the increased wages, improved working conditions, and better integration of work and family life that mean real economic improvement for the majority.

Welfare reform that adequately addresses the low-wage labor market and the high levels of aid to dependent corporations has to be part of a larger national struggle for social change. Enacting such social and labor policies will require, for a start, passing a campaign-finance reform bill that reduces the influence of corporations on lawmakers. It will also require organizing people at the local, state, regional, national, and international levels to keep politicians accountable once elected. Until the state represents a wider sector of political opinion, it will support those who monopolize economic power and put national governments and their citizens in competition with one another in order to make the highest profits for corporate investors. Until the state becomes accountable to a wider economic spectrum, it will not raise the revenues needed to restructure the labor market and provide authentic national security in a postindustrial world.

The struggle for genuine welfare reform in the United States must be part of a larger international struggle to protect jobs, communities, democracy, and the planet itself against the imperatives of global economic expansion. Until the few who run the international corporate and financial institutions that are destroying national and regional economies and the environment are challenged, the vast majority of people on the globe will become landless and homeless, fighting one another for increasingly fewer jobs as we are poisoned by a ravaged planet. National and international networks and coalitions engaged in disciplined, sustained mass pressure against the status quo are necessary to reshape the structures of political economy so that they embody such goals as ecologically sustainable development and community control over land, jobs, resources, and cultural institutions.

While as yet there are no massive social movements to achieve these goals, there are increasing numbers of ordinary people who believe in their right to a better life and who struggle to create structures for keeping government accountable to people rather than profits. The seeds of such movements may be found in the revitalization going on in labor unions and community organizing across the country and in various feminist, environmental, consumer, human-rights, antiracist, and economic justice organizations. The best of these are developing forms of gender, race, and class analyses that are international in scope. When these groups and organizations create national and international alliances with one another, hope is kept alive in the power of courageous collective action to challenge the status quo of white supremacist, male-dominant, global corporate feudalism.[77]

What Can Churches Do?

At its best, ethics is a discernment process which is done in the context of communities doing liberating praxis, communities that are enacting the restoration. While many of the churches are a long way from engagement in such liberating praxis, those of us involved in the construction of welfare ethics can at least pay attention to three things.

First, as a necessary prelude to becoming their allies, we need to listen to what the poor are up against, and portray people on welfare as they describe themselves. Moreover, a just welfare policy requires that poor women be active participants in the political project of defining what they need. As struggles over the interpretation of the new federal legislation are waged at the state level, the Catholic bishops are needed as allies of local welfare groups who represent these women. The voice and authority of the bishops can support these and other social justice organizations as they put pressure on state legislatures to enact better welfare policy.

In addition, the churches might do what states are not required to do: document the success or failure of such programs from the point of view of the women, children, and other poor people that they are intended to serve.[78] By gathering and publishing information of this kind, the bishops would give ongoing support to their own 1995 welfare policy proposals. Such activity would also confirm continuing commitment to the central concern of their 1986 letter on the economy, "Economic Justice for All," which asked about the impact of economic policy on people, especially the people at the bottom.[79]

Finally, if we are to actualize religious values of justice and mercy, Christian social ethicists must begin to use more boldly and more consistently the resources of critical social analysis to identify the power relations at work in the political economy. Only then will we be able to clarify the ethical principles at stake in the structural violence of poverty and increasing economic insecurity for the majority. This insistence, that accurate analysis of the socioeconomic arena is an indispensable requirement to responsible theological ethics, is also a mandate of the bishops' 1986 letter.[80] We must deepen our understanding of the material relations that intimately (though invisibly) bind us together, or more to the point, allow some to enjoy privilege out of the sacrifice of others. That knowledge must not stop with church leadership but must find its way into the parishes and congregations. Only the churches can offer the necessary resistance to the deceptive and myth-ridden public story of the blameworthy poor.

However much the bishops protest blaming those on welfare, people will continue to do so if they are not offered a new and better welfare story, a story that tells what welfare looks like from the point of view of women struggling for survival and dignity at the bottom of the economy. Without a story that is more faithful, not only to the poor but also to the experiences of those who suffer increasing economic insecurity, Christians will lack altogether the necessary theoretical base for a liberating social praxis. Without an alternative story, the faithful are not able to understand their own collective vulnerability in an economy hostile to workers.

Christian social ethics and social policy formation need to challenge the dominant view of welfare; identify its historical, political, and economic distortions; and offer people a more complex and accurate view of social relations. The renewal of Christian identity through critical awareness of the society in which we live is no substitute for moral agency and the hard work involved in collective political action for genuine welfare reform. But justice in this area, as in all others, will not be done without it.

Notes

1. United States Catholic Conference Administrative Board (USCC), "Moral Principles and Policy Priorities on Welfare Reform," *Origins* 24, no. 41 (1995): 667–77.

2. Ibid., 675–77.

3. There are also other agendas fueling welfare reform, such as deficit reduction, and as I discuss below, the need to punish women who have children without husbands.

4. USCC, "Moral Principles," 677.

5. Peter Edelman, "The Worst Thing Bill Clinton Has Done," *The Atlantic Monthly,* March 1997, 48.

6. Michael Albert and Robin Hahnel, *Quiet Revolution in Welfare Economics* (Princeton, N.J.: Princeton University Press, 1990), 128.

7. David Harvey, *The Condition of Postmodernity* (Cambridge, Mass.: Blackwell, 1989), 141–239.

8. Holly Sklar, *Chaos or Community: Seeking Solutions Not Scapegoats for Bad Economics* (Boston: South End, 1995), 26.

9. Ibid., 26–27.

10. Ibid., 32.

11. Ibid., 26.

12. Between January 1993 and December 1995, 9.4 million workers over the age of twenty lost or left jobs because their position or shift was abolished or because their plant or company closed or moved (U.S. Dept. of Labor, Bureau of Labor Statistics [BLS], "Worker Displacement during Mid-1990s," *Displaced Workers Summary*, USDL 96-446: 1–2).

13. Sklar, *Chaos or Community*, 26, 51.

14. Herbert J. Gans, *The War against the Poor* (New York: Basic Books, 1995), 107; Sklar, *Chaos or Community*, 60–64.

15. Sklar, *Chaos or Community*, 31.

16. Juliet B. Schor, *The Overworked American* (New York: Basic Books, 1991), 17–41.

17. Ibid., 21, 38.

18. Ibid., 20. Nancy Fraser, *Justice Interruptus: Critical Reflections on the Postsocialist Condition* (New York: Routledge, 1997), 47–48.

19. For the top United States corporations, profits increased by 19 percent in 1992, 20 percent in 1993, and 40 percent in 1994 (Council on International and Public Affairs [CIPA], "Why Today's Big Profits Mean Big Trouble," *Too Much* [fall 1995]: 1).

20. Ibid.

21. Sklar, *Chaos or Community*, 69.

22. Katherine Newman, "Working Poor, Working Hard," *The Nation* 263, no. 4 (1996): 20–23.

23. Coalition on Human Needs, *How the Poor Would Remedy Poverty* (Washington, D.C.: Ford Foundation, 1986–87), 12.

24. Randy Albelda, "The Welfare Reform Debate You Wish Would Happen," *Feminist Economics* 1, no. 2 (summer 1995): 82.

25. Ibid.

26. Warren R. Copeland, *And the Poor Get Welfare: The Ethics of Poverty in the United States* (Nashville: Abingdon, 1994), 56.

27. Sklar, *Chaos or Community*, 14.

28. Barbara Bergmann and Heidi Hartmann, "Get Real! Look to the Future, Not to the Past," *Feminist Economics* 1, no. 2 (summer 1995): 111. Gans, *War against the Poor*, 70.

29. Roberta Spalter-Roth and Heidi Hartmann, "Small Happiness: The Feminist Struggle to Integrate Social Research and Social Activism," in *Feminism and Social Change: Bridging Theory and Practice*, ed. Heidi Gottfried (Urbana: University of Illinois Press, 1996).

30. USCC, "Moral Principles and Policy Priorities," 675.

31. Ibid., 667.

32. Gans, *War against the Poor,* 107, 129.

33. It is not only the corporate elite and the national politicians and think tanks funded by the elite who support an agenda that is hostile to the welfare state and the environment. The organized right in the churches and in state and local politics harnesses the collective energy of hundreds of thousands of ordinary people who use legitimate tactics to implement regressive policies (Sara Diamond, *Facing the Wrath: Confronting the Right in Dangerous Times* [Monroe, Me.: Common Courage Press, 1996]).

34. Sklar, *Chaos or Community,* 41.

35. Donald L. Bartlett and James B. Steele, *America: What Went Wrong?* (Kansas City, Mo.: Andrews & McMeel, 1992), 47. Charles M. Sennott, "The $150 Billion Welfare Recipients: U.S. Corporations," *Boston Sunday Globe,* July 7, 1996, A1.

36. Sklar, *Chaos or Community,* 144.

37. Aaron Zitner, "Tax Codes Give Companies a Lift," *Boston Globe,* July 8, 1996, A6.

38. Marc Bayard, conversation with the author, January 30, 1997. Bayard is an organizer with Share the Wealth, a nonprofit organization in Boston; Gans, *War against the Poor,* 82.

39. Richard Deaton argues that pension reform could gradually socialize key sectors of advanced market economics in the public interest if corporate control over inadequate pensions were replaced by adequate pensions and public control over capital formation (Richard Lee Deaton, *The Political Economy of Pensions: Power, Politics and Social Change in Canada, Britain and the United States* [Vancouver: University of British Columbia Press, 1989], 306–51).

40. Albelda, "Welfare Reform Debate," 82.

41. Nancy Fraser, *Unruly Practices: Power, Discourse and Gender in Contemporary Social Theory* (Minneapolis: University of Minnesota Press, 1989), 149.

42. Linda Gordon, "The New Feminist Scholarship on the Welfare State," in *Women, the State, and Welfare,* ed. Linda Gordon (Madison: University of Wisconsin Press, 1990), 12–13.

43. Joel F. Handler and Yeheskel Hasenfeld, *The Moral Construction of Poverty: Welfare Reform in America* (Newbury Park, Calif.: Sage, 1991), 12–13, 20–22.

44. Gwendolyn Mink, "Gender, Race and the Origins of the American Welfare State," in *Women, the State, and Welfare,* ed. Gordon, 102–4.

45. Teresa L. Amott, "Black Women and AFDC: Making Entitlement Out of Necessity," in *Women, the State, and Welfare,* ed. Gordon, 288.

46. Handler and Hasenfeld, *Moral Construction,* 15–43.

47. Sklar, *Chaos or Community,* 94.

48. About 39 percent of families receiving AFDC have been white, 37 percent black, 18 percent Latino, 3 percent Asian, and 1 percent Native American. Ibid.

49. Lise Vogel, *Marxism and the Oppression of Women* (New Brunswick, N.J.: Rutgers University Press, 1983), 150.

50. Fraser, *Unruly Practices*, 161.

51. Gans, *War against the Poor*, 70; Sklar, *Chaos or Community*, 99.

52. Katherine Sciacchitano, "Wageless in Wisconsin," *In These Times*, May 27, 1996, 14–17.

53. The increasing economic instability experienced by men is only one reason for the increase in black female-headed families from 18 percent in 1950 to 44 percent in 1985. Other reasons include the lower ratio of black men to black women due to higher disease rates and accidents on the (dangerous) job; the racism of criminal justice system, which removes a disproportionate number of men of color (especially black and Latino) from the community; black women's higher (relative to white women) labor-force participation; and women's choices to live independently or with other women (Amott, "Black Women and AFDC," 284–87).

54. Carol S. Robb, *Equal Value: An Ethical Approach to Economics and Sex* (Boston: Beacon, 1995), 144.

55. Thomas Aquinas, *Summa Theologiae*, IIaIIae 66.7, trans. Fathers of the English Dominican Province (Westminster, Md.: Christian Classics, 1981), 3:1256–72.

56. Prentice L. Pemberton and Daniel Rush Finn, *Toward a Christian Economic Ethic* (Minneapolis: Winston, 1985), 36–40.

57. Robb, *Equal Value*, 142–59.

58. Beverly W. Harrison, "Theological Reflection in the Struggle for Liberation," in *Making the Connections: Essays in Feminist Social Ethics*, ed. Carol S. Robb (Boston: Beacon, 1985), 255. For an ethical assessment of "needs," including enhancement needs and luxuries, see Dennis Goulet, *The Cruel Choice: A New Concept in the Theory of Development* (New York: Atheneum, 1973); Agnes Heller, *The Theory of Need in Marx* (London: Allison & Busby, 1978). For the politics of need interpretation, see Fraser, *Unruly Practices*, 144–60.

59. Gans, *War against the Poor*, 89.

60. Walter Brueggemann, "Voices of the Night—Against Justice," in *To Act Justly, Love Tenderly, Walk Humbly*, ed. Walter Brueggemann, Sharon Parks, and Thomas H. Groome (New York: Paulist Press, 1986), 5–6.

61. Robb, *Equal Value*, 136–37.

62. Ibid., 137.

63. Fraser, *Justice Interruptus*, 62.

64. Teresa L. Amott and Julie A. Matthaei, *Race, Gender, and Work: A Multicul-*

tural Economic History of Women in the United States (Boston: South End, 1991), 183–91.

65. Jacqueline Jones, *Labor of Love, Labor of Sorrow* (New York: Basic Books, 1985).

66. What has risen is the proportion of black children born to unmarried mothers (most of whom are not teens). This reflects the dramatic decline (for reasons made evident in this chapter) in the proportion of married black women. However, throughout the United States population, out-of-wedlock birth rates are rising because of a decline in childbearing among married women and an increase in the number of unmarried women in the population (Rebecca Blank, "Teen Pregnancy: Government Programs Are Not the Cause," *Feminist Economics* 1, no. 2 [summer 1995]: 47–48; Amott, "Black Women and AFDC," 284; Sklar, *Chaos or Community,* 90).

67. Joe Klein, "The Predator Problem," *Newsweek,* Apr. 29, 1996, 32; Mike Males, "Poor Logic," *In These Times,* January 1995, 12–15.

68. Gans, *War against the Poor,* 117; Copeland, *And the Poor Get Welfare,* 56.

69. Barbara Bergmann and Heidi Hartmann, "A Welfare Reform Based on Help for Working Parents," *Feminist Economics* 1, no. 2 (summer 1995): 85–89.

70. Handler and Hasenfeld, *Moral Construction,* 132–200.

71. Ibid., 42.

72. Ibid., 198–99.

73. Katha Pollitt, "Village Idiot," *The Nation,* February 5, 1996, 9.

74. Susan Jhirad, "Ready for the Long Haul," *The Women's Review of Books* 14, no. 5 (Feb. 1997): 21.

75. The belief that lack of participation in public work forfeits one's right to participate in the economy contradicts the notion in neoclassical economic theory that work is a private commodity that one is free to exchange or not in the marketplace.

76. Fraser, *Justice Interruptus,* 46.

77. John Anner, *Beyond Identity Politics: Emerging Social Justice Movements in Communities of Color* (Boston: South End, 1996); Joel Bleifuss, "Reforming the Beast: Campaign Finance Reform," *In These Times,* June 24–July 7, 1996, 12–15; Jeremy Breecher, John Brown Childs, and Jill Cutler, *Global Visions: Beyond the New World Order* (Boston: South End, 1993); Kevin Danaher, ed., *Fifty Years Is Enough: The Case against the World Bank* (Boston: South End, 1994); Gary Delgado, *Organizing the Movement: The Roots and Growth of Acorn* (Philadelphia: Temple University Press, 1986); Paulo Friere and Myles Horton, *We Make the Road by Walking: Conversations in Education and Social Change* (Philadelphia: Temple University Press, 1990); Gottfried, ed., *Feminism and Social Change;* Mary Ann Hinsdale, Helen M. Lewis, and S. Maxine Waller, *It Comes from the People: Community Development and Local Theology*

(Philadelphia: Temple University Press, 1995); Biorn Maybury-Lewis, *The Politics of the Possible: The Brazilian Workers' Trade Union Movement* (Philadelphia: Temple University Press, 1994); David Moberg, "State of the Unions: AFL-CIO's Aggressive New Strategies," *In These Times,* April 1–13, 1996, 22–23; John Nichols, "Labor Gets It Together," *The Progressive,* August 1996, 22–24; Mary Beth Rogers, *Cold Anger: A Story of Faith and Power Politics* (Denton: University of North Texas Press, 1990).

78. Between March 1994 and February 1997, welfare caseloads dropped by 18 percent nationwide. However, none of the states knows the economic status of the families that are no longer on the welfare rolls (Jason DaParle, "A Sharp Decrease in Welfare Cases Is Gathering Speed," *New York Times,* February 2, 1997, 1, 18).

79. National Conference of Catholic Bishops (NCCB), "Economic Justice for All" (Washington, D.C.: United States Catholic Conference, 1986), 130, 319.

80. Ibid., 134.

[10]

Face to Face

Transforming Faith-Based Outreach

Joan Sakalas

"If I were a welfare recipient, what would I ask of the church?"[1] Would I trust that people know or even care about my life when they have not asked what I need? Would men and women in congregations welcome me at worship even though my clothes come from the Goodwill box? Do they want to help me so that I will stay away from their neighborhood, their church? As a woman, I am troubled by these questions. As a feminist, I believe that women must speak for themselves—especially women whose voices have been missing from public discourse. Church congregations have tried to address poor mothers' problems by imagining what might be needed and generally by making goods available. Communities and churches, in particular, have directly impacted families lacking basic resources. The many church-run shelters, soup kitchens, and pantries in New York City attest to the effectiveness of this grassroots approach. However, even faith-based groups with the best of charitable intentions often neglect to involve recipients directly in decision making, in the process of articulating their needs, and in program design. One obstacle to this involvement, Thomas Szasz argues, is our tendency to portray recipients of public assistance as morally inferior.[2] We need to ask ourselves whom this kind of image serves. Do we excuse ourselves from effective redress and direct contact by accepting images of mothers receiving public assistance as hopelessly impaired?

From these questions, two related themes emerge. First, how can we structure outreach programs in ways that empower poor mothers? And second, how can churches support such empowerment? With these questions in mind, in the summer of 1997 I began to design a program that would create a different paradigm for outreach to poor mothers. With Mothers Together I created a model that shifts the power to make decisions, set the pace, and define content to the women involved. The model engages a feminist methodology placing the participants, mothers receiving public assistance, at the center and assumes that they know their aspirations and needs best. By involving women in a cooperative entrepreneurial business, Mothers Together rejects stereotypical images of mothers receiving public assistance and suggests that the broad entrepreneurial possibilities available to middle-class women could be appropriate for poor women as well. By providing the opportunity to create and market their own goods, participants prove to themselves that they can enter an economic and social realm generally unavailable to them. In this case, a successful business experience moves women toward greater economic and social stability by expanding their vision of possible work and of themselves as creative, successful women.

The program creates a team effort enlisting the support of metropolitan faith-based congregations and business people to expose mothers receiving public assistance to the world of work and entrepreneurship. Further, it creates coalitions with other business, child care, training, and educational programs and resources in each community, maximizing opportunities for participating women to connect upon completion of the program with further training, education, or work.

The business cooperative offers hands-on experience in textile design and product production, in basic business accounting, and desktop publishing as they design and create the program newsletter. Mothers Together assumes that one size does not fit all women. Instead it begins with each woman's perception of her own needs, interests, and talents. To this end the training seeks to help women discern their needs, build confidence, and develop communications skills necessary to work effectively toward their goals. For many women this is their first positive experience of working cooperatively with other women. Participants are recruited through metropolitan churches, tenants' associations, neighborhood shelters, and social service agencies. Graduates of the program also make referrals. Working together, the women create and implement a business plan, develop a sales plan, design and produce their goods, and share the profits of their work.

I use this program as a case study for several reasons: first, I am intimately in touch with its genesis and development; second, the program represents an effort to engage congregational goodwill and resources in practical measures to prepare poor women to move toward increased economic and social stability; third, the program provides an example of a paradigm shift from "charity" to outreach.

In this chapter, I place the stories and testimonies of women enrolled in Mothers Together at the center, allowing their words to suggest a different vision of responsive and relevant outreach for faith-based communities.[3] The women's stories serve three purposes. First, they illustrate the problematic dimensions of welfare charity. Second, they articulate the mothers' needs as they see them. Third, they demonstrate the insights of mothers struggling to be independent of public assistance when their own agency is affirmed.

Finally, in order for the reader to understand the difference between a charity and a neighbor model of outreach, I include three composite stories of congregations making the decision to support Mothers Together. I define neighbors as people with whom we expect to come in contact frequently, people who will impact our lives and whose lives we expect to impact. They are people for whom we take some responsibility and whom we expect to take some responsibility for us. Neighbors are not anonymous; they have faces and names, problems and passions. Although we may not like all of our neighbors, we cannot ignore them and may indeed view them as an extended family. The stories that follow illustrate how our sense of relationship to the objects of our outreach defines the quality of our involvement.[4]

Content and Structure—Seven Vignettes

The following vignettes are based on my experience facilitating weekly leadership training groups and coordinating the business workday at the shelter-based site of Mothers Together. The vignettes raise issues regarding the content and structure of outreach and demonstrate the wealth of participating mothers' insight in their own words.

Monday—Leadership Training

SACRED SPACE—IS THIS A HOLY PLACE? We arrived at the shelter early. This week Mary was to lead the opening ritual. At Mothers Together, meetings begin with a simple ritual, the creation of a circle, to recognize that this is a special time and place for the women gathered. The circle metaphorically represents a space of safety, a space where we have deliberately gathered to spend special time together. All materials used in the ritual must be free, found, or of special significance to the woman beginning the ritual. By placing a higher value on found objects, we are agreeing that many of the most meaningful resources have no price and are already held by us.

As Mary entered, Ashley, the facilitator, asked whether she was ready with the opening. Mary responded, "No, I can't think of any way to begin." Ashley asked if she had any item in her room that might become the focus of the opening ritual. She asked whether she could use two photos of Cherokee chiefs that were very important to her. None of us knew that Mary was part Cherokee.

When she returned carrying the photos, Mary told Ashley, "They remind me that my people were once free and happy." Ashley asked if Mary felt free in the shelter. Mary replied, "No." Ashley pursued the issue of freedom, asking, "Do you feel free anywhere?" Mary's answer surprised both of us. "Yes, I feel free in this room when we meet." When Ashley asked why, Mary replied, "Because when we gather here we say what we think and what we feel. Here I am free."

By now the other women had arrived. Following the circle-ritual custom, Mary prepared to pass the photos around. Today to open she asked each woman to say what she saw as they looked at the photos.

THE CIRCLE CONTINUES—THIS IS NOT JUST A BASEBALL GLOVE. The creation of the circle became an integral part of our Monday leadership groups. When the women planned their graduation ceremony, they decided to begin with the circle. They wanted to set a tone and show their guests how we do things. At graduation, Carmen volunteered to plan the ritual. As we settled in our chairs, she held out a baseball glove and ball. She told us that they were Christmas gifts she had bought for her five-year-old daughter with the money she earned in the Mothers Together business. Before she passed them around she told us that she gave a glove and ball to her daughter because as a little girl she never had one. Carmen wanted these gifts to say to her daughter that anything is possible.

THE WHAT-IF GAME. How will you sell your hats? That was the question for our role-play exercise today. The challenge was to imagine approaching a minister of a neighborhood church to ask whether a group of mothers could sell hats after the Sunday service. Shawna drew the slip this time. She read it and looked distressed. In response she said she couldn't do it. She would not speak to a minister. Half of the women in the group agreed. When asked why, Shawna said she would not feel comfortable. "Ministers judge you; he will look at my clothes and think they aren't good enough." Alice added, "Yes, he wouldn't like us. He'd say, 'You don't belong here.'" When I asked whether the other women agreed, they said, "No." Helen said, "I'd talk with a minister. After all they're just like the rest of us. They're not really perfect; they make mistakes. I'd feel comfortable."

BARBARA'S COLLAGE.   Ashley wanted action this week, not words. We were continuing our Monday exploration of how women would move toward their goals. Her choice, a collage that shows our journey toward our dreams, created from magazines, newspapers, and catalogs.

The floor was strewn with the raw materials and the tools: scissors, glue sticks, paper. The shelter had left no tables for us today, so we worked on chairs, the floor, and the broad windowsills. Sometimes a woman asked for a picture. "Does anyone have a picture of a baby? Anyone found animals?" Otherwise we worked silently.

After about one hour, we were ready. Each woman in turn interpreted her combination of words and pictures, describing how they represented her vocational journey. For some like myself, the journey was very immediate, for some like Teresa, long-term.

We had completed our stories, except for one, Mary. She said, "I don't want to show you mine." Thinking that she was embarrassed, we encouraged her, reminding her that we all had shown ours. Her response, however, took us by surprise. "I don't want to show you my collage because it is very important to me. I'm going to put it up in my room. I'm not ready to share it yet." At her graduation she reiterated that she still had the collage on her wall and that it represented the beginning of her realization that she could do something.

Thursday—Business Day

I CAN'T SEW.   There were three tables. At one, two women pinned and cut the patterns for the children's hats. At another, three others were carefully assembling and sewing. At the third, two discussed the flyer they were designing to advertise their work. In the midst of all this busyness, Carmen sat unoccupied. Her attendance in the program was 100 percent and her enthusiasm clear, yet she sat unoccupied. Martha, the volunteer who created the patterns, noticed Carmen and asked if she wouldn't like to help with a new hat design. Carmen said, "No, I'm afraid of the machine. I've never sewn. You don't want to work with me. I'll just mess up." Martha said, "Sit down. We'll work through it together. Then you'll make your own."

Forty-five minutes later, as the women put the fabric away and set tables for lunch and their business meeting, Carmen was still at her machine. Martha asked her whether she was ready to stop and eat lunch. As she cleaned up, Carmen held up two hats, "I made these by myself. You know, sewing isn't that hard. I think I like it."

MOTHERS' STORIES. It was the first week of the program. The women agreed that although they might feel more comfortable cutting or hand-sewing or keeping the books, they would all try every job. As they circulated around the room, two women showed particular skill at machine sewing. Speaking as she sewed, Teresa told us, "My mother was a seamstress. She died a long time ago but always supported us with her sewing. I forgot how much I learned from her."

Carla, who sat at the next machine, was smiling. She said, "Yes, me too, I forgot how much fun I had with my mother. When I was a little girl, she taught me to sew. We don't get along anymore. I forgot that we did have fun."

Postscript: Three weeks later Teresa announced that she asked her husband to buy her a sewing machine for Christmas this year. We talked about brands, about new or used, about business possibilities.

GETTING DOWN TO BUSINESS. At the business meeting Carla asked, "How will we describe the goal of our business? That's the question." Mary answered, "We'll tell them that we are trying to establish a work record. We are building a sense that we can do something successfully. And we are learning to work together and help each other."

"Presence is everything. We need to know what we want to accomplish, and we need to stand tall so people will see that we are proud of what we do. That's what's important when we meet people who might buy our hats," Carmen added. Carmen was the organizer, the woman with a sense of how to structure the business to make it work. "But how will we organize ourselves when it comes time to sell our hats?" she asked. Teresa had a plan. "Each of us will have a job. One will carry and show the hats, one will carry and distribute the flyer, and one will carry the clipboard and speak about the business. The clipboard should have a list of things we want to accomplish so we don't forget what we need to do."

"Yes, a group, that makes sense." agreed Mary. "After all, we are Mothers Together."

Neighbors and Others

A Story of Three Congregations

In order to understand the proposed shift in how we develop outreach, it is helpful to look at examples. This is a story of the responses of three groups—in reality, three modes of faith-based outreach. The first describes a refusal to help. In one conversation I had with the director of a church-sponsored shelter, I was told that she would not refer any women to Mothers Together because the women in her shelter were incapable of following through with a program lasting for four months. I wondered how this director could make this judgment about every resident in her shelter. What message did her judgment give to her residents? Certainly it was not one of hope and empowerment.

A hierarchical model that presumes that the staff of programs and shelters or members of congregations know best has not worked and is not respectful of either the recipients or the providers of services. The approach is a dead end for both parties in that it encourages arrogance on the part of the provider and belligerence, helplessness, or hopelessness on the part of the recipient. We need to pay more attention to what nourishes those of us who are economically and socially more secure. Those nourishing experiences need to become commonplace and frequent for shelter residents as well as for mothers on welfare.

For instance, in Mothers Together, although we use sewing as a vehicle for a business, the goal of the program is not necessarily to produce significant numbers of seamstresses. For a small number, sewing and textile design may open a career path. However, for most, the sewing machines serve as a vehicle for successful mastery of a skill. When mothers learn to sew and create marketable items, that accomplishment proves to them that they can do something well. For women who have no work history or an interrupted one, they need experiences that build or rebuild their confidence in themselves and their capabilities. Integral to the work is reflection on insights and concerns that rise from the work. The specific context of a sewing business provides a vehicle for airing and addressing fears and dreams together. The wisdom of the staff is not privileged. The assumption is that all women present know a great deal from their own life experience and that through the act of sharing we grow and support one another.

In the second and third encounters, I made appointments to speak to the appropriate parish committees, forwarding a proposal, budget, and timetable for the Mothers Together program to each. My hope was that the congregations would make a commitment to offer both material and volunteer support to the program. Realistically, however, I knew that finances were often tight and that jobs and family obligations made volunteer work difficult. The women the program was proposing to serve were not members of the congregation, and in fact, though they were a part of the neighborhood surrounding these churches, they never participated in church activities.

At the second group, a wealthy congregation, representatives had a clear sense of their financial resources. They spoke of how wonderful it would be to do something together and how authorization of financial support was quite probable in that this was clearly the kind of "mission work" they wanted to encourage. They also saw it as a possible vehicle for creating a link with the neighborhood. Initially they provided seed money, and their sense of solidarity with the developing project became evident as members of the congregation regularly inquired about its progress.

Eventually, several women decided that they wanted to accompany their charitable gifts with direct involvement. They wanted to visit Mothers Together to help out with the program as volunteers. However, their resolve gave rise to another practical problem. How could their involvement become more than a voyeuristic exercise where they were either doing good for the needy or attending the program as charitable tourists? Even when the resolve is there to meet face to face, how we construct that meeting is critical.

First the churchwomen were asked what they had to offer the program. Could they sew? Did they have business skills? After discussion, they agreed that their strength lay in fundraising. The challenge then was to structure a meeting in which Mothers Together participants and the women with fundraising skills could develop a strategic plan together. In fact, the participants are the experts on the program, its strong points and its processes. Participating mothers could learn from the churchwomen just how a fundraising event is planned. Both groups of women could speak to one another from their own experience. Thus the meeting held the possibility of both groups becoming neighbors, of moving beyond recipients and donors.

In another community not very far from the second, the third committee gathered. This time several congregations were represented. They asked me to describe the program and made it clear that they were looking for a project through which they might revitalize their neighborhood and respective congregations. As they discussed the program, they described their congregations as aging and with little money. Once they were told that participants in Mothers Together would be sewing hats as their first business, they began to name specific members of the community who were retired seamstresses. They suggested that the seamstresses might be interested in working as mentors and might benefit from the new relationship as well. They named sources such as local shelters and welfare offices where we could recruit participants. One woman expressed concern that poor women would feel uncomfortable entering their church. They asked that we consider holding a workshop where they could consider ways to make women feel welcome. Their answer to my request was a commitment to recruit, provide space, and interact with the participants regularly.

In fact, the financial support of the second church and other individuals made possible the purchase of needed materials, and the support of a small staff. However, this financial support needed to be combined with the direct involvement of the third group of congregations for the program to thrive.

The questions asked at the third church illustrated the difference in their sense of relationship to potential participants. Why would mothers who don't know us feel welcome here? How can we make women feel welcome? What should we say when they walk in the door? All of these questions speak to the congregation's desire to make a positive connection with the mothers involved. Until the participants of Mothers Together become neighbors, become mothers with faces and hopes and aspirations, both parties, the donors and the participants, remain "others." The third group reached toward the women; they committed themselves to listen and trust the dreams and wishes of the mothers. Without active contact, outreach remains something we do for others. With active contact, we begin to create the possibility of transformation, of both parties becoming neighbors, of both parties being transformed.

The Process of Becoming Neighbors

Proposing how church congregations can address poor mothers' problems is a difficult challenge marked often by a focus on service delivery rather than process. Although it may sound outrageous, I find that what congregations do as outreach is not really as important as how the outreach is done. My stories are intended to demonstrate that though the problems to be addressed are complex, attention to process in conjunction with attention to the needs and insights of the subjects of our outreach is as important as the nature of our outreach.

When addressing issues of welfare in the United States, faith-based communities must set empowerment, employment, and economic security as goals for outreach programming, not just service delivery. We need to reframe our focus from welfare to *well fare*. To fare well includes economic, social, and spiritual well-being. It means that congregations must come in contact with one another to be neighbors. Reaching out cannot simply involve mailing a check accompanied by an encouraging letter. Many people are aware of the poor from reading or watching news and videos that graphically portray stories of poverty, but again, that is at a distance. In order to become neighbors, we must meet face to face. And we must be willing to walk in one another's neighborhoods to speak and hear one another directly. Jesus did not minister from a distance; he ministered face to face.

If we believe that congregations must be responsive to our neighbors' needs, then one of the few ways we can know what those needs are is by direct contact with our neighbors, including mothers receiving public assistance. Further, we must trust what we hear and not dismiss their perceptions as any more distorted than our own. Programming which honors the competency of our neighbors is essential if transformation is to take place. For too long, social service, governmental, and faith-based agencies have offered assistance and programs that presume the recipients of services are incompetent or infantile. For instance, some congregations speak of "adopting" a poor family. Yet in the United States we do not adopt adults; we adopt children. We need then to examine whether, by using a term generally applied to children, we are infantilizing the families we wish to help. Perhaps the word "mentoring" is a more accurate representation of the assistance we wish to offer. Even our choice of words makes a difference.

The suggestions listed below are offered as a framework for developing faith-based outreach support.

Suggestions—Outreach

First, congregations must move toward being neighbors as well as benefactors. This means that men and women such as the mothers enrolled in Mothers Together must be made to feel welcome in our churches *as they are.* Although we hope people will arrive at church looking their best, Christianity is not about wealth or expensive clothing. Shawna's concern that her clothes would not be appropriate for church needs to be overcome.

Second, the subjects of outreach must be participants and definers of the shape and substance of that outreach. Once poor men and women feel welcome in our churches, they must be invited to participate on boards and committees and recognized as integral to the effectiveness of any outreach. This does not mean that they must officially join the congregation. Our churches cannot hold our neighbors hostage to the requirement of membership.

Third, once our neighbors feel welcome, their suggestions for modifications to program design must receive serious consideration. Actually, maybe we should rename Christian outreach as "Christian inreach." In other words, we embrace our neighbors, bringing them into our homes, into our churches, so that we can build together better, more effective ways of life for our whole community.

Fourth, privileged negative myths about poor men and women must be replaced with more complex understanding of factors and forces in their lives. As Christians we cannot give in to the popular myths which hold injustice in place. We need to understand why Mary felt free in our room at the shelter. We need to hear what makes poor women feel welcome in a church. We do not know the answer without their insight.

Fifth, in the delivery of faith-based outreach programs we must understand work as an exchange of learning and growth. Although the financial gift of the first congregation in the story, "Neighbors and others," offered critical support, more valuable for both the congregation and the objects of the outreach is a direct encounter where neighbors become people whose faces we know. And it was the exchange of information between the churchwomen and mothers about the program and fundraising in the second story that leveled the playing field, making it possible for the women to appreciate one another as neighbors.

Sixth, congregations need to abandon programs that recreate an authoritarian model where participants are told what to do by presumed experts. Volunteers and staff must model leadership and mutuality. For instance, in Mothers Together it was critical that Ashley and I create and share a collage along with participants. Only as we were willing to participate could we deepen the level of trust. As Christians we expect transformation in our lives. Our outreach must be structured to encourage mutual transformation.

Seventh, men and women can move forward when given freedom to be honest about fears and needs. Mary described a sense of freedom in the leadership group that hinged on a sense of being able to say and think what she felt. An atmosphere in which she was not judged and where her experience was valued created an environment where change and growth were possible. Space for work can be sacred space, and the sacred is everywhere we do our work. Without imposing a particular faith tradition on programs, we can still acknowledge values central to our faiths. The stories of the opening ritual offer one example of the use of simple ritual to acknowledge the sacredness of the world and the places where we work and grow. At the first Mothers Together graduation, participants all placed God and God's work in their lives at the center of their success.

Eighth, skills are taught best when the gifts of wisdom, dignity, and leadership of the women involved are respected. When Carmen voiced her fear of sewing, she was not excused from the work. Instead, Martha worked with her. This respectful cooperation is critical to success in overcoming obstacles to the new experiences of learning.

Face to Face

"If I were a welfare recipient, what would I ask of the church?"[5] The designers of faith-based outreach need help in order to answer this question. The elimination of long-term public assistance programs in the United States heightens the needs of mothers receiving public assistance. As we consider how we can effectively respond to these new, less secure, less responsive social, political, and economic circumstances, we must pay particular attention to how we design and implement responses.

Our congregations must be places where judgment and a sense of superiority are not the salient attitude driving outreach, where our outreach is given to "others." As Christians, we are called to live in relation to the world, to minister to one another, and to love one another. That means that we need to remove ourselves from our own eyeballs and admit that we cannot claim to love men and women with whom we are unwilling to talk. We need to hear the wisdom of the men and women who understand that ministers "make mistakes" and are human like them. We need to be neighbors who "make mistakes" and who are willing to share our gifts, wisdom, and expertise with our neighbors who also bring gifts, wisdom, expertise, and dreams. *Well fare* must become the central concern of our outreach, and a sharing of gifts our methodology.

Notes

1. Teresa Amott, as quoted by Julian Shipp in "Economist Says U.S. Churches Must Brace for the Impact of Welfare Reform," *PCUSA News,* November 5, 1997, 1.

2. Szasz sets poverty relief in historical context, arguing that in the twentieth century, poverty has been criminalized and addressed in a "quasi-therapeutic" manner, which reinforces the vision of the poor as criminal, morally depraved, or insane (Thomas Szasz, *Cruel Compassion: Psychiatric Control of Society's Unwanted* [New York: Wiley, 1994], 21).

3. The Mothers Together program is currently housed in a transitional shelter for homeless families, a Methodist church in Harlem and in a Protective Services suite in a housing project. Besides producing hats and storage bags for sale, participating women develop basic business, computer, and leadership skills. The program is supported by one Union Theological Seminary field intern, Garen Murray, who edits the newsletter; two skilled volunteers, Margaret Watt and Dorothy Lashley; and six trained coordinators (five are graduates of the program). For purposes of this chapter, the names of participants have been changed. The statements they make, however, are based on actual conversations in the leadership and work sessions.

4. Shipp, "Economist Says U.S. Churches Must Brace," 1.

5. The stories are, in fact, aggregates, composites of experiences that shape the outreach of faith-based groups and represent two distinct modes of engagement of congregations with their neighborhoods.

AFTERWORDS

Economics, Ethics, and the Everyday

Reflections from Another Shore

Ada María Isasi-Díaz

In Cuba

I was standing in line for twenty minutes waiting to get into this small grocery shop surprisingly set up, not as the old *bodegas,* with a long counter and all the goods in a storage area behind it, but as a tiny supermarket with the goods on open shelves.[1] I waited outside because there was no room for anyone else inside. As I waited, I watched the waves crashing over the wall of El Malecón, the graceful avenue that borders the sea along much of La Habana. Car traffic on this main road of the capital of Cuba is minimal, and the cars are so old that one wonders time and again how those motors still propel the scarred metal bodies which the paint seems to be holding together.

My melancholic reminiscence was interrupted continuously by what I was able to see—much of it happening under the cover of a surprisingly quiet surface. There was a man holding a couple of pairs of gym shorts in such a casual way that it made the conspicuous inconspicuous as he softly said, pronouncing it in Spanish, "Nike, Nike." There was a woman who looked down at her hands as folks went by and whispered "chocolate balls," calling attention to the candy she was selling. A man came up to the woman behind me and very softly asked her to buy something. She said she had to wait and see if she had

215

enough dollars. Yes, this was a small *bodega* where you could pay only in dollars.

There were all kinds of people in line: some were dressed better than others, and I took that to mean that they were economically better off than the others. There were young people who bought beer and snacks. There was a grandmother with her grandson who bought a couple of pieces of bread and a liter of milk. In line waiting to get to the modern register to pay, the talk from all sides had to do with whether they had enough money to pay for what they had taken from the shelves. The two times I visited this *bodega*, I was the only one who paid with five-dollar bills. Everyone else I saw had only one-dollar bills and the coins the Cuban government has minted that inside Cuba are worth the same as U.S. coins.

Pepe, whom I had contracted to drive me around La Habana, like the owners of the dollar *bodega*, is a *cuentapropista*, a person who works on his own. The owners of the *bodega* have to pay taxes on the income from their business; Pepe does not pay taxes because he is part of the vast underground economy in the island. If he held a regular job, he would have taxes to pay. Cristóbal sells secondhand books and magazines in a park in La Habana. I asked him if he makes enough money to survive. Well, he explained, he has a small radio program for which he gets the equivalent of six dollars a month. (An economist who is a member of the Communist party had told me that one needs at least the equivalent of twenty dollars a month to make ends meet.) Cristóbal assured me that he does get the rest that he needs by selling books, which he buys mostly from elderly people. Since part of the small amounts of books he sells are paid for in dollars, and since there are some things that one can get only with U.S. dollars, Cristóbal seemed to be happy with this little business he has on the side.

Though in 1998 I have noticed an increase in buying and selling, Cuba seems to remain more a direct-exchange-of-goods economy than a money economy, *permutar* (to exchange) instead of *comprar* (to buy) is what you hear about when it comes to durable goods. I stayed in La Habana in the apartment of a friend. I asked him how he had gotten that apartment. "Well," he told me, "I exchanged it for a car!" Another friend of mine wanted to *conseguir* (to get) a small, rather dilapidated house occupied by more than one family. My friend had access to dollars, but the people she was buying from did not want money. They did not want to continue living together, so what they asked for in exchange for the house was two separate places in which to live. Another friend lives in a small house in La Habana with her daughter and grandchild. "I exchanged this house for my daughter's apartment plus the one I used to live in."

Housing is a great problem in Cuba. Houses are dilapidated, and many are being kept standing by wood "crutches," scaffolding that holds them up; the need for paint is very obvious. Everywhere you can see the sign, *se permuta* (for exchange). I called a friend, and a man answered the phone. When my friend called me back, I asked her who had answered the phone. "That is my ex-husband." Though divorced, they live in the same household simply because there is no place for him to move.

Much has been said in the United States about the *jineteras,* the numerous young sex workers that are so visible around the hotels. These women do not want to be called prostitutes for they insist that what they do is not a way of life they have opted for but what they need to do to *resolver*—the ever-present Spanish word that means to solve the situation at hand. Yes, at the personal as well as at the national level, the economy in Cuba is not a matter of planning but of fixing, solving, handling, as well as one can.

Three conversations I had about the economy in Cuba were very illuminating. One economist was furious with me for pointing out that any and all systems have to pay attention to *lo cotidiano* (the daily life of the people). If *lo cotidiano* is unbearable, if people have to spend several hours a day obtaining what they need to survive, then the system has to take a look at itself and it has to change. The economist was angry because, as he blurted out at one point, "*lo cotidiano* is destroying our socialist project." I had the sense that he was not willing to take into consideration the heavy burden people shoulder to solve their needs day in and day out, and what this says about the project of the government. I understood him to be insisting on some sort of abstract idea of a socialist project, which is very far from the reality of the Cuban people in the closing years of the twentieth century.

The other economist recognized that the ad hoc nature of the economy at present is a great danger for the socialist project. But instead of blaming the people as the previous economist had done, he understood the need for the socialist project to respond to what was happening. "Many of our ills can be blamed on the embargo; but we also made mistakes by adopting a model that was foreign to us," he said, referring to the centralization and the bureaucratization of the economy that Castro's government copied from the Soviet model. He was very open about the fact that there is no way of keeping a market economy out of Cuba. "The challenge for us is how to introduce the market in a rational way so it does not destroy our project," he explained.

He told me that there are two main concerns for them right now. One is how to introduce some agility into the economy. This they are doing by decentralizing the economy and by putting business people in charge instead of government functionaries. "Business people know that they have to be effective, and government bureaucrats do not know that," he said. Their other problem is how to get capital, which is where the embargo has such a negative effect.

From many different people I heard that this attempt to allow a market economy to develop carries many dangers. In 1997 and now in 1998, I saw differences in economic status that I certainly had not seen during my previous visit in 1987. The person who explained this to me perhaps most clearly was a worker in a hotel where people who come to Cuba for medical treatment stay. He recognizes that there is a need for free elections in Cuba. "The problem is that if Fidel opens his iron fist, the Americans will swallow us whole," he said worriedly. "The Americans will allow no other system but theirs," he continued, "and we do not want to be subservient to them."

To emphasize the will of many Cubans to resist American control, a friend told me the following story. "Several years ago I had the opportunity of being in Chile and was having a conversation with miners. This man approached me and gave me a one-dollar U.S. bill. Since this is not the currency that is used in Chile, he had to go out of his way to get it. As he gave it to me, he told me this was for me to give to the Cuban government so Cuba could continue to maintain its independence from the United States. This is why we keep trying to survive against such great odds: we do not want to be controlled by the United States."

Tourism in Cuba today is the second source of hard currency, the first one being the dollars the Cuban exiles send to their relatives and friends on the island.[2] However, as long as the U.S.-imposed and -monitored embargo is not rescinded, "all that we get is cheap tourism, which buys a cheap package deal and spends little outside what that purchases for them," an accountant explained. "When the embargo is lifted, we know that expensive tourism—American tourism—will come," he concluded. Everybody dislikes the apartheid that has developed in Cuba: a two-tier system in which all kinds of goods are available for the tourists but not for the Cubans. This system extends to all aspects and levels, and separates those who have access to U.S. dollars from those who do not. My friend the economist told me that 50 percent of the population is believed to have access to between twenty and one hundred dollars a month. How do Cubans get U.S. dollars? Many receive them from their families who live abroad; others work in an industry where incentives are paid to the workers in dollars. According to my friend, construction workers, those who work in the sugar industry, in communications, in oil industries, and in tourism receive U.S. dollars from the government as incentives.[3]

A man whose observation skills I came to value enormously, and whose analyses I respect, knowing that they are not meant to paint a false picture, told me he believes that one-half of the people have no jobs or do not go to work. Another friend told me that she thought that was a bit high, but she did not offer any other number. "The fact is that many people can do better hustling than working at a steady job." A man who tried to sell me alligator steaks as I walked through the less-touristy areas of famous Varadero Beach confirmed this. He insisted that he fared better economically hustling a few dollars here and there from tourists than working very hard as a construction worker. What do they mean by "hustling"? Well, for this construction worker, it meant somehow getting alligator meat and then trying to sell it; he also tries to recruit tourists for a boat ride that is not licensed by the government. Then there was the man on a bicycle who offered to sell me towels. I was sitting with a friend in her house, and since it was warm, we had the door open. I saw the bicycle rider go by. He backtracked when he saw us, to try to sell us towels. When I asked where he had gotten the towels, my friend said that "most probably he stole them."

After fourteen days of keen observation and asking everyone I could every question possible, I used the last three days to test one of my hypotheses. Somewhat afraid that I would be chided for rash judgment, I said to a friend, "I have the sense that every Cuban commits ten illegal acts a day." "No," he replied quickly, "most probably, we commit fifteen illegal acts a day." This led me to a conversation with two pastors. One told me about how difficult it is to preach given this situation. According to him, people come to church in search of some sort of transcendence that allows them to escape the situation at hand. "It is very difficult to preach about anything concrete," he said. "They do not want to hear it, and we do not know what to say." Another pastor explained, "I do not know how to tell the people in my church that, as Christians, they have to be honest. I know that to survive one has to do illegal things such as not go to work, work on your own, underground, so you do not have to pay taxes, take anything you can from the workplace so you can sell it and get some needed cash."

"What about the church's responsibility to denounce injustice?" I asked. These two pastors certainly acknowledged that the situation is not without injustices, but at the same time they think that the government is doing the best it can, given the situation. But, should they not change the system? For these pastors, that is not a solution, for they support the socialist project and believe that if the political system were changed, unbridled capitalism would come into the island and undo much of what the social projects have been able to achieve.

When one comments that the only time the socialist projects worked better was when Cuba was depending on the Soviet Union, and that to rely on the United States is the same as relying on the Soviet Union, the response is that Cuba was not that dependent on the Soviets. Cubans insist that if they had been that dependent, the present Cuban government would have fallen when the Soviet Union fell, and it did not. But then, they also tell you that Cuba was able to survive for so long because it traded sugar for oil and many other goods with the USSR and the Soviet bloc—sugar always being valued in such a way that there was no trade deficit. They also agree that the present economic situation is undoing the socialist project.

Some Reflections on the U.S. Economy Using the Cuban Reality as a Starting Point

I have attempted to structure this chapter in a way that decentralizes the United States while realistically accepting the fact that everything that happens in the economy of the United States has an effect on Cuba and all other Two-Thirds countries. What follows, then, are some reflections about the economy prompted by the chapters in this book and using the Cuban reality I have described above as the starting point.

First, as an ethicist, I must insist on the fact that we are responsible as individual U.S. citizens for immediate and foreseeable-future effects of the policy decisions that are taken and implemented at present in this country. The promotion of economic value as the only value that guides this nation's policies negatively affects Cuba and many other places, and we cannot but denounce the lack of human values that rules the U.S. government, U.S. and U.S.-controlled economic organizations, and U.S. and U.S.-controlled businesses. Therefore, we cannot judge what happens elsewhere if we do not understand how it is driven by what the United States has done and does all around the world. I am in no way absolving Cuba or any other nation of its responsibilities, but those responsibilities are ameliorated, I believe, by the lack of control that Two-Thirds World countries have over the situation they face.

This leads me to my second point. We in the United States have a moral responsibility to realize and act according to the fact that the economic situation we enjoy and the privileges it gives us are at the expense of two-thirds of the people of the world. Our world has finite resources, and what we have is related to the fact that the majority of people do not have enough. The neoliberal economic policy of the United States hides this reality from the majority of its citizens. And those of us who do see the way our country exploits other people are incapable of bringing about change. Perhaps what Cuba and other Two-Thirds World countries challenge us to do is to see the broader picture and build solidarity with them across geographic frontiers so our struggle against economic exploitation can become effective. Maybe the cry "economically exploited people of the world, unite" will gather enough of us to shake the present world order. Cubans see very clearly that the struggle against neoliberal policies will be long and arduous. "The United States will never allow us to have a system different from theirs because that would change theirs," a woman who supports the socialist project in Cuba told me. She insists that with the economic changes that have taken place on the island lately, Cuba is ready to take off economically, "and this will show the rest of Latin America that there is a different model than the one of the United States. This is why there is so much opposition to removing the embargo," she concludes.

Third, it is painfully poignant to realize that whether governmental cuts are due to structural-adjustment policies required by neoliberal economic policies or whether they are imposed because of failed governmental economic policies and the U.S. embargo, women in the United States as well as Cuba are the ones who bear the brunt. This is so because the cuts affect mostly the essentials of life—food, shelter, health, education—essentials for which women have been made responsible through the ages. In Cuba, according to professors in the Women's Studies program of the University of La Habana, the division of roles and tasks between women and men continues to be quite traditional. They indicate, however, that changes are noticeable when it comes to attributing human qualities such as tenderness, caring, assertiveness, firmness of character. So, though one finds endearing men, figuring out how to make do with the very limited amount of groceries that are available falls still mainly on women.

The issue of the youth in Cuba came up repeatedly. Two remarks were central for me. One was made by a man supportive of the regime who believes that "the nation is in peril because the young think there is a need for annexation to the United States. They do not see any other way out of the present economic situation." The friendly economist from whom I learned much made the other remark. "The young people have aspirations that cannot be fulfilled in the present situation of our society. What the youth does not understand is that they have those aspirations because of what this socialist society has given them." I then engaged him in a discussion about motivations and finished by saying to him that the regime in Cuba has the same problem the churches have everywhere—how to motivate people to follow a vision that does not necessarily lead to accumulation of material goods.

Also important to point out when talking about youth in Cuba is the relationship between autonomy and interdependence, between the social and the personal. Usually, in the United States it is the exaggerated emphasis on individualism that leads to ignoring or rejecting social responsibility and interdependence. In Cuba one also notices, especially among the youth, a rejection of social responsibility and interdependence. There, however, it seems to be a reaction to the obliteration of the personal, to the collapse of individual thought, aspirations, and projects. In other words, there is no space for individual expression, because the people, the concept of nation, and the government all are spoken for by the Cuban Communist party.

For me, solidarity continues to be the main expression of justice. I believe that we have great need to continue to insist on the commonality of interests that exists across frontiers in our world today. For me, this commonality of interests, based on a healthy self-love, is central to all the struggles for justice in our world today. Negative understandings such as spiritual poverty or ascribing positive value to destructive self-sacrifice and self-abnegation contribute, I believe, to keeping the poor oppressed and to devaluing a Christian sense of solidarity which really can promote justice in our world.

It is from this perspective that I think we need to indict the U.S. Congress and the Clinton administration for the undoing of the welfare laws. I saw the welfare laws as the only effective means within the present system that could question and, in a tiny but real way, modulate the unbridled capitalism which is bringing so much misery to so many in this country and abroad. The welfare laws were also a different kind of system, in which economic value was not the only value, in which there was a sense of moral responsibility that extended to all in society and not only to those who can contribute to the riches of the few. These were the laws that made the government work for the whole of society and not just for those who can turn a profit. Many in the United States now criticize the present regime in Cuba for turning to the churches for help, especially with the elderly. I believe that the Cuban regime needs to look for effective ways to change its political and economic system so that it can take care of the elderly. But I also realize that this is precisely the same thing that the U.S. Congress did when it suggested that private charities could take care of the needy in the U.S. society. Even if they could, which they cannot, it is immoral for the government to attempt to relieve itself of this responsibility. At least the Cuban regime does so begrudgingly after insisting for decades that taking care of the poor and weak in society was the responsibility of the government.[4]

I find that we have to work avidly at highlighting the importance of *lo cotidiano;* we have to emphasize the intrinsic connections between structural changes and *lo cotidiano.* The undoing of welfare policies points precisely to the opposite. Most welfare policies have been understood to deal with the private sphere, and their undoing has been given little importance, I would like to suggest, because it is seen as relating mainly to *lo cotidiano.* However, *lo cotidiano* is precisely the first horizon of our lives, of the materiality of life. It is in *lo cotidiano* that we first meet and deal with the ethical world, that we form, uphold, and live out our morality. The relegation of *lo cotidiano* to the private sphere is one of the main reasons why the world of women is considered unimportant. The relevance of this is not difficult to guess when one realizes that women constitute more than one-half of the world's population and yet we receive less than 10 percent of the world's income.

Years ago when I was studying in college, one of the professors said that the reason why the United States was willing to drop a bomb on Hiroshima and not, let's say, on Mississippi is because the latter was part of this nation and the former was not. What this rather simplistic example taught me when I had just arrived in the United States is that almost all issues are, in the long run, issues of inclusion or exclusion. I think that this is applicable to the relationship of the United States with Cuba as well as to the undoing of welfare policies. Basically, what the embargo and aggressive policies against Cuba mean is that Cuba is excluded because it is not willing to follow the lead of the United States, to be a pawn in U.S. hands, to sacrifice autonomy and the welfare of the Cuban people so that less than 20 percent of the world can consume over 80 percent of the world's goods. What the undoing of welfare policies points to is the exclusion of women from the common good, from the world that matters. This is why our women's perspectives as ethicists, as Christian ethicists, are so important.

Notes

1. No matter how many parenthetical remarks I introduce in this article, what I say will be read whichever way the reader chooses, greatly determined by her or his ideology, whether she or he is aware of it or not. But, regardless, I need to state my perspective. I am in many ways a social democrat, which means that I support many of the social projects promoted by the Cuban government, such as education and health care. I adamantly oppose, however, the political measures that the Cuban government has used and continues to use to implement these and other social projects. I oppose the lack of free elections, the lack of freedom of speech and information (which go hand in hand with not allowing a free press), and the violation of human rights of anyone who dares to oppose the government. I understand perfectly how vulnerable Cuba is to being swallowed by the United States, and I will always energetically denounce any such attempts. I do not believe that capitalism and democracy are the same thing—a myth that is as much alive in Cuba as it is in the United States, read in each of these countries from two different sides. Furthermore, I do not believe that true justice can exist within capitalism, though I do see the need for some sort of market economy.

2. I know that this is also true of several nations in Central America and most probably in other parts of the world. Those with least resources continue to be the ones who help the poor throughout the world. Though there are a noticeable number of Cubans living in the United States who are not poor, in the majority of those cases, their families and friends also left Cuba. The Cubans who live in the United States who have family and friends back in the

island to whom they send money are mostly those of us with the least economic resources.

3. Freedom of speech is very limited in Cuba, but the jokes weave a deeply insightful narrative. The jokes are funny, but since many are a critique of society, they are also extremely sad. Here is one of them: The police arrested a drunk, whose only answer to all questions was "I am a bellboy at the Riviera Hotel." Finally, in the early hours of the morning, the police were able to get him to tell them the name of his wife. When she came to pick him up, the police asked her why he was so fixated on being a bellboy at the Riviera. Her answer, which points to the need for access to U.S. dollars, was, "When he gets drunk, he gets delusions of grandeur. In reality, he's a neurosurgeon."

4. I believe also, however, that the Cuban government has not allowed the churches to help until now because this gives them a space and importance in civil society that the government has not been willing to give them. I believe that only because it is faced with the desperation of the present situation has the Castro government allowed the churches to begin performing some social action, acting beyond their own doors.

Welfare in the Age of Spectacles

Emilie M. Townes

IT WAS EARLY 1981. NANCY REAGAN wanted new china for the White House. The cost of the Lennox pattern with a raised gold presidential seal was $209,508 for 220 place settings. Ronald Reagan was talking about cutting welfare eligibility as the misery index (inflation plus unemployment) was more than 20 percent.

Our culture has developed a fascination and admiration for power and status. Nothing is more important to this culture than its symbols. Reagan inherited an America in shock from a decade of humiliation. We had lost the longest war in our history as a nation. A president had resigned in disgrace. Our economy was in shambles. Only one-fourth of the voting-age population felt that they could trust government to do what was right most of the time. Jimmy Carter had talked about malaise; Ronald Reagan's response was to talk about power and status. The 1960s spawned the civil rights movement, the antiwar movement, and Woodstock. Reagan talked about the magic of the marketplace—with trickle-down and tax cuts.

Money words, "yuppie," "buppie," "upscale," "privatization," "takeover," became the key language of the 1980s. In the culture of power and status, the past was modern because it held the key to the future. Getting rich was justified because it left the nation better off. Cutting aid to the poor was humane because welfare hurt initiative. The Reagan administration cut personal taxes and established Justice Department guidelines that all but ended antitrust activity.

On Wall Street, we created a paper economy in which the buying and selling of companies were more profitable than running them. Leveraged buyouts and junk bonds made the hostile takeover possible. "Greenmail" was paid to avoid takeovers. Companies were attacked by "raiders" and saved by "white knights." Fired executives floated into retirement on "golden parachutes." While Ronald Reagan spoke of "welfare queens," national attention was diverted away from the looting of the nation's savings and loans by wealthy white men.

In our foreign policy, there was a revival of the Imperial America. We became committed to showing our power. From 1980 to 1987, the military budget more than doubled, to $282 billion annually. Reagan called for us to abandon our "Vietnam syndrome."

The 1983 Grenada invasion came less than seventy-two hours after Lebanese terrorists killed 241 Marines in their barracks. It refocused our attention on a part of the world that has been an American sore spot since the 1979 Nicaraguan revolution. The fighting was over in days. Casualties (as wars go) were light: 19 killed; 115 wounded; 8,612 medals awarded. Many in the land experienced an enormous sense of release of tension: we were no longer a helpless giant.

Yuppies and buppies became dream consumers. The Laffer curve was tailor made for this group, and a new bootstrap was invented: All we have to do is lower tax rates at the upper level, and the rich will try to get richer. In so doing, they would improve the economy and government revenues through their investments and business activities. Jokes abounded about the materialism of yuppies and their passion for brand names. But many of us would only buy Louis Vuitton, Gucci, Mercedes, Liz Claiborne—or at least we wished we could.

The essence of who we were as a nation was image—the extravaganza (grand cultural/master narratives writ large). Reagan's first inauguration cost $8 million for four days (an $800,000 fireworks display at the Lincoln Memorial, two nights of show-business performances, nine inaugural balls). But these extravaganzas were not concerned with the work ethic of small-town America; they were advertisements for America the Grand. The beautiful was the expensive; the good was the costly.

The 1984 Olympics in Los Angeles saw the new patriotism evidenced in the crowds chanting "U.S.A." every time a U.S. athlete competed. The resurgence of national pride Reagan advocated was captured in the $6 million opening and closing ceremonies directed by Hollywood producer David Wolper.

The two hundredth anniversary of the Statue of Liberty saw an opening night in which the faces of the president and his wife were superimposed on the relit statue. Later, Reagan spoke of his tax bill putting a smile on Liberty. Wolper was the director again, this time with a $30 million budget.

And of all the various messages that we, as a nation, drew from this, at least one message was clear: to be an American was to be powerful and to be powerful was to be rich. Reagan assured us that the social safety net for the elderly, needy, disabled, and unemployed would be left intact in this new culture of power and status. However, the crucial point was that the safety net was to be kept out of sight. The problem, it seems, was that our concern for the poor actually crippled them.

Charles Murray, in *Losing Ground* (a 1984 book that was mandatory reading in the Reagan administration), told us that because of relaxed welfare standards and liberal court rulings, the 1960s made it easier for the poor to get along without jobs and to get away with crimes. Murray's methodology was—and is—a conservative individualistic analysis of poverty and welfare policy. For him, the only impulse that is dependable is self-interest. Therefore, he argues for individual freedom unrestrained by government intervention. Murray understood poverty as a personal failure compounded by government-created bad incentives. For him, the only welfare program is one that does not exist at all, as individuals should be left alone to make their own way in life or depend on the charity of their families or neighbors.

Murray's view of poverty offered Reagan the perfect reason to cut back on aiding the poor. The denial of compassion became respectable as the standard of living for the people living in the bottom one-fifth of the economic strata dropped by 8 percent while the top one-fifth rose 16 percent. All this while, Irangate, the 1987 stock market crash, EPA scandals, influence-peddling trials of White House aides (something that remains a feature in the Clinton administration) had little or no effect on the culture of power and states.

In the 1970s, we jogged our way to health. By the 1980s, we powered our way to health with the Nautilus machine or liposuction. The point of this new elegance was to make it clear that what lay beneath all the surface luxury was raw power.

What happened to us is a classic shell game. If the past could be appropriated, it is a powerful weapon for discrediting anyone who opposes the culture of power and status—and, what is more important, all its traditions and values. Make no mistake, those who voted for Reagan and Bush in the 1980s were not voting out of simple self-interest. In 1984, the Reagan-Bush voting bloc comprised 54 percent of blue-collar workers, 59 percent of white-collar workers, and 57 percent of those with incomes between $12,500 and $24,999. They were voting for a culture they saw as hopeful and with which they identified—even though it did not benefit them directly. Part of the cost of that identification was a $2 trillion federal debt and a $500 billion-plus savings-and-loan scandal.

The 1990s have been no better. The current drive for tax cuts and spending reductions is due, in some measure, to Bill Clinton's attempt to shift the balance slightly in 1992. The wealthy paid 16 percent more in taxes the following year as a result, and the antiwelfare rhetoric began in earnest once again. As the dust settles from the Personal Responsibility and Work Opportunity Reconciliation Act of 1996, it is becoming increasingly clear that low-income and poor people are the ones who must bear the weight of balancing the budget. The only deep and/or multiyear budget cuts that were actually enacted as a part of the tax reform of 1996 affect poor and low-income folks.

The moralization of poverty in the age of spectacle is a gruesome and death-dealing pageant for poor and low-income women, men, and children. The poor in U.S. culture and society are often ignored, rendered faceless, or labeled "undeserving"; they are considered an eyesore, their own worst enemy, or simply down on their luck. The recent welfare reforms were crafted with these negative images playing a tremendous (sub)conscious role. These degrading images tell us that poverty is an aberration of the grand narrative of progress and success which fuels much of our culture, or it is an end produced by the poor themselves—they have simply brought this on themselves. In a rather curious circular logic, media portrayals of poverty point out the ways in which the poor suffer from forms of deprivation and then loop back to define those differences as the cause of poverty itself.

The results are all too predictable: there is something fundamentally wrong with the victims. Pundits point to biology, psychology, family environment, community, race, or, more often, to combinations of these in order to map out the reasons for poverty. They also point to these influences in plotting strategies to deal with the gross assumption (which turns into conviction) that the poor are failures because they have not lifted themselves out of poverty. This cesspool of ideologies ignores the fact that poverty in the United States is systematic and the direct result of political and economic policies that deprive people of jobs, subsistence wages, and access to health care.

To speak of "the poor" in U.S. society is to attempt to synthesize a variety of highly diverse people who need different kinds of help. This has, can be, and will continue to be disastrous as governmental policies continually seek to formulate a single policy to deal with the poor through welfare reforms. Welfare is a complex and interlocking set of dynamics that combine (at bare minimum) education, jobs, housing and homelessness, crime, addictions, race, gender, class, health care, and geography.

The war on welfare recipients is, I believe, a strategy being employed by political leaders—both Democrat and Republican—to shift the attention away from the government's redistribution of wealth to the wealthy. We have become an economically stratified industrial nation. The richest 1 percent of U.S. households (those with a minimum net worth of $2.3 million) nearly equals the wealth of the bottom 95 percent of U.S. households.

What does it mean when more than 93 percent of the budget reductions in entitlements have come from programs for low-income people? When the 104th Congress finished its work in 1996, it had reduced entitlement programs by $65.6 billion in the period from 1996 to 2002. Within this amount, almost $61 billion comes from low-income entitlement programs such as food stamps and the Supplemental Security Income program (SSI) for the elderly and disabled poor, and assistance to legal immigrants. One frustrating reality in this is that although entitlement programs for low-income folks accounted for 93 percent of the reduction in entitlement programs, these same programs accounted for only 37 percent of total expenditures for entitlement programs other than Social Security and only 23 percent of all entitlement spending.

Even those programs for low-income folks that are not entitlements experienced a disproportionate reduction in funding in the 1996 budget cuts that ushered in welfare reform. Although these programs represented 21 percent of overall funding for nondefense discretionary programs, they bore more than one and one-half times their share of the nondefense discretionary cuts. From 1994 to 1996 alone, funding for discretionary programs for low-income households was reduced more than 10 percent while funding for other nondefense discretionary programs shrank 5 percent.

There is something dreadfully wrong here.

The chapters in this book begin to show us the nature and the texture of what is wrong with a welfare policy that has at its core the demonization of poor women, children, and men. This policy sees poverty (and those who endure it) as the problem rather than a socioeconomic system structured to insure inequality while touting its openness to all: one must simply work harder to reap the benefits that are there for the taking.

From a clear and abiding stance of justice and justice-making, the authors point to the very real and concrete public policy issues spawned by neoliberal economic policies that demonize poverty. The result becomes a deadly economic funnel that sucks the lifeblood and life chances out of those of us who live in the bottom and middle tiers of economic life while sanctioning corporate welfare.

They pinpoint the ways in which feminist, *mujerista,* and womanist ethics wed theory and practice. Because the authors have, at the very foundation of their work, a sense of accountability to concrete individuals *and* communities, a moral insistence on the relationality of all things, each offers astute analysis *and* practical suggestions and insights on the nature of welfare and its impact on the lives of children, women, and men. In short, the authors are grounded in the concrete experiences of people and not in distracting abstractions that serve to obscure the real-life suffering and triumphs in living and surviving.

Such attention to concrete living necessitates an interstructured analysis that can balance competing and contradictory claims with ones that are in concert with each other. Such an analysis, as the authors note, can clarify the complexity of our humanness and give us more helpful and liberatory analytical tools. Monocausal and monolithic theoretical or practical frameworks are insufficient and may, in fact, serve to reinscribe patterns of domination and subordination that sanction the moralization of poverty in new and more deadly forms.

Seeking to do a feminist or womanist analysis of the nature of the transformation necessary to deliver us from the fears and hatreds and absolute ignorance that often fuel our understanding of welfare policy, the lives of those who need welfare assistance, and the policies we then shape is much like searching for paradise in a world of theme parks. This can be a maddening search through the maze of socioeconomic inequalities that are spawning theoethical debates that are not anchored in the realities of poverty in the United States. Rather than factor in the cost of dead-end jobs and disposable workers in the social order, welfare reform ignored the fact that real wages for average workers are plummeting to levels below those of 1967: 16 percent between 1973 and 1993. That this is happening in the midst of rising productivity represents irony and obscenity combined. Meanwhile, the average CEO of a major corporation earned as much as 41 factory workers in 1960 and 149 factory workers in 1993.

This age of spectacle, our postmodern culture, suffers from the enormous impact of market forces on everyday life. Everyday life has become commodified as corporate profits shoot through the roof in an ironic but deadly gambol. In 1994 alone, the profits of the Fortune 500 companies shot up 54 percent while growth in sales was only 8 percent. This disjuncture was made possible by slashing payrolls, investing in technology, overhauling assembly lines, and reducing fringe benefits. Companies reduced their work force and became more efficient in creating greater profits. Union jobs, which provide better wages and benefits, are disappearing. The downsizing of corporate America has meant the downsizing of the poor.

This tumbledown economic reality has also ushered in the age of racist, sexist, and classist ideologies which mask the realities of an increasingly morally bankrupt economic climate in the United States. These deadly ideologies function to mask the fact that the majority of the poor and those on welfare are white. Inner-city neighborhoods are viewed as sites of pathology and hopelessness. Rural areas are ignored or painted with the pastoral gloss of rugged individualism as the last vestige of true Americana.

Our views of welfare and welfare reform are rimmed with these inadequate and specious views of life in America. We have created (and now are maintaining) a society that simply refuses to care beyond our narrow self-interests. The 1996 welfare reforms are the institutionalization of this callousness. And worse, we have tied these reforms to the hope that our economy will remain strong and provide the jobs needed to give the reforms enacted a chance to work. This is a dangerous assumption and may prove to be a deadly one. If the conditions in Hawaii in 1998 are any indication, the reforms of 1996 may find a most inhospitable economic climate in which to work. Although most of the country has seen dramatic declines in welfare in our current economic boom, Hawaii is experiencing the opposite because its economy is more closely tied to faltering Japanese markets. Welfare rolls are climbing, and Hawaii may be the test case to see if welfare reform can work in a bad economy. Conservatives and liberals have differing interpretations and predictions of (and prescriptions for) what is happening and what needs to happen in Hawaii. But the bottom line will be: Can these reforms—built on mean-spiritedness, self-interest, stereotypes, and political expediency—work to enhance the lives of those who are living in whirlpools of catastrophe in postmodern America? I think not.

The old welfare law needed reforms because it did not adequately require or provide opportunities for work and parental responsibility to help families to get off the roles. Indeed, it often locked families into dependency that had the potential for becoming generational (although this potential was not necessarily fulfilled). However, the crafting of the recent reforms was built in an atmosphere in which the commodification of lives through spectacle, extravaganza, and political-rhetorical absolutes polarized and obscured lives. For conservatives, federal entitlements were equivalent to irresponsibility and lifelong dependency. For liberals, the replacement of entitlements with block grants was equivalent to work requirements. Left in the middle, as political fodder, are poor children and their families. This is truly obscene.

Resources

Abramovitz, Mimi. *Regulating the Lives of Women: Social Welfare Policy from Colonial Times to the Present.* Boston: South End, 1996.

Albelda, Randy, and Chris Tilly. *Glass Ceilings and Bottomless Pits: Women's Work, Women's Poverty.* Boston: South End, 1997.

Albelda, Randy, Nancy Folbre, and the Center for Popular Economics. *The War on the Poor: A Defense Manual.* New York: New Press, 1996.

Amott, Teresa. *Caught in the Crisis: Women and the U.S. Economy Today.* New York: Monthly Review Press, 1993.

Amott, Teresa, and Julie Matthaei. *Race, Gender and Work: A Multicultural Economic History of Women in the United States.* Boston: South End, 1991.

Browning, Don S., Bonnie J. Miller-McLemore, Pamela D. Couture, K. Brynolf Lyon, and Robert M. Franklin. *From Culture Wars to Common Ground: Religion and the American Family Debate.* Louisville, Ky.: Westminster John Knox, 1997.

Cobb, John, and Herman Daly. *For the Common Good: Redirecting the Economy Toward Community, the Environment, and a Sustainable Future.* Rev. ed. Boston: Beacon, 1994.

Coontz, Stephanie. *The Way We Never Were: American Families and the Nostalgia Trap.* New York: Basic Books, 1992.

Copeland, Warren. *And the Poor Get Welfare: The Ethics of Poverty in the United States.* Nashville: Abingdon, 1994.

Couture, Pamela. *Blessed Are the Poor? Women's Poverty, Family Policy, and Practical Theology.* Nashville: Abingdon, 1991.

Dill, Bonnie Thornton, and Maxine Baca Zinn, eds. *Women of Color in U.S. Society.* Philadelphia: Temple University Press, 1994.

Edin, Kathryn, and Laura Lein. *Making Ends Meet: How Single Mothers Survive Welfare and Low-Wage Work.* New York: Russell Sage Foundation, 1997.

Ferber, Marianne A., and Julie A. Nelson, eds. *Beyond Economic Man: Feminist Theory and Economics.* Chicago: University of Chicago Press, 1993.

Fineman, Martha Albertson. *The Neutered Mother, the Sexual Family, and Other Twentieth Century Tragedies.* New York: Routledge, 1995.

Folbre, Nancy. *Who Pays for the Kids? Gender and the Structures of Constraint.* New York: Routledge, 1994.

Funiciello, Theresa. *Tyranny of Kindness: Dismantling the Welfare System to End Poverty in America*. New York: Atlantic Monthly Press, 1993.

Gans, Herbert. *The War against the Poor*. New York: Basic Books, 1995.

Goldin, Claudia. *Understanding the Gender Gap: An Economic History of American Women*. New York: Oxford University Press, 1990.

Gordon, Linda. *Pitied but Not Entitled: Single Mothers and the History of Welfare*. Cambridge: Harvard University Press, 1994.

———, ed. *Women, the State, and Welfare*. Madison: University of Wisconsin Press, 1990.

Handler, Joel F. *The Poverty of Welfare Reform*. New Haven, Conn.: Yale University Press, 1995.

Handler, Joel F., and Yeheskel Hasenfeld. *The Moral Construction of Poverty: Welfare Reform in America*. Newbury Park, Calif.: Sage, 1991.

Harrison, Beverly W. *Making the Connections: Essays in Feminist Social Ethics*, ed. Carol Robb. Boston: Beacon, 1985.

Hernandez, Donald. *America's Children: Resources from Family, Governments, and the Economy*. New York: Russell Sage Foundation, 1993.

Katz, Michael B. *The Undeserving Poor: From the War on Poverty to the War on Welfare*. New York: Pantheon, 1989.

Kozol, Jonathan. *Amazing Grace: The Lives of Children and the Conscience of a Nation*. New York: Crown, 1995.

Mink, Gwendolyn. *Welfare's End*. Ithaca, N.Y.: Cornell University Press, 1998.

Okin, Susan Moller. *Justice, Gender, and the Family*. New York: Basic Books, 1989.

Oliver, Marvin L., and Thomas M. Shapiro. *Black Wealth/White Wealth: A New Perspective on Racial Inequality*. New York: Routledge, 1995.

Omolade, Barbara. *The Rising Song of African American Women*. New York: Routledge, 1994.

Owensby, Walter L. *Economics for Prophets: A Primer on Concepts, Realities, and Values in Our Economic System*. Grand Rapids, Mich.: Eerdmans, 1988.

Piven, Frances Fox, and Richard A. Cloward. *Regulating the Poor: The Function of Public Welfare*. 2d ed. New York: Pantheon, 1993.

Polakow, Valerie. *Lives on the Edge: Single Mothers and Their Children in the Other America*. Chicago: University of Chicago Press, 1993.

Quadagno, Jill. *The Color of Welfare: How Racism Undermined the War on Poverty*. New York: Oxford University Press, 1994.

Rasmussen, Larry. *Moral Fragments and Moral Community: A Proposal for Church in Society*. Minneapolis: Fortress, 1993.

Robb, Carol S. *Equal Value: An Ethical Approach to Economics and Sex*. Boston: Beacon, 1995.

Rose, Nancy Ellen. *Workfare or Fair Work? Women, Welfare, and Government Work Programs.* New Brunswick, N.J.: Rutgers University Press, 1995.

Sanders, Cheryl J. *Empowerment Ethics for a Liberated People: A Path to African American Social Transformation.* Minneapolis: Fortress, 1995.

Sherman, Arloc. *Poverty Matters: The Cost of Child Poverty in America.* Washington, D.C.: Children's Defense Fund, 1997.

Sidel, Ruth. *Keeping Women and Children Last: America's War on the Poor.* New York: Penguin Books, 1996.

Sklar, Holly. *Chaos or Community: Seeking Solutions Not Scapegoats for Bad Economics.* Boston: South End, 1995.

Sparr, Pamela, ed. *Mortgaging Women's Lives: Feminist Critiques of Structural Adjustment.* London: Zed, 1994.

The Twentieth Century Fund. *Welfare Reform: A Twentieth Century Fund Guide to the Issues.* New York: Twentieth Century Fund Press, 1995.

Williams, Lucy. *Decades of Distortion: The Right's 30-Year Assault on Welfare.* Somerville, Mass.: Political Research Associates, 1997.

Withorn, Ann, and Diane Dujon. *For Crying Out Loud: Women's Poverty in the United States.* Boston: South End, 1997.

Zweig, Michael, ed. *Religion and Economic Justice.* Philadelphia: Temple University Press, 1991.

National Organizations Working on Welfare Reform

Activist/Policy Focus

Catholic Charities USA
National Service Center
1731 King Street, Suite 200
Alexandria, VA 22314
(703) 549-1390
http://www.catholiccharitiesusa.org

Center for Community Change
Rich Stolz
1000 Wisconsin Avenue, NW
Washington, DC 20007
(202) 342-0519

Center for Law and Social Policy
1616 P Street NW, Suite 150
Washington, DC 20036
info@clasp.org

Children's Defense Fund
25 E Street, NW
Washington, DC 20001
(202) 628-8787
http://www.childrensdefensefund.org

National Association of Social Workers
15 Park Row, 20th Floor
New York, NY 10038
(212) 577-5000

National Coalition for the Education of Welfare Recipients
Contact: Pam Bayless (212) 794-5581

Welfare Reform Watch Project
c/o NETWORK Education Program
801 Pennsylvania Avenue, SE, Suite 460
Washington, DC 20003
(202) 547-5556
network@igc.apc.org

Welfare Law Center
275 Seventh Avenue, Suite 1205
New York, NY 10001-6708
(212) 633-6967
wlc@welfarelaw.org
http://www.welfarelaw.org

Wider Opportunities for Women
815 Fifteenth Street, NW, Suite 916
Washington, DC 20005
(202) 638-3143

Research/Monitoring Implementation

AFSCME Information on Welfare Reform
http://www.afscme.org//pol-leg/welftc.htm

American Public Welfare Association
810 First Street, NE, Suite 500
Washington, DC 20002-4267
(202) 682-0100
http://www.apwa.org/index.htm

Business Partnerships: W-t-W
http://www.welfaretowork.org

Idea Central
http://epn.org/idea/welf-bkm.html

Institute for Global Communication
http://www.igc.org

Institute for Women's Policy Research
1400 Twentieth Street, NW, Suite 104
Washington, DC 20036
(202) 833-4362
http://www.ipr.org

National Immigration Law Center
Los Angeles, CA
(213) 964-7930

Political Research Associates
120 Beacon Street, Suite 202
Somerville, MA 02143
(617) 661-9313

The Twentieth Century Fund
41 East 70th Street
New York, NY 10022
(212) 535-4441

Urban Institute
2100 M Street, NW
Washington, DC 20037
(202) 833-7200
http://www.urban.org

Welfare Information Network
http://www.welfareinfo.org

Welfare Mom Homepage
http://www.geocities.com/CapitolHill/1064

Welfare Watch
http://www.welfarewatch.org